לעלוי נשמת
ר' חיים בן ר' קלונומוס קלמן זילבער ע"ה

נפטר בשם טוב - ג' אדר תשע"ז

We are saddened and honored to dedicate the Bright Beginnings *Hachana L'Gemara* Workbook in loving memory of our dear friend Reb Chaim Silber z"l (aka 'LOBO') who was a pillar of *chesed* and kindness in *Klal Yisroel*.

Saddened beyond words at his passing far too young, and honored to be able to present this workbook to many thousands of Jewish children worldwide as a *zechus* for his *neshama*.

Chaim's love for life and *simchas ha'chaim* was remarkable; to know him was to become his best friend. He treated his parents with extraordinary *derech eretz* and shared the gifts Hashem gave him selflessly and without fanfare; supporting needy people year-round and especially for *Yomim Tovim*, helping them marry off their children and pay their mortgages – all done with extreme sensitivity and respect.

Purim celebrations at his home were legendary, and he participated in community charity events such as the *Maos Chitim* appeal at the *Sasregen* shul, and the annual Nachum Segal Radio-thon with the same energy and spirit that he brought to the summer baseball league in the Catskills each summer.

Chaim lived his life "family first" in every sense of the word, always spending time with and expressing his deep love for his wife Eva and their children.

Our lives were enriched by our deep friendship with Chaim, and he will be in our hearts and our minds forever.

Yehi Zichro Boruch – May his memory be for a blessing,

Barbara and Jerry Weissman

לעלוי נשמת

בנימין בן רפאל הלוי ז״ל

נפטר כ״א תמוז תשס״ח

אסתר בת יקותיאל יהודה ע״ה

נפטרה ז׳ אייר תשע״ה

We gratefully acknowledge a gift
to *The Bright Beginnings Haschala Gemara Workbook Project*
in loving memory of

Benjamin and Irene Lowy z"l

Benjamin and Irene came to America after the Holocaust, rebuilt their lives and maintained their faith in Hashem despite the many challenges they faced in their lives.

Though they had no children of their own, they found joy and satisfaction in the accomplishments of the children of their family members, and of all Jewish children.

Our *Chazal* (sages) inform us that one who teaches Torah to children is considered to be similar to a parent (*Sanhedrin* 19a).

With that in mind, we are confident that Benjamin and Irene will have *Nachas* in *Gan Eden* watching many thousands of Hashem's children gain fluency in Gemara and a love for Torah learning as a result of their gift to this project.

May their memories be for a blessing.

Yakov Horowitz

INTRODUCTION

THIS BRIGHT BEGINNINGS HACHANA L'GEMARA WORKBOOK is designed to introduce **all** beginner *Gemara* learners (regardless of which *Mesechta* they begin with) to the beautiful and complex study of *Gemara*. It teaches them about *Torah She'bal Peh*, the history of how it came to be written and how it was transmitted through the generations. It also explains the layout of *Gemara* pages and its page count, the various components of *Gemara Shakla V'tarya* (give and take), and the difference between a *Mishna*, *Gemara* and *B'raysa*.

This unique introductory workbook is a testament to the creativity, devotion and ever-expanding skills of its author, Rabbi Aaron Spivak. It is a pre-*Gemara* workbook, and we encourage you to visit www.thebrightbeginnings.com or email publications@thebrightbeginnings.com to learn about our other workbooks. There, you can also download flashcards with the vocabulary words listed in this workbook and their translation and view sample pages from our *Hascholas Gemara* workbook for *Meseches Brachos* and our Chumash workbooks.

I would like to express my gratitude to Melly and Rochelle Lifshitz for dedicating the **Bright Beginnings Gemara Brachos Project** in honor of their parents Daniel and Claire, to Barbara and Jerry Weissman for dedicating this *Hachana L'Gemara* workbook, and to the estate of Benjamin and Irene Lowy for providing a gracious gift to this project. I am forever grateful to Harry Skydell and Mark Karasick for providing the seed money for the Bright Beginnings curricular projects when we were first getting started.

Getting creative Judaic studies materials like this workbook from concept to final product requires a very significant investment, and I ask those of you who may have the capacity to contribute funds to Bright Beginnings or who would perhaps consider dedicating a future volume to kindly contact me at publications@thebrightbeginnings.com. I also encourage you to email your comments, corrections and suggestions to help us improve future workbooks in this series.

We are grateful to Mrs. Dena Peker and her talented staff at Dynagrafik Design Studio for creating this beautiful workbook, and to Mr. Philip Weinreich of Noble Book Press for its printing. I would also like to express my deepest appreciation to Mrs. Chaya Becker, administrative director of CFJFL/Project YES, for all the incredible work she does to make these publications possible.

We are honored that Torah Umesorah distributes all of our Bright Beginnings curricular materials and thank them for all they do to spread Torah around the world.

To our dear children; thank you for sharing me so graciously with the *Klal* and for giving Mommy and me such unending *Nachas* over the past thirty-five years.

Over the past thirty-eight years, my wife Udi has been my full partner, confidant and closest friend, and she utilizes her incredible range of talents to help me actualize my dreams. May Hashem repay her with our greatest wish – that we grow old together and share *Nachas* from our wonderful children and grandchildren.

Finally, and most importantly, I would like to humbly give thanks to Hashem for allowing me to, "dwell in His House," (*Tehillim* 27:4) and to teach His Torah for the past thirty-seven years.

Yakov Horowitz
Monsey N.Y.

25 Adar 5777
March 23, 2017

Introduction to גמרא

LESSON 1

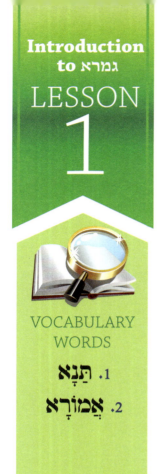

VOCABULARY WORDS

1. תַּנָּא
2. אֲמוֹרָא

Introduction

On שָׁבוּעוֹת[1] in the year 2448 (from the creation of the world) מֹשֶׁה רַבֵּינוּ went up to הַר סִינַי and stayed there for 40 days. While he was there, Hashem taught him all of the הֲלָכוֹת of the תּוֹרָה. Hashem then had מֹשֶׁה write many of the הֲלָכוֹת in a סֵפֶר תּוֹרָה. This was the beginning of what we call תּוֹרָה שֶׁבִּכְתָב (Torah that was written). This part of the תּוֹרָה would be copied by hand many times, so that any member of the בְּנֵי יִשְׂרָאֵל could simply take a סֵפֶר תּוֹרָה and read what ה' had said.

However, for some of the הֲלָכוֹת, Hashem instructed מֹשֶׁה to only write a hint in the תּוֹרָה שֶׁבִּכְתָב (such as an extra letter or word). For these הֲלָכוֹת, the actual הֲלָכָה would be part of תּוֹרָה שֶׁבְּעַל פֶּה (Torah that was taught orally).[2] This part of the תּוֹרָה was not written and could only be learned by listening when מֹשֶׁה (or one of his תַּלְמִידִים) taught it.

Additionally, there were still other הֲלָכוֹת that were not included in תּוֹרָה שֶׁבִּכְתָב at all (not even with a hint). These הֲלָכוֹת were called הֲלָכָה לְמֹשֶׁה מִסִּינַי.

---

[1] For the sake of simplicity, we stated that מֹשֶׁה went up "on שָׁבוּעוֹת." However, it should be noted that according to Rashi (שמות ל״ב,א׳), he actually went up the day after שָׁבוּעוֹת.

[2] For example: ה' taught מֹשֶׁה that just as a person must honor his parents, so too, he must honor his older brother. However, in תּוֹרָה שֶׁבִּכְתָב Hashem instructed מֹשֶׁה to only write "כַּבֵּד אֶת אָבִיךָ וְאֶת אִמֶּךָ – Honor your father and your mother." The הֲלָכָה of honoring an older brother remained in תּוֹרָה שֶׁבְּעַל פֶּה. Hashem had מֹשֶׁה write the word "אֶת" (which isn't really needed to understand the פָּסוּק) as a hint to the הֲלָכָה.

to גמרא

When מֹשֶׁה came down from הַר סִינַי, he began teaching the בְּנֵי יִשְׂרָאֵל all of the הֲלָכוֹת of the תּוֹרָה. He brought down the תּוֹרָה שֶׁבִּכְתָב in written form and taught them the תּוֹרָה שֶׁבְּעַל פֶּה.

At that time, מֹשֶׁה also began to make certain גְּזֵירוֹת and תַּקָּנוֹת (decrees and rules) about which ה' did not command him. ה' gave this ability to מֹשֶׁה and the חֲכָמִים. These laws are called הֲלָכוֹת מִדְרַבָּנָן. The חֲכָמִים of following generations added many more הֲלָכוֹת מִדְרַבָּנָן. These are also part of תּוֹרָה שֶׁבְּעַל פֶּה.

The הֲלָכוֹת of the תּוֹרָה can be divided into four categories:

1. הֲלָכוֹת taught to מֹשֶׁה and written in תּוֹרָה שֶׁבִּכְתָב
2. הֲלָכוֹת taught to מֹשֶׁה and hinted to (but not specifically written) in תּוֹרָה שֶׁבִּכְתָב
3. הֲלָכָה לְמֹשֶׁה מִסִינַי – Taught to מֹשֶׁה but not included in תּוֹרָה שֶׁבִּכְתָב at all
4. הֲלָכוֹת מִדְרַבָּנָן – Instituted by the חֲכָמִים

תּוֹרָה שֶׁבְּעַל פֶּה is made up of the last three of these categories.

REVIEW QUESTIONS:

1. Who taught the תּוֹרָה to מֹשֶׁה רַבֵּינוּ?
2. What are the two parts of the תּוֹרָה called?
3. Which part (from question #2) was מֹשֶׁה taught on הַר סִינַי? (Trick question.☺)
4. What is תּוֹרָה שֶׁבִּכְתָב?
5. Which three types of הֲלָכוֹת make up תּוֹרָה שֶׁבְּעַל פֶּה?

LESSON 1 Review

Introduction to גמרא

KNOW YOUR FACTS:

1. To whom did ה׳ teach all of the הֲלָכוֹת of the תּוֹרָה? _____

2. Where did He teach the הֲלָכוֹת to him? _____

3. To whom did this person teach the הֲלָכוֹת when he came back from this place? _____
   _____

4. What is a הֲלָכָה לְמֹשֶׁה מִסִינַי? _____

5. What is a הֲלָכָה דְרַבָּנָן? _____

6. Which of the following are considered תּוֹרָה שֶׁבִּכְתָב (check all that apply)?
   ☐ הֲלָכוֹת taught to מֹשֶׁה and written in the חוּמָשׁ
   ☐ הֲלָכוֹת taught to מֹשֶׁה and hinted to in the חוּמָשׁ
   ☐ הֲלָכָה לְמֹשֶׁה מִסִינַי
   ☐ הֲלָכָה מִדְרַבָּנָן

7. Which of the following are considered תּוֹרָה שֶׁבְּעַל פֶּה (check all that apply)?
   ☐ הֲלָכוֹת taught to מֹשֶׁה and written in the חוּמָשׁ
   ☐ הֲלָכוֹת taught to מֹשֶׁה and hinted to in the חוּמָשׁ
   ☐ הֲלָכָה לְמֹשֶׁה מִסִינַי
   ☐ הֲלָכָה מִדְרַבָּנָן

8. Which of the following were taught by ה׳ (check all that apply)?
   ☐ הֲלָכוֹת taught to מֹשֶׁה and written in the חוּמָשׁ
   ☐ הֲלָכוֹת taught to מֹשֶׁה and hinted to in the חוּמָשׁ
   ☐ הֲלָכָה לְמֹשֶׁה מִסִינַי
   ☐ מִצְוֹת מִדְרַבָּנָן

MULTIPLE CHOICE:

	תּוֹרָה שֶׁבִּכְתָב		תּוֹרָה שֶׁבְּעַל פֶּה		Taught by Hashem		Originated from חֲכָמִים
הֲלָכוֹת taught to מֹשֶׁה and written in the חוּמָשׁ	☐	or	☐		☐	or	☐
הֲלָכוֹת taught to מֹשֶׁה and hinted to in the חוּמָשׁ	☐	or	☐		☐	or	☐
הֲלָכָה לְמֹשֶׁה מִסִינַי	☐	or	☐		☐	or	☐
מִצְוֹת מִדְרַבָּנָן	☐	or	☐		☐	or	☐

MATCHING:

____ 1. The One who taught מֹשֶׁה   א. ה'

____ 2. הֲלָכוֹת made by the חֲכָמִים   ב. **הַר סִינַי**

____ 3. הֲלָכוֹת taught by ה' but not even hinted in the חוּמָשׁ   ג. **הֲלָכָה לְמֹשֶׁה מִסִינַי**

____ 4. The ones to whom מֹשֶׁה taught the תּוֹרָה   ד. **מִדְרַבָּנָן**

____ 5. The place where מֹשֶׁה learned the תּוֹרָה   ה. **בְּנֵי יִשְׂרָאֵל**

VOCABULARY REVIEW:

_____ תַּנָא

_____ אֲמוֹרָא

© 2017 Bright Beginnings | 7

Introduction to גמרא
LESSON 2

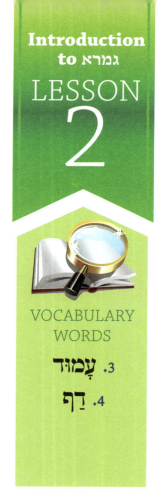

VOCABULARY WORDS

3. עַמּוּד
4. דַּף

Although מֹשֶׁה taught all of the הֲלָכוֹת to all of the בְּנֵי יִשְׂרָאֵל, he had one main תַּלְמִיד with whom he entrusted the task of teaching the תּוֹרָה after מֹשֶׁה was no longer living. This תַּלְמִיד was יְהוֹשֻׁעַ בֶּן נוּן. If we keep in mind that תּוֹרָה שֶׁבְּעַל פֶּה was not written anywhere, we can begin to realize just how important יְהוֹשֻׁעַ's job really was. Any הֲלָכָה that would be forgotten would be extremely difficult to ever get back. However, יְהוֹשֻׁעַ proved worthy of his position and during his life לִימוּד הַתּוֹרָה flourished.

After יְהוֹשֻׁעַ was נִפְטָר, the job was left to פִּינְחָס בֶּן אֶלְעָזָר הַכֹּהֵן who, in turn, passed it on to the חֲכָמִים of the next generation. This began a chain which linked each generation back to הַר סִינַי. Each generation had one or two leaders who would lead the חֲכָמִים of their time in teaching תּוֹרָה to the בְּנֵי יִשְׂרָאֵל. They would teach the הֲלָכוֹת the way they had learned it from their רֵבִּי going all the way back to מֹשֶׁה רַבֵּינוּ.

In those days, learning תּוֹרָה was very different than it is today. A child would learn with his father or a רֵבִּי and master all of the פְּסוּקִים of תּוֹרָה שֶׁבִּכְתָב between the ages of five and ten years old. Then, if he was lucky enough, he would continue learning תּוֹרָה and memorize הֲלָכוֹת until he was fifteen years old. If he had the privilege of continuing after that, he would begin to learn the underlying principles for the הֲלָכוֹת and how they are learned from the פְּסוּקִים (whether directly or from a hint). There were no סְפָרִים in the בֵּית הַמִּדְרָשׁ other than סִפְרֵי תּוֹרָה (and perhaps the סְפָרִים of נְבִיאִים and כְּתוּבִים). When the רֵבִּי gave a שִׁיעוּר, he would tell everyone what he learned from his רֵבִּי and then they would review it until they knew it.

8 | © 2017 Bright Beginnings

AGE:	LIMUD:
5 - 10	תּוֹרָה שֶׁבִּכְתַב of פְּסוּקִים
10 - 15	תּוֹרָה שֶׁבְּעַל פֶּה of הֲלָכוֹת
15+	Underlying principles of הֲלָכוֹת and how they are learned from פְּסוּקִים

This system worked well for many years and many generations. This was how תּוֹרָה was learned when we came into אֶרֶץ יִשְׂרָאֵל, during the days of the שׁוֹפְטִים, through the first בֵּית הַמִּקְדָשׁ, in גָּלוּת בָּבֶל, and during the first half of the second בֵּית הַמִּקְדָשׁ.

Towards the middle of the time of the second בֵּית הַמִּקְדָשׁ, however, problems first began to arise.

The two גְדוֹלֵי הַדוֹר at that time were הִלֵּל and שַׁמַּאי. For the first time, they began to disagree about what the הֲלָכָה was in certain situations. Although the cases in which they had a מַחֲלוֹקֶת (disagreement) were limited, they each founded a יְשִׁיבָה (called בֵּית שַׁמַּאי and בֵּית הִלֵּל) and the יְשִׁיבוֹת had many more מַחֲלוֹקוֹת with each other over the years.

In the following generations, the Roman persecution made it more difficult for the חֲכָמִים to study with proper peace of mind. As a result, the disagreements increased. It was becoming more and more difficult to learn תּוֹרָה and have a clear picture of what the original הֲלָכָה was, as taught by מֹשֶׁה רַבֵּינוּ. This problem only became worse when the בֵּית הַמִּקְדָשׁ was destroyed and the סַנְהֶדְרִין was exiled from יְרוּשָׁלַיִם (and finally disbanded altogether).

REVIEW QUESTIONS:

1. Who was the main תַּלְמִיד of מֹשֶׁה רַבֵּינוּ?

2. Why was יְהוֹשֻׁעַ's job so important?

3. How was תּוֹרָה learned in the early generations? What would it be like to learn in יְשִׁיבָה back then? How is it different from the way that you learn today?

4. What major change happened in the days of הִלֵּל and שַׁמַּאי? What impact did this have on those who learned תּוֹרָה? What happened in the years immediately following שַׁמַּאי and הִלֵּל?

Introduction to גמרא

LESSON 2 Review

KNOW YOUR FACTS:

1. Who was the main תַּלְמִיד of מֹשֶׁה רַבֵּינוּ? _____

2. What responsibility did this תַּלְמִיד have? _____
   _____

3. How was the תּוֹרָה transmitted to each future generation? _____
   _____

4. What would a child learn at each age?
   - א. 5 yrs. old – 10 yrs. old _____
   - ב. 10 yrs. old – 15 yrs. old _____
   - ג. 15 yrs. old _____

5. Describe the main difference between the way that תּוֹרָה was learned in those days as opposed to the way we learn today. _____
   _____
   _____

6. What problem began to occur in the days of הִלֵּל and שַׁמַאי? _____
   _____

7. What made this problem get worse? _____
   _____

MATCHING:

_____	1. The main תַּלְמִיד of מֹשֶׁה רַבֵּינוּ	עָמוּד	א.
_____	2. The main סֵפֶר they had	הֲלָכוֹת	ב.
_____	3. What a child learned from 5 until 10	סֵפֶר תּוֹרָה	ג.
_____	4. What a child learned from 10 until 15	דַף	ד.
_____	5. What a person learned from 15 and on	פְּסוּקִים	ה.
_____	6. Began happening in the days of הִלֵּל וְשַׁמַּאי	יְהוֹשֻׁעַ בֶּן נוּן	ו.
_____	7. Problem got worse when they disbanded	תַּנָא	ז.
_____	8. One side of a page	סַנְהֶדְרִין	ח.
_____	9. A full page (both sides)	אֲמוֹרָא	ט.
_____	10. חָכָם from the מִשְׁנָה	מַחֲלוֹקֶת	י.
_____	11. חָכָם from the גְמָרָא	Underlying principles of הֲלָכוֹת	יא.

VOCABULARY REVIEW:

_____ עָמוּד

_____ אֲמוֹרָא

_____ דַף

_____ תַּנָא

Introduction to גמרא

LESSON 3

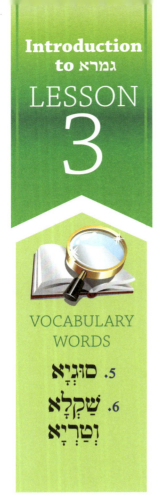

VOCABULARY WORDS

5. סוּגְיָא
6. שַׁקְלָא וְטַרְיָא

The future of תּוֹרָה looked like it was in trouble. As always, 'ה saved us. This time, 'ה sent the יְשׁוּעָה (salvation) through the hands of a great צַדִּיק named רַבִּי יְהוּדָה הַנָּשִׂיא. (Because of his greatness, he is sometimes just referred to as "רַבִּי.")

Although the תּוֹרָה שֶׁבְּעַל פֶּה was not supposed to be written down, רַבִּי יְהוּדָה הַנָּשִׂיא applied the פָּסוּק of "עֵת לַעֲשׂוֹת לַה' הֵפֵרוּ תּוֹרָתֶךָ" – "It is a time to do for Hashem so they have nullified your תּוֹרָה." This פָּסוּק means that at certain times of extreme need, a גָּדוֹל הַדּוֹר may violate a הֲלָכָה in order to save the generation from spiritual catastrophe. With this in mind, רַבִּי יְהוּדָה הַנָּשִׂיא wrote the מִשְׁנָה which was a collection of the הֲלָכוֹת and other teachings that were taught by the חֲכָמִים from הִלֵּל and שַׁמַּאי until his own time. The חֲכָמִים from those generations became known as the "תַּנָּאִים*." Simply stated, הִלֵּל and שַׁמַּאי were the first תַּנָּאִים and רַבִּי יְהוּדָה הַנָּשִׂיא was the last.

---

*For the purpose of this work, we have defined the period of the תַּנָּאִים as having begun with הִלֵּל and שַׁמַּאי. It should be noted that there are those who use the term תַּנָּאִים to refer to a broader group of חֲכָמִים which began at an earlier time.

The מִשְׁנָה was divided into six sections called סְדָרִים. All of them together are known as the שִׁשָׁה סִדְרֵי מִשְׁנָה:

The הֲלָכוֹת of planting and growing food	זְרָעִים
The הֲלָכוֹת of שַׁבָּת and יָמִים טוֹבִים	מוֹעֵד
The הֲלָכוֹת of marriage and divorce	נָשִׁים
The הֲלָכוֹת of monetary issues and בֵּית דִין	נְזִיקִין
The הֲלָכוֹת of the קׇרְבָּנוֹת and the בֵּית הַמִקְדָשׁ	קׇדָשִׁים
The הֲלָכוֹת of טוּמְאָה and טׇהֳרָה	טׇהֳרוֹת

Each סֵדֶר was then divided into מַסֶכְתּוֹת, each מַסֶכְתָּא was divided into פְּרָקִים and each פֶּרֶק was divided into מִשְׁנָיוֹת. For example, if a person wanted to find out what בְּרָכָה to make on fruit, he could look in סֵדֶר זְרָעִים, מַסֶכֶת בְּרָכוֹת, פֶּרֶק ו׳, מִשְׁנָה א׳.

REVIEW QUESTIONS:

1. What great problem was threatening the future of the תּוֹרָה?

2. Who did ה׳ send to save us from this problem?

3. What did he do to help the situation? Why was this a questionable thing to do? What reasoning did he have to explain why he could do this?

4. What is the מִשְׁנָה? Who wrote it?

5. Who were the תַּנָאִים? Who were the first ones? Who was the last one?

6. What are the שִׁשָׁה סִדְרֵי מִשְׁנָה? What does each one discuss?

7. What is a מַסֶכְתָּא? How is each מַסֶכְתָּא divided up?

© 2017 Bright Beginnings | 13

LESSON 3 Review

Introduction to גמרא

KNOW YOUR FACTS:

1. What great problem was threatening the future of the תּוֹרָה? _____
   _____

2. Whom did ה׳ send to save us from this problem? _____

3. What did that person do to fix this problem? _____
   _____

4. Why were his actions considered questionable? _____
   _____

5. If so, why did he do this? _____
   _____

6. What are תַּנָאִים? _____

7. Who were the first תַּנָאִים? _____

8. Who was the last תַּנָא? _____

9. Please describe the subject of each of the שִׁשָׁה סִדְרֵי מִשְׁנָה:

   א. זְרָעִים _____
   ב. מוֹעֵד _____
   ג. נָשִׁים _____
   ד. נְזִיקִין _____
   ה. קָדְשִׁים _____
   ו. טָהֲרוֹת _____

MATCHING:

_____	1. Laws of marriage and divorce	סֵדֶר נְזִיקִין	א.
_____	2. Laws of טַהֲרָה and טוּמְאָה	רַבִּי יְהוּדָה הַנָשִׂיא	ב.
_____	3. Justification (why was it okay) to write down תּוֹרָה שֶׁבְּעַל פֶּה	סֵדֶר נָשִׁים	ג.
_____	4. Laws of planting and food	סֵדֶר זְרָעִים	ד.
_____	5. First תַּנָאִים	סֵדֶר קָדָשִׁים	ה.
_____	6. Laws of קָרְבָּנוֹת and בֵּית הַמִקְדָשׁ	הִלֵּל וְשַׁמַאי	ו.
_____	7. Last תַּנָא	סֵדֶר טְהָרוֹת	ז.
_____	8. Laws of יוֹם טוֹב and שַׁבָּת	עֵת לַעֲשׂוֹת לַה׳	ח.
_____	9. Laws of money and בֵּית דִין	סֵדֶר מוֹעֵד	ט.
_____	10. First סֵפֶר of תּוֹרָה שֶׁבְּעַל פֶּה to be written	מִשְׁנָיוֹת	י.

VOCABULARY REVIEW:

עַמוּד _____

אֲמוֹרָא _____

דַף _____

סוּגְיָא _____

שַׁקְלָא וְטַרְיָא _____

Introduction to גמרא
LESSON 4

VOCABULARY WORDS

7. שְׁאֵלָה
8. קַשְׁיָא

Rebbi Yehudah HaNassi had many great תַּלְמִידִים. Two of these תַּלְמִידִים were named רַב and שְׁמוּאֵל*. These two גְדוֹלֵי הַדוֹר (leaders of the generation) went to בָּבֶל to open יְשִׁיבוֹת for the people there. רַב opened a יְשִׁיבָה in the city of סוּרָא and שְׁמוּאֵל did the same in נַהַרְדְעָא.

For the next few generations, people learned מִשְׁנָיוֹת. However, learning מִשְׁנָיוֹת alone was not enough. For, although the מִשְׁנָיוֹת taught the הֲלָכוֹת, they did not include the reasons for the הֲלָכוֹת. They also didn't teach how these הֲלָכוֹת are learned from פְּסוּקִים. This part of the תּוֹרָה remained בְּעַל פֶּה with each רֶבִּי teaching it to his תַּלְמִידִים. And just as it happened with the הֲלָכוֹת themselves, the reasons and sources were in danger of being forgotten.

Once again, ה' sent the right people to save the situation. רָבִינָא and רַב אַשִׁי put together all of the teachings beginning with שְׁמוּאֵל and רַב all the way to their own time. This collection of teachings was called "תַּלְמוּד" or "גְמָרָא". (רַבִּי יוֹחָנָן had done something similar in אֶרֶץ יִשְׂרָאֵל

*This follows the opinion of the Rambam

16 | © 2017 Bright Beginnings

several generations earlier. To differentiate between the two works, the גְּמָרָא written in אֶרֶץ יִשְׂרָאֵל is called "תַּלְמוּד יְרוּשַׁלְמִי" and the one written in בָּבֶל is called "תַּלְמוּד בַּבְלִי". Our focus will be on the תַּלְמוּד בַּבְלִי.) The חֲכָמִים from these generations became known as the "אָמוֹרָאִים".

REVIEW QUESTIONS:

1. Which two תַּלְמִידִים did רַבִּי יְהוּדָה הַנָּשִׂיא send? Where did he send them?

2. What was the main thing that people learned in those days?

3. What did that סֵפֶר include? What didn't it include? How were these parts taught? What problem arose with that system?

4. Whom did 'ה send to save us from this problem? What did they do to help?

5. Who were the אָמוֹרָאִים? Who the first ones? Who were the last ones?

6. What is the difference between תַּלְמוּד יְרוּשַׁלְמִי and תַּלְמוּד בַּבְלִי? Which one is primary (the main one)?

© 2017 Bright Beginnings | 17

LESSON 4 Review

Introduction to גמרא

KNOW YOUR FACTS:

1. Which תַּלְמִידִים did רַבִּי יְהוּדָה הַנָשִׂיא send to בָּבֶל? _____

2. What part of תּוֹרָה שֶׁבְּעַל פֶּה was not included in the מִשְׁנַיוֹת? _____
   _____

3. What happened to this part of תּוֹרָה שֶׁבְּעַל פֶּה? _____
   _____

4. What is גְמָרָא? _____

5. Who wrote the גְמָרָא?   א. תַּלְמוּד בַּבְלִי   _____

   ב. תַּלְמוּד יְרוּשַׁלְמִי   _____

6. Which גְמָרָא do we focus on more? (Circle) one)   תַּלְמוּד יְרוּשַׁלְמִי   תַּלְמוּד בַּבְלִי

   E.C. Why? _____

7. What are אֲמוֹרָאִים? _____

8. Who were the first אֲמוֹרָאִים? _____

9. Who were the last אֲמוֹרָאִים? _____

VOCABULARY REVIEW:

_____ סוּגְיָא

_____ שַׁקְלָא וְטַרְיָא

_____ אֲמוֹרָא

_____ עַמוּד

18 | © 2017 Bright Beginnings

MATCHING:

_____ 1. a question asking for information	אֲמוֹרָאִים	.א
_____ 2. the first אֲמוֹרָאִים	תַּלְמוּד בַּבְלִי	.ב
_____ 3. גְמָרָא of the חֲכָמִים	תַּלְמוּד יְרוּשַׁלְמִי	.ג
_____ 4. a topic of discussion in the גְמָרָא	שְׁאֵלָה	.ד
_____ 5. the last אֲמוֹרָאִים	רָבִינָא וְרַב אַשִׁי	.ה
_____ 6. the back and forth discussion of the גְמָרָא	קֻשְׁיָא	.ו
_____ 7. included in the גְמָרָא but not in the מִשְׁנָה	רַב וּשְׁמוּאֵל	.ז
_____ 8. גְמָרָא written by רַבִּי יוֹחָנָן	שַׁקְלָא וְטַרְיָא	.ח
_____ 9. a question that something does not make sense	סוּגְיָא	.ט
_____ 10. the main גְמָרָא	Underlying principles of הֲלָכוֹת	.י

VOCABULARY REVIEW:

שְׁאֵלָה _____

תַּנָא _____

דַף _____

קֻשְׁיָא _____

© 2017 Bright Beginnings | 19

Introduction to גְמָרָא
LESSON 5

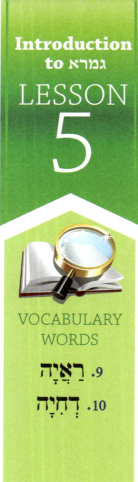

VOCABULARY WORDS

9. רְאָיָה
10. דְּחִיָּה

Before we start learning גְמָרָא we have to know how to "get around." In order to make learning easier, most גְמָרוֹת have an identical page layout. This means that if you look in your גְמָרָא at a certain word on a certain line on a certain page, almost anyone in the world will find the same word in that place. To make this possible, the גְמָרָא has a special page numbering system. Every page in גְמָרָא is called a דַף (בְּלַאט in Yiddish). A דַף is one sheet of paper that is made up of two sides. Each דַף is numbered beginning with דַף ב. Each side is called an עָמוּד. If you hold up a page in the גְמָרָא, the front side is called עָמוּד א and the back side is called עָמוּד ב. It seems simple enough, but be careful to remember that when your גְמָרָא is lying open, the first side you will read (the right-hand page) is עָמוּד ב and the second side (the left-hand page) is עָמוּד א. For example, in the picture above, the right hand page is דַף כ עָמוּד ב and the left hand page is דַף כא עָמוּד א. The number of the דַף (using Hebrew letters) can be found on the top-left corner of each עָמוּד א.

20 | © 2017 Bright Beginnings

Very soon, we will start learning גְמָרָא from the beginning of the second פֶּרֶק of מַסֶּכֶת בָּבָא מְצִיעָא. This פֶּרֶק begins in the middle of דַּף כא עַמּוּד א. To make it easier to write, we abbreviate עַמּוּד א with a "." and עַמּוּד ב with ":". Therefore, if I wanted to write the same עַמּוּד in short-hand, I could write "בָּבָא מְצִיעָא כא.".

To see if you understand this all, open your גְמָרָא בָּבָא מְצִיעָא to :ל. If the first word on the page is "לא", you've got it!

REVIEW QUESTIONS:

1. What is a דַּף? What is a בְּלַאט? What is an עַמּוּד?

2. What is the difference between עַמּוּד א and עַמּוּד ב?

3. How do I know which דַּף and עַמּוּד I am learning?

4. I looked in my notes and it said the following: "בָּבָא מְצִיעָא כט.". What does that mean?

5. What is the first דַּף in each מַסֶּכְתָּא?

LESSON 5 Review

Introduction to גמרא

KNOW YOUR FACTS:

1. What is a דַף? _____

2. What is a בְּלַאט? _____

3. What is an עַמוּד? _____

4. How do I know what דַף I am learning? _____
   _____

5. The first side of each דַף is called _____

   The second side of each דַף is called _____

6.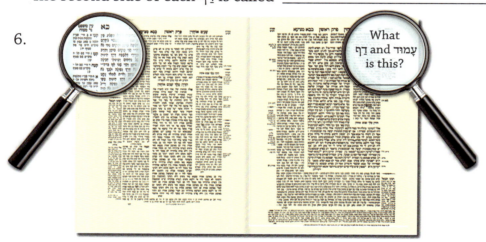

   What עַמוּד and דַף is this?

7. What do the following abbreviations mean?

   א. קידושִין לה. _____

   ב. זְבָחִים ב: _____

   ג. בָּבָא בַּתְרָא קמג. _____

8. Please abbreviate the following:

   א. מְסֶכֶת עֲרָכִין דַף יג עָמוּד ב _____

   ב. מְסֶכֶת תְּמוּרָה דַף כ עָמוּד א _____

   ג. מְסֶכֶת כְּתוּבוֹת דַף קב עָמוּד ב _____

TRUE OR FALSE:
(Circle T or F)

1. דַף and בְּלַאט are the same thing.

2. There are two דַף on every עָמוּד.

3. מְסֶכֶת בָּבָא מְצִיעָא עָמוּד כא דַף א means בָּבָא מְצִיעָא כא.

4. 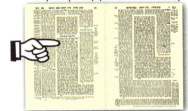 The hand is pointing to עָמוּד ב.

5. For עָמוּד ב דַף מג שַׁבָּת I would write: שַׁבָּת מג.

6. The first page of גְמָרָא is דַף א.

7. To know which דַף I am learning, I look at the top of עָמוּד א.

8. Every דַף has עָמוּד א and עָמוּד ב.

9. Most גְמָרוֹת have the same page layout.

10. The second פֶּרֶק of מְסֶכֶת בָּבָא מְצִיעָא begins in the middle of דַף כא עָמוּד א.

VOCABULARY REVIEW:

רְאָיָה
_____
דְּחִיָּה
_____
שְׁאֵלָה
_____
קֻשְׁיָא
_____
סוּגְיָא

Introduction to גְמָרָא
LESSON 6

VOCABULARY WORDS

11. סְתִירָה
12. תֵּירוּץ

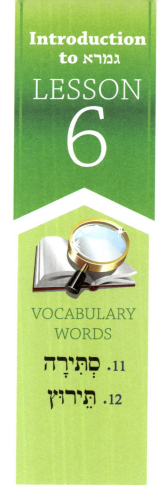

Once you start learning גְמָרָא, you will notice that the style of גְמָרָא is extremely different from the style of the מִשְׁנָה. Most מִשְׁנָיוֹת list הֲלָכוֹת without any discussion. The גְמָרָא, on the other hand, is nothing but discussions. One discussion will be trying to figure out what the הֲלָכָה would be in a particular situation and another might be trying to understand why the מִשְׁנָה said a certain הֲלָכָה. The one thing that they all have in common is that they are all discussions. Each topic of discussion is called a סוּגְיָא. In fact, once you start learning גְמָרָא, you might be asked (either by a friend, relative, or anyone in shul) "What סוּגְיָא are you learning?" What the person means to say is "What is the גְמָרָא (that you are learning) discussing?"

Illustration by Gadi Pollack for Beth Medrash Govoha © 2012

A סוּגְיָא is made up of שַׁקְלָא וְטַרְיָא. This is another way of referring to the discussion of the גְמָרָא. The שַׁקְלָא וְטַרְיָא can be divided into "steps." Each step is one piece of the discussion. If the גְמָרָא begins with a שְׁאֵלָה and then gives a תֵּירוּץ and then proves the תֵּירוּץ with a רְאָיָה, that would be three steps. If the גְמָרָא then gives a דְחִיָה to the רְאָיָה followed by a new רְאָיָה, we would have a total of five steps. Consider the following example:

Dovid asked his brother Chaim, "Do you know what Mommy is making for supper?" Chaim answered, "We are having hamburgers. I know this because I saw Mommy take some ground beef out of the freezer this morning." "Well," responded Dovid, "that doesn't mean anything; maybe we will be having meatballs!" Chaim ended all doubt when he said, "That's true, but she also went to the store and bought hamburger buns."

Look at the above story and find the same five steps described in the paragraph before it. Write the words of the story that show each of these five steps:

1) שְׁאֵלָה _____

2) תֵּירוּץ _____

3) רְאָיָה _____

4) דְּחִיָּה _____

5) רְאָיָה _____

REVIEW QUESTIONS:

1. What is the main difference in style between גְּמָרָא and מִשְׁנַיוֹת?

2. What is a סוּגְיָא?

3. What is שַׁקְלָא וְטַרְיָא? What are "steps"?

4. Can you think of an example of a discussion that is made up of steps?

Introduction to גמרא

LESSON 6 Review

KNOW YOUR FACTS:

1. How is the style of גְמָרָא different from that of מִשְׁנַיוֹת? _____
   _____

2. Define the following terms:
   א. סוּגְיָא _____
   ב. שַׁקְלָא וְטַרְיָא _____
   ג. A step _____

3. Please write a discussion that has 3 steps.
   _____
   _____
   _____
   _____
   _____

4. Please describe the 3 steps (ex. question, answer, statement, proof, etc.).
   Step 1 _____ Step 2 _____ Step 3 _____

VOCABULARY REVIEW:

_____ סְתִירָה
_____ דְּחִיָה
_____ תֵּירוּץ
_____ שְׁאֵלָה
_____ רְאָיָה

26 | © 2017 Bright Beginnings

MULTIPLE CHOICE:

A) facts	B) discussion	מִשְׁנַיוֹת:
A) facts	B) discussion	גְמָרָא:

MATCHING:

_____ 1. The entire discussion of the whole topic   A Step   א.

_____ 2. The back and forth of the discussion   שַׁקְלָא וְטַרְיָא   ב.

_____ 3. One piece of the discussion   סוּגְיָא   ג.

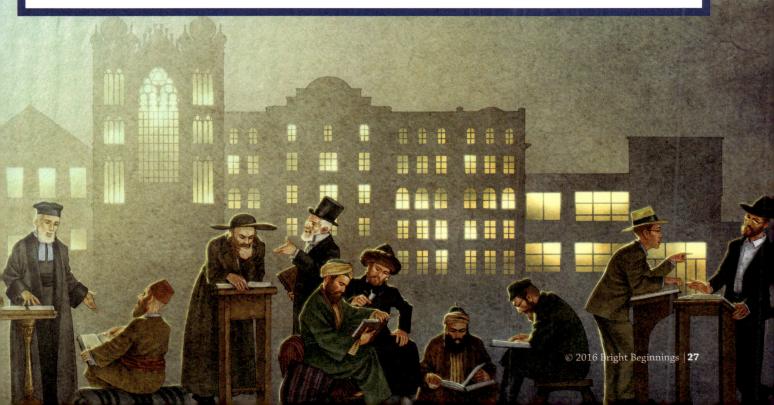

Introduction to גמרא
LESSON 7

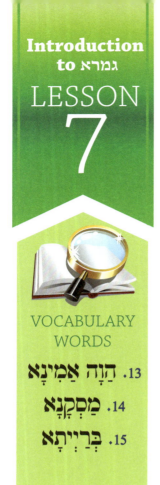

VOCABULARY WORDS

13. הֲוָה אַמִינָא
14. מַסְקְנָא
15. בְּרַיְיתָא

There are times, though, while learning גְמָרָא that you will be given straight הֲלָכוֹת with no discussion. This will usually be in one of two cases. Either you are learning a מִשְׁנָה (every גְמָרָא begins with a מִשְׁנָה because, after all, the גְמָרָא is just the explanation of the מִשְׁנָה) or you are learning a בְּרַיְיתָא. What is a בְּרַיְיתָא? I'm glad you asked:

When רַבִּי was putting together the מִשְׁנָיוֹת, it was not possible for him to collect each and every teaching of each and every תַּנָא. Some things had to be left out. Any teaching of a תַּנָא that was not included in a מִשְׁנָה is called a בְּרַיְיתָא. It is very common for the גְמָרָא to cite and quote בְּרַיְיתוֹת. A בְּרַיְיתָא is very useful because of the following rule: An אֲמוֹרָא is never allowed to argue with a תַּנָא unless there is another תַּנָא that agrees with him. Therefore, if one אֲמוֹרָא wants to prove himself right he will present a רְאָיָה (a proof) by quoting a מִשְׁנָה or בְּרַיְיתָא that says what he says. If the גְמָרָא wants to ask a קֻשְׁיָא on something that an אֲמוֹרָא has said, it will quote a מִשְׁנָה or a בְּרַיְיתָא that seems to say the opposite. One common type of תֵּירוּץ that can be given is to find another מִשְׁנָה or בְּרַיְיתָא that says the same thing as the אֲמוֹרָא.

Another time that a בְּרַיְיתָא will be brought is to ask a סְתִירָה. Often, we will find that a תַנָא says one thing in a מִשְׁנָה and he seems to say the opposite in a בְּרַיְיתָא. The גְמָרָא can answer by saying that our הֲוָה אָמִינָא of what the תַנָא is saying is incorrect. Instead, the גְמָרָא will correct our misunderstanding and if the idea is accepted, we call it the מַסְקָנָא.

It may sound confusing, but if you learn to take the גְמָרָא, one step at a time, you will see that you will not only understand the גְמָרָא but you will also enjoy it!

REVIEW QUESTIONS:

1. What are the two types of teachings of תַנָאִים?

2. What is a בְּרַיְיתָא? How is it different from a מִשְׁנָה?

3. Why is it important to know which teachings were taught by תַנָאִים and which were taught by אָמוֹרָאִים?

4. What restriction is there on an אָמוֹרָא?

5. What are some reasons why a גְמָרָא might quote a בְּרַיְיתָא?

Introduction to גמרא

LESSON 7 Review

KNOW YOUR FACTS:

1. A teaching of a תַּנָא can either be a _____ or a _____ .

2. With whom can an אֲמוֹרָא not argue? _____

3. He may only argue if _____ .

4. Explain how the teaching of a תַּנָא can be used for each of the following:

   קֻשְׁיָא _____

   רַאֲיָה _____

   תֵּירוּץ _____

   סְתִירָה _____

5. When the גְמָרָא assumes that a תַּנָא's statement is talking about a certain situation or case, it is called the _____ .

6. When the גְמָרָא comes to the proper conclusion about what the תַּנָא meant, it is called the _____ .

VOCABULARY REVIEW:

_____ סוּגְיָא

_____ תֵּירוּץ

_____ מַסְקְנָא

_____ שְׁאֵלָה

30 | © 2017 Bright Beginnings

TRUE OR FALSE:
(Circle T or F)

1. T F   Every teaching of a תַּנָא is found in a מִשְׁנָה.

2. T F   A בְּרַיְיתָא is a teaching of a תַּנָא.

3. T F   An אֲמוֹרָא may argue on a תַּנָא if there is another תַּנָא that supports him.

4. T F   A תַּנָא may not argue with a בְּרַיְיתָא.

5. T F   If we find a תַּנָא who said the same thing as an אֲמוֹרָא, it is a רְאָיָה for the אֲמוֹרָא.

6. T F   What we think at first is called the מַסְקָנָא.

7. T F   A מַסְקָנָא corrects a הֲוָה אֲמִינָא.

8. T F   The words of a תַּנָא can be used as a דְחִיָה.

VOCABULARY REVIEW:

_____ דְחִיָה

_____ בְּרַיְיתָא

_____ הֲוָה אֲמִינָא

_____ קֻשְׁיָא

This workbook is dedicated

to my dear wife, Rikki. Your wisdom, insight, and support enable me to strive for excellence. Our partnership in life permeates and brightens everything that I do. On behalf of all of the students who use this book, thank you for making it possible.

May the לימוד התורה which comes forth from this book, be a זכות for us to see נחת from our children, as we watch them develop into עובדי השם and לומדי תורה.

Aaron

RTI in Action

Oral Language Activities for K–2 Classrooms

Froma P. Roth, PhD, CCC-SLP

Dorothy P. Dougherty, MA, CCC-SLP

Diane R. Paul, PhD, CCC-SLP

Deborah Adamczyk, MA, CCC-SLP

The **American Speech-Language-Hearing Association (ASHA)** is the national professional, scientific, and credentialing association for audiologists, speech-language pathologists, and speech, language, and hearing scientists. ASHA works to promote the interests of these professionals and to advocate for people with communication disabilities.

RTI in Action: Oral Language Activities for K–2 Classrooms is published by the American Speech-Language-Hearing Association. ASHA publications are designed to support practitioners in their efforts to keep their knowledge and skills current in a broad range of administrative and clinical areas.

The opinions contained herein are the views of the contributors and are not to be construed as reflecting the official view of the American Speech-Language-Hearing Association.

ASHA grants permission, without request, to make and share up to 25 copies of particular activities featured in this product for professional use in classrooms and other work settings. Information provided in the book and on the CD may be printed and/or photocopied, providing that ASHA is credited as the publisher and copyright holder and that no alterations are made to the text for such use unless otherwise stipulated in content itself as being permissible. No other use, including translation, storage in a retrieval system, microfilming, recording, or posting to any site or page on the World Wide Web, or otherwise, is allowed without written permission from the publisher. For any such requests, contact permissions@asha.org.

Copyright 2010, American Speech-Language-Hearing Association
ISBN-10: 1580412335
ISBN-13: 9781580412339
Copies may be ordered from:
ASHA Product Sales: 888-498-6699
www.asha.org/shop

RTI in Action: Oral Language Activities for K–2 Classrooms
Table of Contents

About the Authors.. v

Acknowledgments.. vi

Introduction vii

Response to Intervention: Overview 1

Role of the Speech-Language Pathologist in Response to Intervention.. 5

Classroom Modifications to Support an RTI Instructional Model.......... 8

Instructional Strategies 14

Web Resources Related to RTI.. 22

Kindergarten Activities (Tiers 1, 2, and 3) 25

    Basic Concepts... 26

    Vocabulary 30

    Listening and Speaking.. 54

    Phonological Awareness... 102

    Print Knowledge... 114

    References.. 132

Grade 1 Activities (Tiers 1, 2, and 3) 135

    Basic Concepts... 136

    Vocabulary 140

    Listening and Speaking.. 170

    Phonological Awareness... 218

    Print Knowledge... 226

    References.. 230

Grade 2 Activities (Tiers 1, 2, and 3) 233

    Basic Concepts... 234

    Vocabulary 236

    Listening and Speaking.. 276

    Phonological Awareness... 336

    Print Knowledge... 340

    References.. 342

Appendices **345**

Appendix A: Cultural Competence Checklist 346

Appendix B: Developmental Milestone Checklist 347

Appendix C: Progress Monitoring for Individual Students 350

Appendix D: Progress Monitoring for Groups 351

Appendix E: Intensity Grid 352

Appendix F: Graphic Organizer—Spider Map 353

Appendix G: Graphic Organizer—Venn Diagram 354

Appendix H: Graphic Organizer—Story Map 355

Appendix I: Graphic Organizer—Definition Map 358

About the Authors

Froma P. Roth, PhD, CCC-SLP, is a Professor in the Department of Hearing and Speech Sciences at the University of Maryland, College Park. Her research program is directed at specifying relationships between oral language, emergent literacy, and early literacy. She is also engaged in implementing an RTI model of tier-based instruction in preschool settings. She serves as ASHA's liaison to the National Joint Committee on Learning Disabilities. Her publications emphasize issues related to the assessment and treatment of language and literacy problems from preschool through adolescence. She is the co-author of a basic textbook on speech and language intervention, entitled *Treatment Resource Manual for Speech-Language Pathology* (4th ed.; 2011, Delmar Cengage Learning).

Dorothy P. Dougherty, MA, CCC-SLP, is a speech-language pathologist who has worked with children and adults in school, clinic, and private practice settings for more than 30 years. Mrs. Dougherty has published more than 50 articles on speech and language development in magazines and newspapers both in the United States and internationally. She is the author of three other best-selling books to help parents enhance speech and language development of their children: *How to Talk to Your Baby: A Guide to Maximizing Your Child's Language and Learning Skills* (2001, Perigee Trade); *Teach Me How to Say It Right: Helping Your Child With Articulation Problems* (2005, Harbinger Publications); and *Talking on the Go: Everyday Activities to Enhance Speech and Language Development* (2007, American Speech-Language-Hearing Association).

Diane R. Paul, PhD, CCC-SLP, is the Director of Clinical Issues in Speech-Language Pathology for the American Speech-Language-Hearing Association (ASHA) and an ASHA Fellow. Dr. Paul provides professional consultation for speech-language pathologists, tracks speech-language pathology trends, develops education programs and products, and assists with the development of speech-language pathology practice policy documents. Dr. Paul is co-author of *Talking on the Go: Everyday Activities to Enhance Speech and Language Development* and the DVD, *Speech, Language, and Hearing Milestones: Birth to Age Five*, both best-selling ASHA products.

Deborah Adamczyk, MA, CCC-SLP, has worked as a practitioner, administrator, state consultant, and state compliance monitor in the school setting. She was a member of ASHA's Legislative Council, a site visitor for the Council on Academic Accreditation in Audiology and Speech-Language Pathology, and a member of other ASHA committees and national boards before joining the ASHA staff as the Director of School Services. She received her undergraduate degree from Edinboro State University of Pennsylvania and her master's degree and supervisory certification from the University of Pittsburgh.

Acknowledgments

Many people contributed their expertise, talent, and time to the preparation of this book. The authors greatly appreciate the work of Leslie Katz, Karen Taus, Andrea Moxley, Tarja Carter, Rebecca Bachman Smith, Donna A. Vernon, Jeremi Jones, Olga Zografos, Michael Cannon, Kathleen Halverson, Peter Hoffman, Brent Jacocks, Kathleen Whitmire, and Amy Albert.

Introduction

RTI in Action:
Oral Language Activities for K–2 Classrooms

The implementation of Response to Intervention (RTI) models is increasing across schools nationwide, from preschool through secondary grades. RTI uses multi-tiered instruction to improve student performance, prevent learning and behavior problems, and more accurately identify those students who may be eligible for special education services. In the past few years, the number of books about RTI also has multiplied dramatically. What makes this book unique?

This book is unique in four primary ways:

1. Designed to enhance K–2 students' oral language skills critical for literacy and academic learning

2. Offers practical oral language activities based on general education curricular standards

3. Provides specific, straightforward strategies to help speech-language pathologists (SLPs) and teachers modify instruction to meet the learning needs of students

4. Capitalizes on the power of collaboration between SLPs and teachers by using their combined expertise to maximize student learning

The American-Speech-Language-Hearing Association (ASHA) developed this book because of the strong, reciprocal connection between communication and learning. Effective communication skills are essential for literacy acquisition and learning in the primary grades. In turn, the ability to read and write advances higher level language and communication attainments in areas such as vocabulary, figurative language, and complex syntax.

Power of Collaboration

Collaborative instruction is a problem-solving process used by professionals to guide and refine educational practices. RTI provides the natural context for meaningful collaboration among classroom teachers, other school professionals, and SLPs (Coleman, Buysse, & Neitzel, 2006; Coleman, Roth, & West, 2009; National Joint Committee on Learning Disabilities, 2005). Working together, SLPs and teachers can give students the support they need to improve their communication skills. Improved communication enhances reading, writing, and academic skills. Language is not learned in a vacuum and therefore must be enhanced and reinforced on a daily basis, throughout a student's school day. SLPs and teachers form a critical partnership in student language learning. This book creates a framework for using the combined talents of SLPs and teachers in developing and strengthening students' oral language and literacy skills. It also provides explicit activities and instructional strategies that demonstrate the connection between oral communication and print knowledge.

Oral Language Activities Within an RTI Model

This book provides practical activities to build oral language skills in five major areas critical to success in language, literacy, academics, and social skills:

1. Basic Concepts
2. Vocabulary
3. Listening and Speaking
4. Phonological Awareness
5. Print Knowledge

We designed the book for SLPs and teachers to help all students in K–2 general education classrooms, including students at different developmental levels, monolingual and multilingual speakers, English language learners (ELLs),[1] and students with different learning styles, strengths, challenges, and disabilities.

Modifications may be needed in specific activities or instructional strategies depending on the needs and performance of individual students. Some of the activities within the book may be influenced by linguistic and cultural variances and familial norms (e.g., interpreting facial expressions, turn taking in conversation). We've included a cultural competence checklist to heighten awareness when working with students from diverse cultural backgrounds (see Appendix A).

---

[1] Several terms are used to refer to students who are learning English as a second language, including *English learners*, *dual language learners*, and *English language learners*. For the sake of clarity and consistency, the term *English language learners* will be used throughout this book to refer to these students.

Activities Organized by Grade and Curricular Standards

The oral language areas targeted in this book are mastered by the mid-elementary school grades and enable students to use language to acquire reading and writing skills and academic content knowledge. This book, therefore, is divided into three elementary grades—kindergarten, first, and second. Activities within each grade are aligned with language arts standards in the general education curriculum (i.e., state standards of learning/standards of performance). We reviewed the common core standards that are being adopted by many states as the foundation for instruction (www.corestandards.org) and many different K–2 curricula. We selected those communication skills that most commonly appeared and those that are predictive of achieving adequate yearly progress, academic success, and social competence (e.g., phonological awareness, vocabulary, summarization skills, and adapting messages for different listeners and situations).

We've also included a developmental milestone checklist for listening, talking, reading, and writing for students in kindergarten through second grade. The checklist will give you an idea about what to expect for students at each grade (see Appendix B). Communication tips at the end of the checklist can be shared with families, caregivers, and day care providers.

Tiers of Instruction

The activities are presented within an RTI model with multiple tiers of instruction. The book provides an overview of RTI and describes the role of the SLP within an RTI model.

For each activity, we describe three tiers of instruction:

Tier 1 activities are geared for the whole classroom. The activities are based on research about the way students learn language. Tier 1 activities provide high-quality instruction and cover a breadth of learning opportunities. Tier 1 activities may be tailored to meet the learning needs of individual students.

Tier 2 activities are designed for in-class instruction with small groups. Instruction at this level is more differentiated and intended for students who require additional support to successfully access the curriculum.

Tier 3 activities provide further differentiated instruction for smaller groups or one-on-one instruction. Activities and supports at this level are more intensive, frequent, and individualized than Tier 1 and Tier 2.

Instructional Strategies

Students at Tier 2 or Tier 3 may need more prompting, visual or auditory scaffolds, or other supports to enhance instruction. The book offers examples of ways each Tier 1 activity can be systematically and intentionally modified for Tier 2 and Tier 3 instructional levels. Two Tier 2 and two Tier 3 modifications are provided for each Tier 1 activity. A comprehensive list of instructional strategies is included in the book (see pp. 14–21). These strategies offer numerous ways to scaffold instruction according to student needs. SLPs and teachers may use the strategies suggested for a particular activity or select others from the list. All of the strategies also can be used for general instruction at the Tier 1 level. SLPs and teachers work together at all tiers of instruction to provide instruction, observe students in class, modify or create new activities, select new strategies, and evaluate student performance. We've included charts to assist with progress monitoring for individual students and for groups of students (see Appendices C and D).

Where to Use Activities

The activities offer a variety of ways that SLPs and teachers can work together in the classroom. The activities also can be used in the lunchroom, on field trips, or in any setting where students interact. We give suggestions for children's books, offer academic subject–specific examples (e.g., science, math, social studies, art), and show ways to incorporate different themes (e.g., holidays, weather, transportation) into daily lessons. We include some bonus activities that supplement instructional activities. Sometimes we provide links to related websites. At the time of publication, all links were active. However, if the links do not work for you, you may design a similar activity or search for other links that address the objective.

Universal Design for Learning and Classroom Modifications

The book provides additional information to help SLPs and teachers build students' oral language skills:

- Overview of principles of universal design for learning (UDL) that demonstrates the connection between UDL and an RTI instructional model.
- Specific ways to adapt the classroom environment to enhance learning. This section includes modifications to improve classroom acoustics, suggests accommodations for students who may benefit from assistive technology, and highlights the importance of instructional feedback.

Other Ways to Use This Book

SLPs can use information from this book for in-service training in schools about RTI. A sample PowerPoint™ presentation and handouts are included on a CD as a resource with the book to help you with in-service training about RTI, the role of the SLP, and the link between oral language and learning. The introductory material, list of instructional strategies, and RTI activities provide a source of information for teachers and other education professionals. Information also may be shared with administrators to advocate for more collaborative opportunities between SLPs and teachers. The activities and instructional strategies also may be useful for families, caregivers, and day care providers. We've included a list of ASHA and other web-based resources on page 22 related to RTI to supplement the information from this book. You may change the PowerPoint® presentation to fit the needs of your audience (e.g., staff, parents, families, caregivers, day care providers).

References

Coleman, M. R., Buysse, V., & Neitzel, J. (2006). *Recognition and response: An early intervening system for young children at-risk for learning disabilities* [Full report]. Chapel Hill: The University of North Carolina, Frank Porter Graham Child Development Institute.

Coleman, M. R., Roth, F. P., & West, T. (2009). *Roadmap to Pre-K RTI: Applying response to intervention in preschool settings*. New York, NY: National Center for Learning Disabilities.

National Joint Committee on Learning Disabilities. (2005). Responsiveness to intervention and learning disabilities. *Learning Disabilities Quarterly, 28*, 249–260. Available from www.asha.org/policy.

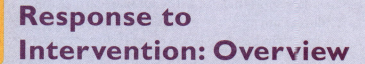

Response to Intervention: Overview

Response to Intervention (RTI) is a multi-tiered approach used to identify students at risk for poor learning outcomes and to provide specialized instruction and strategies to address learning needs within the general education setting. Within an RTI model, teams provide evidence-based interventions, monitor student progress, and adjust interventions depending on student responsiveness. RTI is a process of support for all students and is sanctioned in the re-authorization of the Individuals with Disabilities Education Improvement Act of 2004 (IDEA 2004).

The rationale for an RTI approach is based on converging evidence that an aptitude–achievement discrepancy model is a wait-to-fail approach, does not reliably distinguish between specific learning disabilities and low achievement, does not predict student response to remediation efforts, and does not adequately guide instructional planning and implementation (Fuchs & Fuchs, 1998; Fuchs, Mock, Morgan, & Young, 2003). In contrast, the focus of RTI is on student learning over time rather than strictly on a student's achievement at a single point in time. Thus, RTI aims specifically at prevention, early identification of struggling students or students at risk for learning and other disabilities, and above all, quality education for all students. These aims are achieved through the delivery of high-quality classroom instruction to all students that is implemented with fidelity (a practice is used as intended), with ongoing progress monitoring, and by providing differentiated classroom instruction for students to avert or mitigate the need for special education services.

RTI is a collaborative problem-solving team process; teachers, speech-language pathologists (SLPs), and other related service providers work in concert with families to identify a concern, analyze the learner's problem, develop and implement a support plan, and monitor its effectiveness so that continuous adjustments can be made. Its multi-tiered design provides the appropriate intensity of instruction necessary to improve each individual's achievement. The most widely used RTI model includes three tiers (Coleman, Roth, & West, 2009).

Tier 1

At the Tier 1 level of instruction, all students receive high-quality, classroom-wide instruction in the general education setting with an evidence-based core curriculum. The classroom teacher uses differentiated instruction to teach the core curriculum concepts and skills. Differentiated instruction is responsive instruction rather than "one-size-fits all" teaching (Tomlinson, 2003). It involves the use of varied approaches and degrees of scaffolding to teach the same core concepts to meet the learning needs of different children.

The aim of differentiated instruction is to optimize each student's learning potential and increase the likelihood that each student will learn as much as possible about the core curriculum. Universal screenings are administered at the beginning and end of a school year to obtain baseline levels of each student's performance and to guide classroom instruction. Progress monitoring is used on an ongoing and frequent basis (e.g., weekly, biweekly, monthly) to assess student learning progress toward mastery of important learning outcomes. These measures also provide objective data for evaluating the effectiveness of instruction/intervention. In progress monitoring, the assessments are brief; the criteria for "adequate" and "inadequate" progress are preset, and the results are charted and analyzed regularly by the collaborative school team (sometimes called the collaborative problem-solving team) to inform instruction and a student's need for additional services.

Tier 2

In Tier 2, students with known risk factors or whose performance or rate of progress lags behind their peers receive more intensive and specialized prevention and remediation (i.e., differentiated instruction) within the general education classroom. Sometimes, instruction may involve teaching prerequisite skills from an earlier developmental stage. These additional learning opportunities are provided in both large and small group formats with increased emphasis on differentiated instruction. Progress monitoring is generally conducted more frequently to inform instructional and behavioral modifications.

Tier 3

Tier 3 is designed for students who do not make the expected progress with the support of Tier 2 interventions. Two activities generally occur at this tier, either sequentially or simultaneously: (1) More intensive, frequent, and individualized interventions are implemented and may be conducted on a one-to-one basis with the student. Frequently, instruction may involve teaching prerequisite skills from an earlier developmental stage. Repeated progress monitoring continues to guide decisions about the student's educational program; (2) The student is referred for a comprehensive evaluation conducted by a multidisciplinary team to determine eligibility for special education services.

According to Fuchs (2003), Speece and Case (2001), and others, an RTI model has the potential of reducing classification errors of sensitivity and specificity that have plagued the aptitude–achievement discrepancy approach. Lack of sensitivity results in overidentification of students because the assessment methods do not adequately differentiate between students who have disabilities from those who do not (e.g., English language learner [ELL] students, or students from economically impoverished backgrounds). Lack of specificity results in underidentification of students, as the testing procedures fail to identify students who have disabilities.

Through its emphasis on prevention and early prereferral educational intervention, it is projected that 80% of at-risk students can meet educational achievement expectations through Tier 1; an additional 10% will attain grade-level performance with Tier 2 assistance, and approximately 10%–15% will require Tier 3 supports, which may include a referral for special educational testing (Fuchs, 2003). In sum, RTI is based on a "dual discrepancy;" that is, despite high-quality instruction *and* remedial instruction, a student does not progress at the expected rate (Fuchs, 2003).

Principles of Universal Design for Learning

The Universal Design for Learning (UDL) framework is consistent with an RTI model as both embody the provision of equal learning opportunities for all students, including those with disabilities, different cognitive profiles, and students who are ELLs (Rose & Meyer, 2000).UDL provides a way of thinking about instruction that calls for modifying and shaping strategies to address a wide range of differences seen in today's students. Indeed, today's classrooms are enormously diverse, with students from various cultures who present a wide range of learning styles, attitudes, specialized needs, and life experiences. Three main principles provide the basis of UDL:

1. **Multiple means of representation**: Various methods must be available to the student to access curriculum content (e.g., traditional textbooks, CD-ROMs, talk-to-text media, digital media, word processing).

2. **Multiple means of expression:** Various methods and modalities must be available to assess a student's mastery of curriculum content (e.g., oral expression, written expression, talk-to-text computer programs, signs).

3. **Multiple means of engagement:** Students must be provided with enough successful learning opportunities to maintain adequate motivation for learning.

UDL strongly advocates for the use of technology-based educational resources (e.g., assistive technologies) to expand the learning opportunities for all students (Dalton, Pisha, Eagelton, Coyne, & Deysher, 2002; Strangeman, 2003). These principles call for the reconceptualization of curriculum from the "one size fits all" model to curricula that are flexible enough to accommodate the unique learning needs of individual students.

References

Coleman, M. R., Roth, F. P., & West, T. (2009). *Roadmap to Pre-K RTI: Applying response to intervention in preschool settings.* New York, NY: National Center for Learning Disabilities.

Dalton, B., Pisha, B., Eagleton, M., Coyne, P., & Deysher, S. (2002). *Engaging in the text* [Final report to the U.S. Department of Education]. Peabody, MA: CAST.

Fuchs, L. S. (2003). Assessing intervention responsiveness: Conceptual and technical issues. *Learning Disabilities Research & Practice, 18,* 172–186.

Fuchs, L. S., & Fuchs, D. (1998). Treatment validity: A unifying concept for reconceptualizing the identification of learning disabilities. *Learning Disabilities Research & Practice, 13,* 204–219.

Fuchs, D., Mock, D., Morgan, P. L., & Young, C. L. (2003). Responsiveness-to-intervention: Definitions, evidence, and implications for the learning disabilities construct. *Learning Disabilities Research & Practice, 18,* 157–171.

Individuals with Disabilities Education Improvement Act of 2004 (PL 108-446), 20 U.S.C. §1400 *et seq.* Available from http://idea.ed.gov/download/statute.html.

Rose, D. H., & Meyer, A. (2000). Universal design for individual differences. *Educational Leadership, 58,* 39–43.

Speece, D. L., & Case, L. P. (2001). Classification in context: An alternative approach to identifying early reading disabilities. *Journal of Educational Psychology, 93,* 735–749.

Strangeman, N. (2003). Strategy instruction goes digital: Two teachers' perspectives on digital texts with embedded learning supports. *Reading Online, 6,* 9.

Tomlinson, C. A. (2003). Differentiating instruction for academic diversity. In J. M. Cooper (Ed.), *Classroom teaching skills* (7th ed., pp. 149–180). Boston, MA: Houghton Mifflin.

Role of the Speech-Language Pathologist in Response to Intervention

The SLP has many skills that are well matched to the RTI process (ASHA, 2010). SLPs use a variety of assessment processes, including curriculum-based assessment, standardized assessment, and dynamic assessment, which uses a pretest–teach–test format that embeds into the assessment process (Lidz & Peña, 2009). The SLP may be instrumental in identifying those students in the general education classrooms who are at risk due to difficulties with phonemic awareness, comprehension, and other spoken and written language skills that affect academic success. The SLP can help teams understand the link between spoken and written language, demonstrate how language weaknesses affect literacy, and plan goals and strategies to address these weaknesses. However, given the demands on SLPs to engage in both general education as well as special education initiatives, it is important that consideration be given to total workload when assuming responsibilities. ASHA has information available regarding a workload approach to managing SLP caseloads in schools at www.asha.org/slp/schools/resources/schools_resources_caseload.htm. A workload approach justifies and gives support for indirect activities and collaboration in addition to direct student services (ASHA, 2002).

The SLP also can be a part of the team creating RTI plans using intensity grids (see Appendix E). An intensity grid designates strategies for different tiers of instruction. The grid also specifies who provides the strategy, how progress will be monitored, and the amount of time students will receive specialized instruction.

The SLP is able to play a role at each tier of instruction.

Tier 1

The SLP can assist the classroom teacher in Tier 1 in the following ways:
- Screen to identify students at risk for academic and social problems that may be a result of communication needs. SLPs assess vocabulary development, phonemic awareness, print knowledge, comprehension, and other oral language skills that influence literacy.
- Interpret other screening and assessment results. An SLP can collaborate with teachers to review achievement tests, curriculum-based assessments, and other data to determine if a student's problems may be related to communication skills.
- Analyze the communication expectations within the classroom. Understanding classroom expectations can help teams in selecting individual adaptations, such as modifying pace, content, or length of instruction.

SLP Role

- Provide suggestions for enhancing the physical learning environment with language- and literacy-rich materials and experiences.
- Help teams understand the links between spoken and written language.
- Model communication-facilitating strategies in the classroom.
- Assist in identifying research-based interventions for classroom goal acquisition.
- Suggest classroom accommodations.
- Provide practice materials for teachers' use in the classroom.
- Assist in creating data collection systems for progress monitoring.
- Participate in literacy audit processes that determine the effectiveness of literacy instruction, and recommend ways to improve instruction.
- Provide staff development programs on topics such as the language basis of literacy and language or communication-facilitating strategies for classroom teachers.
- Assist teachers in breaking down tasks into smaller parts.
- Help teachers identify causal factors and prerequisite skills for students with difficulties with spoken or written language.
- Train classroom assistants/aides to support communication in the classroom.
- Identify language weaknesses that may be contributing to students' behavioral problems.
- Help families understand the connection between language and literacy and ways they can support oral language and literacy in the home.

Tier 2

The SLP can assist the classroom teacher in Tier 2 in the following ways:
- Conduct more in-depth screening for struggling students.
- Analyze curricular materials to determine adaptations and modifications to help students.
- Assist in making decisions about individual students' needs for lesser or greater levels of instructional support.
- Pre-teach or re-teach vital curricular concepts that may be related to language for individual or small groups of students.
- Provide short-term instruction either in the classroom or as a pull-out service for small group or individual students with spoken or written communication needs.
- Participate in the progress monitoring for specific groups or individual students.

Tier 3

The SLP can assist the classroom teacher in Tier 3 in the following ways:
- Provide more frequent or more intense instruction in language-related areas for students with spoken or written communication needs.
- Conduct more intense assessments with struggling students.
- Identify factors that would trigger a referral for a full multidisciplinary evaluation.

The success of RTI depends on strong collaboration and cooperation among all team members. Each member brings different strengths to the team. Those strengths and skills should be identified, respected, and applied to ensure student success. There are no uniform criteria for determining the duration of Tier 2 or Tier 3 services. Criteria vary within and across schools, districts, regions, and states and are frequently influenced by teachers' judgment and learning standards, as well as by characteristics of individual learners. ASHA provides an online resource list with further information about the role of the SLP and RTI at www.asha.org/slp/schools/prof-consult/RtoI.htm.

References

American Speech-Language-Hearing Association. (2002). *A workload analysis approach for establishing speech-language caseload standards in the school: Position statement.* Available from www.asha.org/policy.

American Speech-Language-Hearing Association. (2010). *Roles and responsibilities of speech-language pathologists in schools* [Professional issues statement]. Available from www.asha.org/policy.

Lidz, C. S., & Peña, E. D. (2009). Response to intervention and dynamic assessment: Do we just appear to be speaking the same language? *Seminars in Speech and Language, 30,* 121–133.

Classroom Modifications

Classroom Modifications to Support an RTI Instructional Model

This section of the book provides suggestions for modifying the classroom environment to maximize all students' access, participation, and progress in the general education setting, including students with special needs, students who use assistive technology, and ELLs. Many of the strategies for these populations also are adaptable for any student in need of special modifications and/or adaptations. These suggestions for improving the learning environment support an RTI instructional model and may be foundational to the application of the UDL principles. We conclude this section by discussing ways to use instructional feedback to enhance student performance.

A student's ability to understand what is being said in the classroom is vital for learning. Unfortunately, this ability can be reduced in a noisy classroom. Poor classroom acoustics occur when the background noise and/or the amount of reverberation in the classroom are so high that they interfere with teaching and learning. Noisy ventilation and lighting systems, hard wall and floor surfaces, playground and other outside noise, and classroom activity are typical sources of noise in the educational setting. There are strategies that can help students better understand what they hear. The physical environment also can be modified to improve the classroom and make it more conducive to learning as illustrated in Table 1.

Table 1. Classroom Modifications to Support an RTI Instructional Model

Provide both verbal and written instruction for lessons and homework.
Use gestures to gain a student's attention and clarify what you are saying.
Face students while speaking, but do not stand in front of a bright window that may distract the student's view of your face.
Seat students who need special help near where you teach and away from the noisiest part of the classroom.
Offer "listening buddies"—other students who can help to clarify missed information.
Talk to students about noise and demonstrate how it can be difficult to hear when many children are talking at the same time.

Classroom Modifications

Reduce classroom noise.

- Place rugs or carpet in the room.
- Hang window treatments such as curtains or blinds.
- Hang soft materials such as flags, corkboard, or student art on the walls.
- Place tables at an angle around the room to interfere with the pathways of sound.
- Turn off noisy equipment when it is not in use.
- Keep windows and doors closed when possible.
- Replace noisy light fixtures.
- Place latex-free soft tips on the bottoms of chairs and tables.
- Avoid open classrooms where many classes are taught in a large space.
- Avoid dividing the class into groups where one group is listening to audiovisual equipment such as the TV and the other group is listening to the teacher.
- Remind visitors to the classroom that they should not be talking when the teacher is talking.
- Consider moving the teacher's desk away from the front of the room, into a corner.

Arrange the room to provide the teacher with as much proximity to the students as possible. Create walkways so you can get to any students with as few steps as possible.

Develop a routine for rearranging the classroom for different activities. Once students know the routine, you can give the signal and create a new room arrangement for small group work, full classroom projects, and quiet independent work time.

Post pictorial schedules for the day's activities within the classroom. Post the schedule near a clock to bring attention to the concept of time.

Use visual prompts for journaling. Post a magazine or clip art picture to help students begin the journal entry of the day.

Develop posters to prompt students. For example, make a poster to help students know what to do when they don't understand a word they've read.

Classroom Modifications

Make or find strategy bookmarks and post them on students' desks. The bookmarks can include hints such as *make connections*, *visualize*, *question*, *predict*, and *self-correct* to improve comprehension.

Post symbols or pictures on students' desktops as guides.

- Use a red and green card for students who tend to call out for help. Instruct students to put the red side of the card face up on the desk when they need help, then turn it back to the green side when they receive help.

- Facilitate turn taking by giving students a certain number of tokens on the desk. They turn in a token each time they talk, but can only talk when they have tokens. Students who are reluctant to talk could be encouraged to spend all of their tokens within a specific time period.

- Use individual pictorial checklists for students who have difficulty sequencing or completing tasks.

Make a poster about the "five finger test" for choosing a book that's just right. Tell students to:

- *Choose a book and read the first page or two.*
- *Put one finger up for each word you don't know.*
- *If five of your fingers go up while you are reading, choose another book.*
- *If only 2 or 3 fingers go up, then you've found a book that is just right.*

Provide a graphic summary for directions. In addition, give a whole set of plans—one step at a time with a picture and a few words for each step.

Mouth an unknown word or phrase as a visual prompt. Make the mouth movements but don't say the word(s). This draws students' attention and helps them to recall the target.

Provide verbal prompts, such as the first sound or first word to help with recall of target words and phrases.

**Classroom
Modifications**

Classroom Adaptations for Students With Special Needs

Special educators, including SLPs and audiologists, work collaboratively to understand and implement specific classroom modifications and adaptations for students with special needs. Adaptations may include changing seating, work surfaces, and materials; providing additional wait time for responses; alternating means of demonstrating knowledge; addressing sensory issues; and modifying reading levels. Such adaptations align with the UDL principles. Adaptations that are good for **all** students but specifically for students with special needs include the following:

- Decrease auditory and visual distractions, especially during difficult tasks.

- Provide appropriate seating and place students in close proximity to where most of the teaching takes place.

- Develop a routine for getting students ready for new information.

- Schedule academic tasks earlier in the day.

- Increase structure for initial skill development.

- Increase active participation.

- Provide opportunities for physical activity prior to instructional tasks.

- Modify task and material length.

- Get students' attention before giving directions/instructions.

- Shorten assignments.

- Pair written words with verbal and visual cues.

- Provide frequent repetition.

- Use concrete examples as much as possible.

- Monitor students' comprehension.

- Adjust to students' rate of learning.

- Use manipulatives (e.g., blocks, letter forms)

- Simplify the language of the lesson.

- Provide appropriate feedback and reinforcement at regular intervals.

Assistive Technology in the Classroom

Some students may require assistive technology (AT) to help with learning. UDL principles advocate for needed technology. AT may range from simple adaptations to keyboards and special software to amplification systems or high-tech communication devices with features such as a portable text to speech, graphic/text to speech programmable for individual needs, digitized speech dynamic displays, keyboard communication devices, talking screens, or other software. Students using these devices are most often students with an individualized education program (IEP) or a 504 plan. Work with the team to understand the technology, and to ensure that it is used appropriately. Assist the team to understand how AT can be used to improve classroom performance. It is also important to communicate with the team about communication demands within the classroom that need consideration. All team members need training to understand and use AT appropriately and consistently.

Classroom Enhancements for English Language Learners

The term *English language learner* (*ELL*) refers to a broad group of individuals. You may be working with students who just came to this country with no experience in English and students who were born in this country who have been exposed to small amounts of English. There may be differences in students' development of their "social" language system and their "academic" language system, and there may be a gap between the two systems. Families from different cultures may have a different experience and understanding of traditions, expectations regarding classroom behavior, education, and life activities.

Various classroom accommodations may be used to engage ELLs more and help them access the curriculum:

- Pre-teach specific key words and concepts.

- Provide dictionaries of a student's native or primary language.

- Consider the background of the students when planning appointments, outings, holiday celebrations, and snacks.

- Use classroom materials that show various cultures.

- Have books available in the classroom in a student's native language.

- Provide materials in the parents' preferred language so that they may assist their child in oral language and literacy development at home.

- Assign a peer buddy.

Instructional Feedback

Teacher feedback often is identified as the most important instructional practice affecting student learning and student success (Bohn, Roehrig, & Pressley, 2004; Topping & Ferguson, 2005). Effective instructional feedback has the following characteristics:

1. It is target-specific (Roth & Worthington, 2005), providing a student with specific information about why a response is correct or incorrect (e.g., "*Very good, you described the story events in the order in which they happened*");

2. It is stated in positive terms, even when a student's answer is incorrect, creating a welcoming classroom climate (Rubies-Davies, 2007);

3. It invites students to elaborate/explain their contributions. This increases student participation in learning and decreases the proportion of teacher-driven instruction (high rates of directive and closed-ended questions), a characteristic of highly effective teachers (Rubies-Davies, 2007); and

4. The verbal and nonverbal aspects (e.g., facial expressions, body language, volume, emphasis) of feedback messages are consistent with one another to avoid ambiguity and misunderstanding.

Consistent with an RTI instructional model and UDL principles, providing instructional feedback is another means of motivating students and helping them access the curricular content.

References

Bohn, C. M., Roehrig, A. D., & Pressley, M. (2004). The first days of school in the classrooms of two more effective and four less effective primary-grades teachers. *Elementary School Journal, 104,* 269–287.

Roth, F. P., & Worthington, C. K. (2005). *Treatment resource manual in speech-language pathology* (3rd ed.). New York, NY: Delmar Cengage Learning.

Rubies-Davies, C. M. (2007). Classroom interactions: Exploring the practices of high- and low-expectation teachers. *British Journal of Educational Psychology, 77,* 289–306.

Topping, K., & Ferguson, N. (2005). Effective literacy teaching behaviors. *Journal of Research in Reading, 28,* 125–143.

Strategies

Instructional Strategies

Scaffolding Instruction

This section presents instructional strategies, or scaffolds, for all tiers to help students learn and retain information. A scaffold is simply a bridge between what the student knows and what the student is learning. Scaffolds can be used individually or in combination, with the amount of scaffolding decreasing gradually as the student's level of mastery increases.

The activities presented throughout this book illustrate all of the listed strategies for scaffolding instruction, but this list is not an exhaustive one. Teachers should select appropriate strategies based on an analysis of a student's skills that identifies problem areas, determines the cause of the problems, and identifies specific skills that need to be mastered.

Although these strategies are provided primarily for Tier 2 and Tier 3 levels of instruction for students who need more help, they also may be used at the Tier 1 level for general instruction for the whole classroom. In some cases, teachers may choose activities and strategies from another grade level. The tiering of instruction is flexible and movement across tiers is bidirectional; for example, some students may benefit from a Tier 2 level of instruction after receiving Tier 3.

Providing Instructional Feedback

Regardless of the strategies used, teachers should provide immediate, frequent, and relevant feedback to students. By correcting student errors when they are first made, it is less likely that errors will become internalized and therefore repeated. The student also should have the opportunity to reflect on the feedback, make adjustments, and then revise information or try the task again.

If students continue to have difficulties following intensive and individualized Tier 3 instruction, they should be referred to a multidisciplinary team for a comprehensive assessment and evaluation.

14 RTI in Action • STRATEGIES

Adjust Pace

Adjust the overall lesson pace so that it is slow and deliberate. Give students more time to respond.

Advance Organizers (Visual/Graphic)

Use a metacognitive technique that enables students to access prior knowledge and understand the basic organization of the material to be learned prior to actually learning the materials. Examples include semantic maps, thinking maps, and story charts. Sample advanced organizers are included in Appendices F, G, H, and I.

Use these organizers to provide a visual tool to help students acquire new vocabulary and concepts. Examples include:

- **Attribute Web:** Use a "web" type of diagram to list and organize attributes that go with a concept as a way of helping students learn vocabulary words.

- **Venn Diagram:** A Venn diagram is made of intersecting circles that have separate as well as overlapping sections and demonstrates similarities and differences between two concepts or events.

- **Sequence Map:** A sequence map is filled in with sentences or pictures that represent the sequence of events in learning a concept.

- **Spider Map:** Place the overall topic in the center. Underlying concepts radiate from the overall topic in the center.

Alternative Response Mode

Change response mode to simplify the task. For example, the response can be a change from an expressive to a receptive task by requiring students to demonstrate comprehension rather than expression of a word or concept. Simplify a task by asking students to express thoughts while speaking rather than by writing them on paper.

Assistive Technology (AT)

Use any assistive devices that may help students learn and function more effectively (e.g., hearing aids, individual or classroom amplification devices, glare reduction screens, voice recognition software, tape recorders, or PCs and other computer software).

Strategies

Auditory Cues

Provide auditory cues such as key words, brief oral descriptions, or verbal directions to help students recall information to support information they receive visually. Examples include:

- **Associated word cue**: Provide a word connected by meaning. For example: *fork and _____; old and _____.*

- **Beginning sound**: Provide a written or verbal presentation of the beginning sound or syllable of the target words.

- **Category**: Provide the group or subgroup membership for the target word.

- **Context**: Provide a common usage in a phrase or sentence with the target word omitted.

- **Description**: Provide information describing the attributes of the target words, such as parts, color, or size.

- **Different meaning**: Provide information using the target word in another context.

- **Function**: Provide information concerning the purpose or use of the target word.

- **Rhyming or similar-sound words**: Provide a word that sounds like or rhymes with the target word.

Change Response Length

Ask students to give fewer or shorter answers.

Check for Understanding

Ask questions frequently during the lesson to check understanding and, if necessary, provide immediate instruction. For example, ask questions after students read a few pages rather than after students read the entire book.

Completion/Cloze Questions or Statements

Provide the beginning of a question or statement. Students fill in the blanks with the missing word or phrase.

Comprehension Probe

Ask students for a meaning or example of a key word or concept before, during, or after reading or teaching a new concept.

16   RTI in Action • STRATEGIES

Strategies

Concentrated Instruction

Focus on a small set of skills rather than introducing all of the instructional objectives for a skill at the same time.

Concrete Materials

Present concepts using hands-on learning experiences that actively engage students. The materials are concrete and directly available to the senses. For example, tangible objects can be used to explore sights, sound, smell, movement, or touch.

Connecting to Prior Knowledge

Question students about a new skill or concept before teaching it in order to activate any relevant prior knowledge in the students' minds to help them focus on the materials to be presented.

Different Representations

Connect and integrate different abstract and concrete forms or representations of the same concepts.

Different Stimuli

Provide additional opportunities to practice a new skill with different materials in a variety of contexts.

Double Dose of Instruction

Provide additional instruction time. Introduce skills during the first session and then re-teach with added practice during subsequent sessions.

Elaboration

Give students detailed explanations or additional information about concepts.

Examples and Nonexamples

Provide, or have students generate, examples and nonexamples that do or do not represent the particular concept or skill.

Forced-Choice Questions

Provide two possible answers in question format from which students choose one (e.g., *Is it large or small?*).

Strategies

Imitation

Ask students to copy your gesture(s) or spoken or written word(s) (e.g., students imitate a word or definition).

Independent Practice

Give an assignment to encourage students to practice target skills on their own. Independent practice may be done in class or for homework.

Matching

Produce a stimulus and ask students to respond or choose an answer that is the same or matches the stimuli (e.g., ask students to match a word with its definition).

Memory Aid

Provide methods that assist students in understanding and completing a task or remembering and retrieving information. Examples include:

Mnemonic aids: Simple cueing sounds, letters, or words such as:

- **Acronyms**: Demonstrate an aid in which students use the first letter of a group of words to form a new word.

- **Acrostics:** Demonstrate an aid in which the first letter of each word can make a sentence.

Chunking: Separate lists of words or categories of information into smaller units.

Rehearsal: Instruct students to say the words they need to remember over and over.

Mental Imagery

Encourage students to form visual images of what they are reading or while learning a new concept. For example, ask students to picture a setting or a character described in a text. While teaching homonyms, encourage students to picture *the flour used for making a cake, and a flower that grows in a garden.*

Metacognitive Thinking Stems

Provide students with a structuring mechanism or support to assist in improving organization skills and completing an assignment. Teach students to plan the steps necessary to complete a task, order those steps into the correct sequence, and monitor progress on those steps. Ask students to complete phrases such as *I'm thinking, I'm noticing, I'm wondering, I'm seeing,* and *I'm feeling.* Encourage students to state and complete their own metacognitive thinking stems.

Strategies

Modeling

Provide a demonstration of what students are expected to do or provide the correct response.

Multiple Choice

Ask a question and give students several choices, one of which is correct.

Multiple Modalities

Use multiple modalities (e.g., auditory, visual, tactile) when presenting directions, explanations, and instructional content.

Negative Practice

Give examples that are incorrect and ask students to correct them.

Paraphrasing

Prompt students to restate or reword information presented.

Peer Tutoring

Pair students with similar or dissimilar abilities to practice skills that have been presented earlier.

Previewing

Before reading or presenting a new concept, preview the words and/or concepts the students will be learning. This may help students learn new vocabulary and comprehend the instruction more easily.

Repeated Exposure

Use vocabulary words and concepts often and in various contexts across the curriculum throughout the school day.

Repeated Practice

Give students additional opportunities to practice a new skill or concept using the same stimuli. Make student practice sessions interesting by using game-like activities or incorporating themes or topics that students finds interesting.

Repeated Reading

Reread the same story or text on several occasions rather than switching to a new story or text.

RTI in Action • Strategies 19

Strategies

Restricted-Choice Questions

Expand student knowledge by asking yes/no questions rather than open-ended questions.

Role Play

Assume the roles of characters and use dialogue or actions to portray the roles with students.

Simplify

Reduce linguistic complexity of the instruction or question.

Step-by-Step

Break down complex or conceptually difficult concepts into simple steps. Use a poster or handout that lists the main steps.

Story Starters

Present open phrases such as, *Once upon a time, there was a girl who lived in the city…*, and ask students to add information or make up a story.

Think Aloud

Demonstrate how to talk through the steps of a problem-solving strategy. Encourage students to "think aloud" to improve understanding and internalize the steps.

Turn and Talk

Designate student partners and instruct them to "Turn and talk" to their partner about an issue or idea, or to make a prediction with a partner. Partners listen to each other and focus on the topic, sharing ideas in one minute or less. Ensure that students adhere to the short time frame and signal the students back to the group after the talk.

Visual Cues

Provide visual information (e.g., written directions, instructions) to support the information that students hear. Examples include:

- **Color code**: Use colored highlights or highlighter tape to emphasize important information.

- **Gesture**: Provide a pantomime or hand gesture that demonstrates the target word or concept.

- **Facial Expression:** Use varying facial expressions to cue students.

- **Icon:** Provide a symbol that gives a cue for the word or concept.

- **Written**: Use the word, part of the word, or the initial consonant sound to provide a print cue.

20   RTI in Action • STRATEGIES

Strategies

Visual Dictionary

Use pictures to define words or concepts.

Word Bank

Create a list of words and definitions with students. Lists may be organized by category or subject. Review words often and encourage students to refer to the word bank for assistance.

Selected References for Instructional Strategies

The following sources were useful in identifying and describing the instructional strategies.

Brown-Chidsey, R., & Steege, M. W. (2005). *Response to intervention principles and strategies for effective practice.* New York, NY: Guilford.

Hagan, J. S., McDonald, S. B., & Meyer, J. (1990). *The speech and language classroom intervention manual.* Columbia, MO: Hawthorne Educational Services.

Harmin, M. (1995). *Inspiring active learning: Strategies of instruction.* White Plains, NY: Inspiring Strategy Institute.

Jacobs, G. M., Powers, M. A., & Inn, L. W. (2002). *The teacher's sourcebook for cooperative learning.* Thousand Oaks, CA: Corwin.

Kumin, L. (2001). *Classroom language skills for children with Down syndrome.* Bethesda, MD: Woodbine House.

Landis, K., Woude, J. V., & Jongsma, A. E., Jr. (2004). *The speech-language pathology treatment planner.* Hoboken, NJ: Wiley.

Mastropieri, M. A., & Scruggs, T. E. (2007). *The inclusive classroom: Strategies for effective differentiated instruction.* New York, NY: Pearson.

McCarney, S. B. (1993). *The pre-referral intervention manual.* Columbia, MO: Hawthorne Educational Services.

McCook, J. E. (2006). *The RTI guide: Developing and implementing a model in your schools.* Palm Beach Gardens, FL: LRP Publications.

Richards, R. A. (2003). *The source for learning & memory strategies.* East Moline, IL: LinguiSystems.

Strickland, D. S., Ganske, K., & Monroe, J. K. (2002). *Supporting struggling readers and writers.* Portland, ME: Stenhouse.

Wending, B. J., & Mather, N. (2009). *Essentials of evidence-based academic interventions.* Hoboken, NJ: Wiley.

Web Resources

Web Resources Related to RTI

The following is a list of resources available on RTI. The list is not meant to be all-inclusive.

ASHA Online Resource Packet

Response to Intervention
www.asha.org/slp/schools/prof-consult/RtoI.htm

ASHA Related Policy Documents

American Speech-Language-Hearing Association. (2010). Roles and Responsibilities of Speech-Language Pathologists in Schools [Position Statement]
www.asha.org/docs/html/PS2010-00318.html

American Speech-Language-Hearing Association. (2010). Roles and Responsibilities of Speech-Language Pathologists in Schools [Professional Issues Statement]
www.asha.org/docs/html/PI2010-00317.html

National Joint Committee on Learning Disabilities. (2005). Responsiveness to Intervention and Learning Disabilities [Technical Report]
www.asha.org/docs/html/TR2005-00303.html

Center for RTI in Early Childhood

www.crtiec.org

IDEA 2004

Specific Learning Disabilities
www.asha.org/advocacy/federal/idea/04-law-specific-ld.htm

Early Intervening Services
www.asha.org/advocacy/federal/idea/04-law-early-services/

IDEA Partnership

Go to www.ideapartnership.org. Click on "Many Voices."

Web Resources

International Reading Association

www.reading.org/Resources/ResourcesByTopic/ResponseToIntervention/Overview.aspx

LD Online

www.ldonline.org/indepth/rti

National Association of State Directors of Special Education

Go to www.nasdse.org. Click on "Projects."

National Center for Learning Disabilities

RTI Action Network
www.rtinetwork.org

National Center on Response to Intervention

www.rti4success.org/

National Research Center on Learning Disabilities

www.nrcld.org

Grade K

RTI in Action:
Oral Language Activities for Kindergarten Classrooms

BASIC CONCEPTS
Understand and Use Basic Concepts......................26

VOCABULARY
Understand and Use Nouns 30
Understand and Use Action Words....................32
Understand and Use Adjectives 34
Understand and Use New
 Vocabulary Words 36
Categorize Words and Ideas....................38
Understand Classification 40
Recognize Comparisons and Contrasts 42
Understand and Produce Word Definitions 44
Understand Cause and Effect Relationships..........46
Understand and Use Synonyms 48
Understand and Use Antonyms 50
Understand and Use Similes.....................52

LISTENING AND SPEAKING
Respond to Multistep Directions.............................54
Understand and Use Different
 Types of Sentences.........................56
Use Complete Sentences 60
Speak for Different Purposes: Describe.................62
Speak for Different Purposes:
 Ask Questions.........................64
Speak for Different Purposes: Persuade.................66
Participate in Conversations:
 Change and End Topics........................68
Adapt Messages to Different
 Situations and Listeners.....................72
Understand and Use Nonverbal Signals 74
Understand and Use Tone of Voice
 to Convey Meaning 75
Understand and Express Feelings 78

Ask Questions for Repetition/Clarification............80
Understand and Use Fictional Narratives...............82
Retell a Story or Directions in
 Correct Order...............................84
Understand Setting for Stories....................86
Understand Characters in Stories 88
Understand Key Concepts in Stories....................90
Understand and Use Figurative
 Language: Oral Riddles 92
Understand Humor in Words
 and Situations 94
Summarize Stories and Events 96
Understand and Distinguish Fact
 From Opinion...............................98
Understand and Use Inferences 100

PHONOLOGICAL AWARENESS
Identify Initial/Final Sounds in Words 102
Delete First and Last Syllable of
 Compound Words..........................104
Blend Syllables Into Compound Words 108
Blend Syllables Into Two-Syllable Words.............. 110
Segment Sentences Into Words 112

PRINT KNOWLEDGE
Understand Concept of Letter/Alphabet.............. 114
Understand Concept of Word 116
Understand Concept of Sentence.......................... 118
Understand and Track Conventions
 of Print 122
Recognize Environmental Print.......................... 124
Match Spoken to Written Words.......................... 126
Participate in Shared Book Reading....................... 128
Understand Features of Print........................... 130

Teacher Instruction: Black text on white background   **Student Response:** Black text on shaded background

LANGUAGE AREA:	OBJECTIVE:
Basic Concepts	Understand and Use Basic Concepts

TIER 1 — Basic Concepts

Help students understand and use basic concepts such as spatial relationships, time, and quantity.

Snack time: Give students different amounts of snack food. Talk about who has **more**, **less**, and **equal** amounts of foods.

Lining up: Give directions using basic concept words.

- Line up by **every other** row.
- Stand in the **front/back** of the line.
- Stand **between** _____ and _____.
- Stand **behind** _____.
- Find _____ (name student). **Skip** a student and stand **behind** the next student.

Writing: Talk about letters that go **above** and **below** the lines.

Reading: Find words, sentences, and paragraphs on the **top**, **middle**, and **bottom** of the page.

Science: Talk about animals that fly **above** water and live **below** the water.

Vocabulary: Use body part vocabulary to reinforce basic concept words:

- What is **on** your head?
- What is **above** and **below** your nose?
- What is on the **left** side of your head?
- What is on the **right** side of your head?
- What is **over** your eyes?
- What is **above** your eyebrows?
- What is at the **end** of your hand and foot?
- What is in the **middle** of your leg and arm?

26 GRADE K • BASIC CONCEPTS

Calendar activities: Choose an activity that will happen today. Talk about what will happen *before* this activity and what will happen *after* this activity.

Ask students questions such as the following each day:

- *What day comes **before** today?*
- *What day comes **after** today?*
- *How many days are **before** the weekend?*
- *How many days are in this month? Are there **more than**, **less than**, or **equal to** last month?*
- *Is it the **beginning, middle,** or **end** of the month?*
- ***Skip** a day, and tell me what day it is.*
- *We are _____ (give activity) the day **after** tomorrow; what day will that be?*
- *When is your birthday—in a **few** days or in **many** days?*
- *What holiday is at the (**beginning, middle,** or **end**) of this month?*
- *What month comes **next**? What month came **before** this month?*
- *Tell something we would **never** do in _____ (name of month). Tell something we **always** do in _____.*
- *What days are **between** today and the weekend?*

Respond to the teacher's questions.

TIER 2   Basic Concepts

Grade K

Repeated exposure

- Administer an inventory of basic concepts such as the *Boehm Test of Basic Concepts, Third Edition; Bracken Basic Concept Scale—Revised*; or *Wiig Assessment of Basic Concepts*.

- For the concepts the student has not mastered, determine which ones may be interfering with the ability to follow the general education curriculum without support.

- Throughout the day, provide models and opportunities for the student to practice using targeted concepts.

Practice using basic concepts.

Negative practice

Give students statements with basic concept words used incorrectly. For example:

- *I put my socks on **after** my shoes.*
- *My elbow is at the **end** of my hand.*
- *My nose is on the **side** of my face.*
- *Five is **less** than three.*

Correct the sentences by replacing the incorrect basic concept words with correct ones.

28   GRADE K • BASIC CONCEPTS

TIER 3 — Basic Concepts

Concrete materials

Use manipulatives or actions to illustrate basic concept words. Instruct students to put their hands

- **on** the table
- **under** the table
- **over** the table
- **behind** their head
- **in front of** them
- **between** their knees

Follow the directions using the objects.

Visual dictionary/Alternative response mode

Show pictures and ask students to find a person or object that is **under**, **over**, **above**, **between**, **near**, **far**, and so forth.

Point to the person or object.

LANGUAGE AREA: Vocabulary

OBJECTIVE: Understand and Use Nouns

TIER 1 — Nouns

Explain that a *noun* is the name of a person, place, animal, or thing.

- Before reading *Brown Bear, Brown Bear, What Do You See?* by Bill Martin Jr., ask students to listen for things and people that Brown Bear sees in the story.
- Read the story.
- Brainstorm a list of nouns using the following prompt sentences:
  - *Brown Bear saw _____ in the story.*
  - *Brown Bear would see _____ if he came to our classroom.*
  - *Brown Bear would see _____ if he came to your house.*
  - *Brown Bear would see _____ if he went to the playground.*

Fill in the blanks with a list of nouns.

TIER 2 — Nouns

Auditory cues

- Show the illustrations in *Brown Bear, Brown Bear, What Do You See?*
- Ask students to identify a noun that Brown Bear saw by listening to auditory category cues such as *Is it an animal?* or *Is it a person?*

Identify a noun that fits the category.

Auditory cues

- List persons, places, animals, and things.
- Give students auditory function cues to fill in the categories. For example:
  - *It is the person who cleans our school.*
  - *It is something that we fly in the air with a string.*
  - *It is something that we use to draw a picture.*

Listen to the cues and say a noun that fits the teacher's description.

TIER 3 — Nouns

Forced-choice questions

Ask students which of these words is a noun.

- *hat* or *run?*
- *sit* or *bike?*
- *mother* or *swim?*
- *bear* or *hide?*

Choose the noun.

Visual dictionary/Elaboration

- Randomly display pictures that represent people, places, animals, or things.
- Ask students to sort the pictures.

Separate the cards into four piles representing people, places, animals, or things.

Grade K

LANGUAGE AREA: Vocabulary

OBJECTIVE: Understand and Use Action Words

TIER 1 — Action Words

Help students understand the concept of *action words* and give examples.

- Give examples of actions that the students are currently doing (*sitting, writing, talking*).
- Explain that an *action word* or *verb* is something that we do.
- Trace a life-size outline drawing of a boy or girl and hang it up at the front of the classroom.
- Explain that different body parts can perform different actions.
- Demonstrate an action that you do with your legs, arms, mouth, or other body parts.
- Emphasize the action word and which body part we use to perform this action.
- Write the action words on notecards, and place the notecards in a basket or bag.
- Pick a notecard, demonstrate the action word on the notecard, and ask, *What am I doing?*
- Choose another student to answer the question, and on the body outline, place the notecard on the body part that can perform this action.

⭐ **Bonus:** Build a vocabulary list of body parts.

TIER 2 — Action Words

Simplify

Ask students to demonstrate a specific action word. For example, *Show me* **hopping.**

Demonstrate the action word.

- Talk about how we use our legs to hop.
- Continue making a list of actions (*sing, eat, write, bow,* and so forth).
- Demonstrate the action word.
- Identify the body part that we use to perform this action.

Visual dictionary/Concrete materials

Show pictures of action words.

Pantomime the action word, and say the body part that helps us perform the action.

TIER 3 — Action Words

Forced-choice questions

Ask students questions about action words.

- *What is an action we can do with our legs?* (*run* or *blink*)
- *What is an action we do with our fingers?* (*sit* or *touch*)

Choose the correct action word.

Alternative response mode

Place six pictures of action words in front of students. These words should demonstrate several actions that can be done with our

- legs (*running, hopping*)
- arms (*throwing, playing piano*)
- mouth (*singing, eating*)

Choose the action picture that goes with the body part.

Bonus: Use objects and pictures to make sure students understand the concept of *verbs* and *verb tenses* by having them demonstrate what is happening, what has already happened, and what will happen.

LANGUAGE AREA: Vocabulary

OBJECTIVE: Understand and Use Adjectives

TIER 1 — Adjectives

Explain that *adjectives* are words that tell us about the size, color, or shape of something or what something smells like, feels like, or tastes like. Adjectives make what we say, read, and write more interesting.

- Read *Caps for Sale* by Esphyr Slobodkina.
- Talk about the words that the author uses to describe the hats: *checkered, gray, brown, blue,* and *red*.
- Show students pictures of hats, or bring in different kinds of hats: *sombrero, sports cap, cowboy hat, firefighter hat, bike helmet,* and so forth.
- Brainstorm words that describe each hat.
- Draw a picture of a hat, or bring your favorite hat to school.

Place the hats in the center of the circle.

Use adjectives to describe your hat as classmates guess which hat is being described.

TIER 2 — Adjectives

Different representations

Ask students to find classroom objects that can be described using the following words: *soft, round, long, hard, tiny, blue, sharp, green, rough, red, square, smooth,* and *yellow*.

Find the object that is being described.

Concrete materials

- Write the category words *size, color, shape, smell,* and *feel* on a piece of paper.
- Provide different objects.

Choose an object and talk about a word that would fit into each category.

TIER 3 — Adjectives

Alternative response mode

Place three pictures of hats or real hats in the center of the table and describe the size, color, and shape.

Pick the hat that the teacher described.

Completion/Cloze statements

Show pictures of the peddler's hats. Ask the students to complete the following questions:

- *The color of this hat is _____.*
- *The size of this hat is _____.*
- *This hat feels _____.*

Complete the sentence.

LANGUAGE AREA:	OBJECTIVE:
Vocabulary	Understand and Use New Vocabulary Words

TIER 1 — New Vocabulary Words

Help students understand and use new words using current vocabulary knowledge.

Use a semantic map/web about a science unit (*dinosaurs*). For example, the known word is *dinosaur* and the target vocabulary words are *fossils, extinct,* and *paleontologist*. Put the word *dinosaur* (focus word) at the center of the web. (Select other words if these are too difficult for students.)

- Have students brainstorm words associated with dinosaurs, and write the words on the board under various categories (*what they ate, where they lived, how they were discovered, body parts, types*).
- Connect the categories with lines that branch outward from the focus word to show the relationship between the focus word and the different characteristics of dinosaurs.
- Introduce new words as students generate their ideas. For example, if students state that dinosaurs are *old* or *they have bones*, introduce the word *fossil* and explain its meaning. If students share the word *dead*, introduce the term *extinct* and explain its meaning.
- Highlight the target words on the web and refer back to them frequently.

Learn new words associated with words you already know.

TIER 2 — New Vocabulary Words

Multiple choice

- Provide students with one of the target words and two additional words (one synonym, two nonsynonyms).
- Ask students, *Is _____ another word for _____ (synonym) or (nonsynonym) or (nonsynonym)?* For example, *Is extinct another word for dead or alive or excited?*

Provide correct word choice.

Visual cues

As each new word is introduced, show a picture or object that represents the word.

Show a picture or object of a new word.

36 GRADE K • VOCABULARY

| TIER 3 | New Vocabulary Words |

Forced-choice questions

- Provide students with the original word and two additional words (one synonym, one nonsynonym).

- Ask students, *Is _____ another word for _____ (synonym) or (nonsynonym)?* For example, *Is fossil another word for old bones or old books?*

Provide the teacher with the correct word choice.

Turn and talk

- Review the definition of the target vocabulary word with a small group of students.

- Ask the first student to paraphrase and repeat the definition of the target vocabulary word to the student sitting beside him.

- Ask that student to turn to the next student and repeat the definition.

- Continue until the last student in the group repeats the definition back to you.

Provide definitions of new vocabulary words to other students.

LANGUAGE AREA:	OBJECTIVE:
Vocabulary	Categorize Words and Ideas

TIER 1 — Categorize

Help students understand the relationship between words and ideas by sorting words into groups on the basis of similar characteristics.

- Review a semantic category (*farm animals*) and common items in a category (*cow, horse, pig*). Provide a brief definition of the category (*animals that live on a farm*).
- Introduce a set of 10 words (five examples and five nonexamples) in the category (*cow, pig, horse, chicken,* and *goat* vs. *snake, giraffe, lion, zebra,* and *elephant*).
- Talk about why each word is or is not an example of a farm animal.
- Name animals, and ask students to indicate which animals are farm animals and which are not.

- Respond with a "thumbs up" or "thumbs down" to each example.
- Explain why each item is or is not an example of a farm animal.

TIER 2 — Categorize

Multiple choice/Visual cues

Present sets of four pictures (three farm animals, one non–farm animal).

Select the picture that does not belong.

Present sets of four pictures (one farm animal, three non–farm animals).

Select the picture of the farm animal.

Multiple choice/Visual cues

Present sets of two different pictures (one farm animal, one non–farm animal).

Select the picture of the farm animal.

Present sets of two different pictures (one farm animal, one non–farm animal).

Select the picture of the non–farm animal.

TIER 3 — Categorize

Grade K

Peer tutoring

- Pair one student who has mastered the concept of categorizing with a student who is having difficulty.
- Give each pair two to three sets of objects and ask students to practice sorting them (pennies, blue blocks, short pencils, red crayons).
- Give each pair a set of pictures of animals. Instruct each pair to first decide if each picture is a farm animal or non–farm animal.
- Ask each student to take a turn sorting the pictures, with the other student being the "coach," providing corrections as needed.

Sort the objects and pictures into the correct groups.

Modeling

- Provide students with a variety of objects such as coins, colored blocks, pencils, and crayons.
- Model sorting each group of items into specific categories (pennies, blue blocks, short pencils, red crayons).
- Direct students to sort items in the same categories as modeled.
- Next, provide pictures of a variety of animals.
- Model categorizing pictures by where the animals live (farm, ocean, zoo).
- Direct students to categorize the animals as modeled.

Categorize the objects and pictures into correct groups.

GRADE K • VOCABULARY 39

Grade K

LANGUAGE AREA: Vocabulary

OBJECTIVE: Understand Classification

TIER 1 — Classify

Help students understand that certain things are alike and can be grouped together.

- Read or recite the nursery rhyme, *Hey, Diddle Diddle*.
- Classify animals according to how they move. Demonstrate by flapping your arms and saying, *Birds fly*. Ask students to show how animals move.
    - *Kangaroos hop.*
    - *Fish swim.*
    - *Dogs walk.*
    - *Snakes slither.*
- Ask students to name other animals that move the same way.
- Ask students to raise their hand when they hear the name of an animal.
- Repeat the rhyme, this time substituting *cat, dog,* and *cow* with different animals.
- Raise your hand when the teacher says an animal.
- Show how animals move and name other animals.

TIER 2 — Classify

Multiple choice

- Place four pictures of animals in front of students: three animals that move in the same way and one that moves differently. For example, display pictures of a frog, lion, kangaroo, and rabbit.
- Ask students to find the animal that does not _____. For example, ask, *Which animal does not hop?*

Choose the correct animal picture.

Repeated reading/Connecting to prior knowledge

- Write the rhyme from Tier 1 on the board. As you read the rhyme, underline the names of the animals.
- Reread the rhyme, and revisit each animal, asking students what they know about this animal.
- Discuss the similarities between the animals to help students understand why they are all members of the same group called *animals*.

Discuss your prior knowledge about the animals.

TIER 3 — Classify

Visual cues

- Display pictures of the animals in the rhyme as well as additional pictures that are not animals.
- As you read the rhyme, do not say the animal names.
- Pause, and ask the student to choose the animal picture to fill in the blank.

Choose the animal picture that goes in the blank.

Double dose of instruction/Visual cues

- Review the concepts of *same* and *different*.
- Explain how we put words into groups on the basis of things that are the same.
- Give examples of categories.
- Give students pictures of food, clothes, animals, and musical instruments in random order.

- Group the pictures into categories.
- Say or draw additional members of each group.

 Bonus: Make sure students understand that all objects, people, and actions can be grouped together on the basis of how they are alike. Explain that words can be categorized according to many different attributes, such as size, function, and texture.

Grade K

LANGUAGE AREA:
Vocabulary

OBJECTIVE:
Recognize Comparisons and Contrasts

TIER 1 — Compare and Contrast

Help students answer questions that help them recognize comparisons and contrasts within and across stories.

- Make sure students understand the concept of *alike.* Show two objects that are the same and ask, *Are the two balls alike?* **Same** *means alike. Yes, they are alike; they are the same.*

- Next, show two different cups. *Are these two cups alike? No, they are not alike; they are different.*

- Next, randomly show two objects that are alike and two objects that are different, and ask students to determine if they are alike or different. Explain to the students that when we **compare** two or more things, we talk about how they are *alike.* When we **contrast** two or more things, we talk about how they are *different.*

- Bring two students to the front of the class, and ask them to talk about ways that they are alike and ways that they are different.

- Reinforce how they are alike. (*Yes, you and Tom are alike because you are both wearing red shirts.*)

- Read *Some Things Are Different, Some Things Are the Same* by Marya Dantzer-Rosenthal. In this book, Josh visits Stephen's house and compares how things at this house are alike and different. Show the illustrations to the students, and compare and contrast Josh's and Stephen's houses.

- Look at your classmates, and find someone who has something that is the same as you (*black shoes, red shirt, long hair, bracelet,* and so forth).

- Compare and contrast the characters' houses.

42   GRADE K • VOCABULARY

TIER 2 — Compare and Contrast

Mental imagery/Concentrated instruction

- Show the illustrations, and read the text that shows Stephen's bedroom.
- Ask students to visualize their own bedroom.

> Close your eyes, and think about your bedroom. What is the same about your bedroom and the character's bedroom? What is different?

Concrete materials

Ask students to draw a picture of their favorite toy.

Instruct them to

- look at the illustration in the book, and compare and contrast Stephen's favorite toy and the picture of the student's favorite toy
- do the same with Josh's favorite toy

> Draw a picture, and make comparisons and contrasts.

TIER 3 — Compare and Contrast

Concentrated instruction

Focus only on explaining how Josh's and Stephen's houses are the same.

> Compare the illustrations, and talk about ways in which the characters' houses are the same.

Different stimuli

Compare and contrast familiar classroom objects, such as in the following examples:

- *How are a _____ and a _____ alike?*
- *How are a _____ and a _____ different?*

Some examples include

- pen and pencil
- desk and table
- crayon and marker
- stapler and paper clip

> Talk about how the two items are alike and different.

Grade K

LANGUAGE AREA: Vocabulary

OBJECTIVE: Understand and Produce Word Definitions

TIER 1 — Word Definitions

Help students understand and produce word definitions.

- Select three new vocabulary words in a book to read to the class, such as *Caps for Sale* by Esphyr Slobodkina (*imitate, ordinary,* and *refreshed*).
- Read the book, and provide short definitions of words while reading (*imitate: copy; ordinary: not special; refreshed: feeling better*).
- Provide student-friendly explanations of the meaning of each word using everyday language that students would already know.
    - Imitate: *When someone or something copies something else.*
    - Ordinary: *Something that is not special.*
    - Refreshed: *The way people feel when they have a lot of new energy.*
- Ask students to compare the word to other similar words, compare the definition of each word with the definition provided in a dictionary or glossary, and then define each term in their own words.
- Listen to the story.
- Compare new words to other similar words.
- Compare brief definitions of each word with definitions provided in a dictionary or glossary.

Note: Some students may have difficulty with the concepts of *imitate*, *ordinary*, and *refreshed*. Provide more examples to emphasize the concepts for these words.

TIER 2 — Word Definitions

Elaboration/Simplify

- Repeat the Tier 1 activity.
- Give three examples of simple sentences in which students could use each word.
- Ask students to define each term in their own words.

- Listen to the story and definitions.
- Provide brief definitions of each word.

Concentrated instruction/Visual cues

- Repeat the Tier 1 activity with two new vocabulary words.
- Read the book and provide short definitions of words while reading.
- Provide student-friendly explanations of the meaning of each word.
- Show the appropriate page of the book as each definition is modeled.
- Use each word in three simple sentences that students would use.
- Ask students to define each term in their own words.

- Listen to the story and definitions.
- Provide brief definitions of each word.

TIER 3 — Word Definitions

Alternative response mode

- Repeat book-reading and explanation activities.
- Ask students to point to pictures in the book that show the meaning of the target words.

Point to pictures that show meaning of target words.

Imitation

- Repeat book-reading and explanation activities.
- Ask students to repeat the definitions of the target words while showing the appropriate book page(s).

Repeat the teacher's definitions of the target words as the teacher shows the appropriate book page(s).

LANGUAGE AREA:	OBJECTIVE:
Vocabulary	Understand Cause and Effect Relationships

TIER 1 — Cause and Effect

Help students understand and express the relationship between events and their consequences.

- Explain that *cause and effect* is the relationship between two things when one thing makes another thing happen.
- Use emotions to teach the concept of *cause and effect*.
- Ask a student volunteer to come to the front of the class. Whisper a feeling word (*happy, sad, angry, surprised, worried*) to the student, and ask the student to show how she would look if she were feeling this way.

- Guess how your classmate is feeling.
- Brainstorm situations that would cause her to feel this way.

TIER 2 — Cause and Effect

Completion/Cloze statements

Repeat the Tier 1 activity. After a student demonstrates an emotion, provide a completion statement. After each statement, discuss what happened and why. Here are two examples:

- *Mary was happy because _____.*
- *Shawn is excited because _____.*

Respond to the teacher and complete the sentences.

Forced-choice questions

Repeat the Tier 1 activity. Provide two answers in a question format that express cause and effect. Here are two examples:

- *Mike is happy because (a) he lost his puppy or (b) he got a new bike?*
- *Sue is excited because (a) she is going to the fair or (b) she lost her homework?*

Respond to the teacher and choose the correct response.

TIER 3 — Cause and Effect

Advance organizers

- Instruct the students to make a spider map (see Appendix F).
- In the center, make a face that illustrates an emotion.
- On the lines that generate from the center, draw pictures of events that may cause you to feel this way.
- Repeat with other emotions.

Draw pictures to illustrate the emotion in the center of your spider map.

Visual cues/Different representations

- Present a sheet of construction paper that has a vertical line drawn down the middle with two named columns: *Cause* and *Effect*.
- Read a book that emphasizes cause and effect relationships (such as *If You Give a Pig a Pancake* by Laura Joffe Numeroff and Felicia Bond) using dialogic reading technique.
- Reread the book, and fill in the chart with events from story (*If you give a pig a pancake… it will get all sticky*) for each cause and effect sequence in the book.
- Review chart with students.

Listen to the story, and identify examples of things that made other things happen in the book, calling them *Cause* and *Effect*.

 Bonus: Start to blow bubbles. Explain that blowing through the wand is the cause and the effect is bubbles.

Grade K

LANGUAGE AREA: Vocabulary

OBJECTIVE: Understand and Use Synonyms

TIER 1 — Synonyms

Explain that synonyms are different words that mean the same thing.

- Ask students to show a happy face and a glad face.
- Explain that *happy* and *glad* are different words, but they have the same meaning. Introduce the term *synonym*.
- Continue concrete examples of synonyms: *over/above*, *shut/close*, and *near/close*.
- Replace a word in a sentence with a synonym, and show students that the meaning of the sentence does not change—for example, *I closed the door.* (A synonym for *closed* is *shut.*)
- Repeat the sentence, and ask students to see if it means the same thing: *I will shut the door.* (Yes, *closed* and *shut* are synonyms.)
- Give directions using the following synonyms, showing that both synonyms direct students to do the same thing. See the following examples:
  - *behind/in back*
  - *next to/beside*
  - *below/under*
  - *beginning/first*
- Follow the directions.
- State the synonym pairs.

Note: *Synonym* may be a difficult word for some students. You may have to repeat it several times.

TIER 2 Synonyms

Visual cues

Give directions using synonyms and perform a corresponding gesture.

Follow the directions.

Visual dictionary

- Use pictures to demonstrate synonyms.
- Say a sentence about each picture.
- Repeat the same sentence with a synonym, and stress that the sentences mean the same thing.
- Ask students to tell you the synonyms.

Repeat the synonym pairs for each picture.

TIER 3 Synonyms

Check for understanding

- Ensure that the student understands the concepts of *same* and *different* (these concepts underlie the concepts of *synonym* and *antonym*).
- Emphasize similarities and differences among concrete objects, actions, and pictures.

Demonstrate understanding of *same* and *different*.

Step-by-step

- Say the word *synonym*.
- Say the first part of the definition: *A synonym is a word that means _____.*
- Say the entire definition. Stress the word *same* by saying it louder and longer.
- *A synonym is a word that means the **SAME** thing as another word.*

- Repeat the word *synonym*.
- Repeat: *A synonym is a word that means _____.*
- Repeat: *A synonym is a word that means the **SAME** thing as another word.*

★ **Bonus:** Write a paragraph on the board that describes material in a unit covered in class (such as holidays). Include three to five words that students overuse (*good, happy, nice, sad,* and so forth). Ask students to underline overused words and generate new words that are synonyms for each overused word.

GRADE K • VOCABULARY 49

LANGUAGE AREA:	OBJECTIVE:
Vocabulary	Understand and Use Antonyms

TIER 1 — Antonyms

Explain that *antonyms* are words that are very different. Demonstrate how you can put your hands

- *up* and *down*
- *over* and *under* your head
- *in front of* and *behind* your back

Display a poster of a playground scene, or go to a real playground. Talk about how we can

- swing *forward* and swing *backward*
- see things *under* our feet and *over* our heads
- go *up* the ladder and *down* the slide
- go *high* and *low* on the swing
- *walk* and *run*
- find things that are *rough* and *smooth*
- ride on things you can *push* and *pull*
- hear *loud* and *quiet* sounds
- get *on* and *off* playground equipment

- Close your eyes and pretend to be at your favorite playground.
- Next, pantomime the antonym words.

Note: *Antonym* may be a difficult word for some students. You may have to repeat the definition several times.

Bonus: Think of the opposite of **short** giant, **weak** dragon, **young** mummy, **large** mouse, **visible** ghost, **white** spider, **fat** skeleton, and **beautiful** witch. Give the antonyms for each word.

TIER 2 — Antonyms

Completion/Cloze statements

Give sentence starters such as the following statements:

- *First, I go **up** the ladder; next I go _____ the slide.*
- *I saw an airplane **over** my head and an ant _____ the picnic table.*

Fill in the blank with an antonym.

Multiple choice

- Say one word from a pair of antonyms.
- Give the student a choice of two words to complete the antonym pair. Here are two examples:
  - *What is an antonym for **rough? smooth? far?***
  - *What is the antonym for **sit? fly? stand?***

Choose the antonym.

TIER 3 — Antonyms

Word bank

Call attention to antonyms throughout the curriculum. See the following examples:

- Math: *add/subtract; more/less*
- Social studies: *far/near; north/south; east/west; land/water; mountain/valley*
- Language arts: *happy/sad; laugh/cry; large/small; before/after*

Place antonym picture pairs into a word bank for review and easy reference.

Alternative response mode

- Prepare pictures of antonym sets.
- Place in random order in front of student.

Choose two pictures and find the antonym sets.

Bonus: Students may have difficulty with the concepts of *same* and *different*. Emphasize similarities and differences among concrete objects, pictures, and actions.

Grade K

| LANGUAGE AREA: | OBJECTIVE: |
| Vocabulary | Understand and Use Similes |

TIER 1 — Similes

Explain that a simile is a comparison of two words using *like* or *as*.

- Read *The Mitten* by Jan Brett and talk about how Nicki likes mittens as white as snow.

- Brainstorm a list of words that can be substituted for *snow*, such as

  o *as white as a marshmallow*

  o *as white as a pillow*

  o *as white as a cloud*

- Reread the line in the story that uses the above simile. Change the color of the mitten. See the following examples:

  o *Nicki likes mittens as red as a _____.*

  o *Nicki likes mittens as blue as a _____.*

  o *Nicki likes mittens as yellow as a _____.*

Brainstorm words to fill in the blank.

TIER 2 — Similes

Double dose of instruction

- Brainstorm a list of things that are red, blue, yellow, and white.
- Explain what a *simile* is, and give examples.

- Pick a color and a word from the corresponding list.
- Create a simile using these two words.

Completion/Cloze statements

Say a sentence with a blank followed by a sentence with an incomplete simile.

- *A _____ is blue. The sky is as blue as a _____.*
- *A _____ is red. The mitten is as red as a _____.*
- *The _____ is brown. The bear is as brown as a _____.*

Complete the two sentences in each statement.

52   GRADE K • VOCABULARY

TIER 3 — Similes

Auditory cues

Give students a category cue to complete a simile. See the following examples:

- *The mitten is as red as a _____.* (*kind of fruit*)
- *The mitten is as white as a _____.* (*in the sky*)
- *The mitten is as yellow as a _____.* (*vegetable*)

Fill in the blank to complete each simile.

Visual dictionary/Simplify

Give students pictures of objects that are different colors (*red apple, yellow sun, brown bear*).

- Find an object in the classroom that is as red as the apple, yellow as the sun, and brown as a bear.
- Give a simile for each.

LANGUAGE AREA:	OBJECTIVE:
Listening and Speaking	Respond to Multistep Directions

TIER 1 — Multistep Directions

Explain that being able to follow directions is important to doing well at school and other places. Play a game with students in which they have to remember and follow the directions. Give specific, simple, two-step directions. Gradually increase length and complexity.

- Get the students' attention before giving a direction.
- Use an appropriate and varied tone of voice.
- Speak slowly and clearly.
- To increase complexity, use words such as *before, after, first,* and *finally.* Make sure that students understand concepts in isolation before embedding them in directions.
- Check for understanding throughout the activity.
- Encourage students to ask questions.

Begin the game in which students are directed to place a picture in a given location. Have a set of pictures or objects at the front of the room, and then give a two-step direction to each student. For example, *Pick up the blue ball and place it under Sam's chair; pick up the dog and put it beside the trash can.*

- Give three-step directions for the same activity. Activity books such as *Follow Me! Listen and Do Activities* by Grace W. Frank or *Listening Skills for Young Children* by Trish Vowels provide some good ideas for practicing directions.
- Keep track of students' errors to evaluate where the breakdown occurs.
- Errors with following directions can be attributed to weaknesses in listening, understanding basic concepts or other vocabulary, understanding the complexity of the language, attending, memory, distractibility, sequencing, and possibly hearing loss. When students make errors, attempt to evaluate where the breakdown occurs. Be vigilant about keeping your directions simple during training stages.

Follow directions appropriately for up to three-step directions.

TIER 2 — Multistep Directions

Assistive technology

Use web resources such as the link listed below to allow students to practice following directions.

Can You Follow Directions From Tina's World?
www.earobics.com/gamegoo/games/tina2/tina2lo.html

Follow the directions on the website.

Visual cues

- Draw simple cues of the direction's specific elements on the board. For example, if the directions are *walk in a circle and clap your hands*, then draw a picture of a circle and hands on the board.
- Once students follow the directions accurately, erase the cue and ask them to follow the directions again.

Follow the directions accurately.

TIER 3 — Multistep Directions

Simplify

- Give single-step directions only.
- Once students show competency, gradually add the second element.
- Assess where the breakdown is occurring, and simplify accordingly.

Follow the direction(s) accurately.

Concrete materials

Give students two simple objects and present directions that they can follow using those objects. For example:

- *Put the crayon in the box.*
- *Cover the red crayon with the paper.*
- *Give me the pen and the pencil.*
- *Place the pencil under your chair.*

Follow the directions accurately.

Grade K

LANGUAGE AREA: Listening and Speaking

OBJECTIVE: Understand and Use Different Types of Sentences

TIER 1 — Different Types of Sentences

Explain differences between statements and questions. We use statements to give information, and questions to get information.

- Use a story, or generate a list of statements and questions.
- Explain that a statement ends with a period and a question ends with a question mark.
- Write a few examples of each on the board:
  - *Jose is 5 years old.* [This is a statement because it tells you something and ends with a period.]
  - *How old is Roy?* [This is a question because it has an answer, and it ends with a question mark.]
  - *I had a sandwich for lunch.* [This is a statement because it tells you something.]
  - *What did you have for lunch?* [This is a question because it asks for information.]
- Give each student a card with a period and the letter *S* and a card with a question mark and the letter *Q*.
- Ask students to raise the *S* card for statements and the *Q* card for questions.
- Read a list of statements and questions.
- Ask students to generate their own list.
- Ask other students to indicate which are statements and which are questions.

Raise the appropriate card to show whether a sentence is a statement or question.

TIER 2 — Different Types of Sentences

Grade K

Comprehension probe/Examples and nonexamples

- Review characteristics of questions.
- Give examples, asking if each example is a question.
- Ask students to generate questions. If necessary, prompt with words such as *who, what, where, when, why,* or *how*. Or use prompts such as *What would you say if you don't know a person's name? Birthday?*
- Ask students to say something that is not a question. You may need to prompt with leading statements such as *Tell me what you ate for lunch, Tell me what you did at recess,* or *Tell me who is in your family*.
- Repeat this activity using both statements and questions, first asking students to raise the correct card to say whether the sentence is a statement or question, then asking students for a statement or question when you raise the appropriate card.

- Generate questions when called upon.
- Generate statements when called upon.
- Generate both questions and statements.

Repeated practice

- Use a simple kindergarten book and repeat introductory information about differences between a question and a statement.
- As you read the first few pages of the book, pause after each sentence and tell students whether it is a statement or a question. The following books may be useful for this activity:
  - *Brown Bear, Brown Bear, What Do You See?* by Bill Martin Jr.
  - *Do You Want To Be My Friend?* by Eric Carle
  - *How Many Fish?* by Caron Lee Cohen
  - *Aserrín, Aserrán* by Alma Flor Ada and María del Pilar de Olave
  - *May I Please Have a Cookie?* by Jennifer Morris
- After providing a few examples, read a sentence aloud and ask students to tell you whether that sentence is a statement or a question.

Say whether sentences are statements or questions.

TIER 3 — Different Types of Sentences

Auditory cues

- Create a list of statements and questions to be read to the group. Before reading, tell students that they will hear questions read differently than statements and that your voice will change at the end of a question.
- Read a few questions, changing your voice appropriately to show how a question sounds different from a statement.
- Next, read each sentence in the list, cuing students to listen to the voice change between questions and statements.
- Continue to read sentences, asking students to say whether each sentence is a question or a statement.

Listen to each sentence and correctly identify it as either a question or a statement.

Repeated exposure

- Throughout the day, remind students of the differences between statements and questions.
- As a student uses one or the other, repeat that sentence and ask classmates to say whether it is a statement or a question.

Correctly identify sentences as questions or statements.

Notes:

Grade
K

GRADE K • LISTENING AND SPEAKING   59

LANGUAGE AREA: Listening and Speaking

OBJECTIVE: Use Complete Sentences

TIER 1 — Complete Sentences

Explain that a sentence expresses a complete thought.

- Give examples of complete sentences and incomplete sentences.
- Hold up a puppet, and explain that the puppet wants to meet all the students in the classroom. Students must tell the puppet their full name and something about their clothing.
- Demonstrate by introducing yourself. For example:
  - *My name is Mrs. Burton.*
  - *I am wearing a white shirt.*

Say sentences with your own name and what you are wearing.

- *My name is _____.*
- *I am wearing _____.*

TIER 2 — Complete Sentences

Modeling

Model the sentences for the student, as in the following example:

- *What is your name?*
- *My name is Tommy Brown. What is your name?*

Repeat the modeled sentence.

Completion/Cloze statements

Give students the following sentence starters:

- *My school is _____.*
- *I like to eat _____.*

Complete the sentence starters.

60 GRADE K • LISTENING AND SPEAKING

TIER 3 Complete Sentences

Independent practice

If a student is having difficulty saying her first and last name, ask parents or caregivers to practice at home. Ask these familiar adult(s) to explain to the student why she was given her name.

For homework, practice introducing yourself to family members or to your favorite stuffed animals.

Visual cues/Different stimuli

- Place pictures of nouns into one pile and verbs into another.
- Demonstrate how to say a sentence by using a card from each pile.

Choose a card from each pile, and say a sentence that uses the two words.

LANGUAGE AREA:	OBJECTIVE:
Listening and Speaking	Speak for Different Purposes: Describe

TIER 1 — Describe

Read *A Children's Zoo* by Tana Hoban. In this story, animal photographs are accompanied by three describing words that provide clues to the type of animal.

- Read the clues without showing the illustrations.
- Ask students to guess the type of animal from the clues.
- Brainstorm other describing words for each animal.

- Guess the animal.
- Brainstorm additional describing words for each animal.

TIER 2 — Describe

Auditory cues

- Place several pictures of animals in front of students.
- Tell students that they have to choose the animal being described.
- Give students a category before the description word. For example:
   - A word that describes the animal's size is **large.**
   - A word that describes the animal's color is **gray.**
   - A word that describes what this animal eats is **peanuts.**
   - What is the name of the animal I described?

Guess the animal.

Auditory cues

- Place several pictures of animals in front of students.
- Give students three words that describe one of the animals.
- Give students the beginning sound of the animal's name. For example:
   - It lives in the woods. It is brown. It is big. It begins with a "b" sound. What animal did I describe?

Guess the animal.

TIER 3 — Describe

Alternative response mode

Place several pictures of animals in front of students. Say three words that describe one of the animals and ask students to point to the animal described.

> Point to the animal described by the teacher.

Connecting to prior knowledge

- Talk about a trip to the zoo.
- Discuss animal sizes, colors, and special features.
- Discuss a poster or picture of the zoo.
- Ask students to provide examples of their own experiences at the zoo, in a book about the zoo, or in movie/TV show about the zoo.

> - Talk about animals you have seen at the zoo or in a book about the zoo.
> - Point to familiar animals in a poster or picture.

 Bonus: Make a bar graph of large versus small animals (or other descriptive words) and see which type students prefer.

Grade K

LANGUAGE AREA: Listening and Speaking

OBJECTIVE: Speak for Different Purposes: Ask Questions

TIER 1 — Ask Questions

Talk about how we ask questions to gain information. *Wh-*questions may begin with *who, what, where, when,* or *why*. Give examples of each type of question.

- Read *A Children's Zoo* by Tana Hoban. Ask students to listen for the names and descriptions of the animals that are mentioned in the story.
- Model questions using details from the story.
    - *What did she feed the elephant?*
    - *Who took care of the _____?*
    - *When did she feed the elephant?*
    - *Where did the (name any animal in story) live?*
    - *Why was the elephant happy?*
- Ask students to work in small groups, asking each other questions about the different animals in the story.
- Listen to each group, and model questions if necessary.

Ask appropriate questions about animals in the story.

TIER 2 — Ask Questions

Different stimuli/Auditory cues

Make *wh-*question words visible to students: *who, what, where, when,* and *why*.

Pick a *wh-*question word. Ask a question about an animal; the question should begin with the selected signal word.

64 GRADE K • LISTENING AND SPEAKING

Imitation

- Make *wh*-question words visible to the students: *who, what, where, when,* and *why.*
- Give students a short sentence, and ask a question. Here are some examples:
  - The elephant was gray. (Who is gray?)
  - The elephant lives in the zoo. (Where does the elephant live?)
  - The elephant likes to eat peanuts. (What does the elephant like to eat?)
  - The elephant likes to eat peanuts every day. (When does the elephant eat peanuts?)
  - The elephant is very happy because the children gave him lots of peanuts. (Why is the elephant happy?)

Repeat the teacher's questions.

TIER 3 — Ask Questions

Concentrated instruction

Ask students to ask only two types of *wh*-questions (e.g., *who* and *what*).

Ask questions with the selected signal words.

Simplify/Imitation

- Display the *wh*-question words.
- Choose an animal, and point to a *wh*-question word.
- Model how to ask a question about the animal.

- Repeat the teacher's questions.

Bonus: Each week, when classroom jobs are assigned, ask the students the following questions.

- Who will _____?
- Where will this job take place?
- When will (student's name) do the job?
- Why do we do this job?
- How will (student's name) do this job?

After several weeks, encourage students to ask questions about classroom jobs.

GRADE K • LISTENING AND SPEAKING

 | **LANGUAGE AREA:** Listening and Speaking | **OBJECTIVE:** Speak for Different Purposes: Persuade

TIER 1 — Persuade

Explain that sometimes we try to persuade someone to think, feel, or act in a certain way. One way to persuade someone is to give good reasons.

- Tell students the following story:
  - *Mary wanted to stay up 10 minutes later at night. Mary tried to persuade her parents to let her stay up by giving them these two reasons: "If you let me stay up later, I can eat two bedtime snacks and watch TV longer." Her parents said, "No."*
- Ask students the following questions: *Do you think these were good reasons or silly reasons for staying up late? Why? Why not?*
- Tell students another version of the story:
  - *Mary said, "If you let me stay up 10 minutes longer, I will be able to read an extra book each night." Her parents said, "Yes." Mary persuaded her parents to let her stay up later by giving them a good reason.*
- Ask students the following questions: *Do you think this was a good reason or a silly reason for staying up late? Why? Why not?*
- Read *Where the Wild Things Are* by Maurice Sendak. Ask students the following questions:
  - *What caused Max's parents to send him to his room?*
  - *What could Max have done instead of this behavior?*
  - *What should Max do next time?*
  - *How can Max persuade his parents not to send him to his room for acting wild?*
- Pretend that a new student is coming to school tomorrow. Ask students the following questions:
  - *How can we persuade a new student that he or she wants to be in our class?*
  - *How would you persuade this new student to come to your house and play?*
  - *How would you persuade this new student to play your favorite game or sport?*

- Say whether a reason was good or silly and explain why.
- Respond to the teacher's questions from the book.
- Brainstorm good reasons to persuade a new student.

TIER 2 — Persuade

Examples and nonexamples

Pick one of the *how* questions listed at the end of the previous "Teacher" section. Randomly give examples of good and silly reasons that may be used to persuade.

Indicate whether a reason is a good way to persuade someone to do something.

Advance organizer

- Make a spider map (see Appendix F). Write *My House* in the center. Do the same activity with *My Classroom*.
- Ask students to brainstorm reasons that someone would want you to come to their house/classroom.
- As reasons are named, write them on the lines that radiate from the center of the spider map.

- Brainstorm reasons why someone should come to your house and play.
- Brainstorm reasons why a new student would want to be in your classroom.

TIER 3 — Persuade

Concentrated instruction

Talk about your favorite game. Give the students reasons why it is your favorite. Ask students to think of their favorite game.

Brainstorm reasons why a game is your favorite and give examples of your favorite games.

Completion/Cloze statements

Give students sentence starters to help them persuade a classmate to come to their house.

- *My house is _____.*
- *We will make a _____.*
- *I have _____.*
- *I like to play with _____.*

Finish the sentences.

LANGUAGE AREA: Listening and Speaking

OBJECTIVE: Participate in Conversations: Change and End Topics

TIER 1 — Change and End Topics

Talk about conversations, how they are started, how they are kept going, and why they occur. For example:

- *People have conversations to share thoughts and ideas with one another.*
- *The person who starts a conversation wants you to talk about his or her topic.*
- *We keep conversations going by asking questions or sharing thoughts and ideas about the same topic.*
- *We talk and listen during conversations.*
- *The goal is to keep the conversation going.*

Talk to students about starting and taking turns during conversations. The following websites have some good ideas for conversation starters:

- http://iteslj.org/questions
- www.straightdopeforparents.org/pdf/conversation-starters-elementary-and-middle-school.pdf
- www.dailyesl.com/
- www.canteach.ca/elementary/prompts.html
- www.cindysautisticsupport.com/socialskills/conversationpictures.pdf

The "talking stick exercise" is another way of teaching students to participate in conversations.

- Bring a "talking stick" or a ball of yarn, and tell the students that you're all going to have a conversation together.
- Whoever has the talking stick or ball of yarn has to add to the conversation by saying something about the conversational topic or asking a question about the topic started by teacher. You can talk only when you have the talking stick or ball of yarn in your hands. *Let's practice by having a conversation together about our favorite TV programs. Let me start. I like to watch (name show) every week because…*

- Hand the talking stick or yarn to a student, and prompt the student to say something about her favorite TV programs or to ask a question about yours.

- If a student has trouble, prompt by asking questions, giving suggestions, modeling, or giving feedback (*Jenny, were you saying something about TV shows?*).

- If a student changes the topic or takes too long to get to the point, redirect the student to help her maintain the topic and get to the point.

Change and end topics appropriately.

TIER 2 — Change and End Topics

Multiple modalities

- Design a simple game board, and make enough copies to distribute to small groups. See Holiday and Seasonal Games by Super Duper Publications, or design your own simple board game. See *Make Your Own Board Game* at www.thriftyfun.com/tf71529722.tip.html or download and print from www.abcteach.com/directory/fun_activities/games/folder_board_games/.

- Provide game pieces for each student.

- Divide class into groups of two to four students.

- Give each group a conversation starter phrase, and ask the group to talk about the topic.

- Each time a student appropriately adds to the topic, he moves ahead one space.

- If a student adds an unrelated topic, he moves back one space. Each student is trying to get to the end of the board first.

- Float among groups to ensure that students are staying on topic.

Play the game while engaging in conversation.

Visual cues

Create a visual display of question words to help students think of things to say or questions to ask in conversation. The following website has some suggested visual cues and questions: http://jillkuzma.files.wordpress.com/2008/09/question-words-bn1.pdf

Use the question words to ask a question or contribute to the conversation in another way.

GRADE K • LISTENING AND SPEAKING **69**

TIER 3 — Change and End Topics

Alternative response mode

- Give students a green card and a red card.
- Tell them that you will be talking, and when you stop talking, you want them to hold up a card to show whether the last thing you said kept the conversation going or stopped the conversation.
- Start a conversation, and make another statement.
- Ask students whether that statement kept the conversation going about the same idea or stopped the conversation.
- Continue above steps until the conversation is completed.

Raise the appropriate card to show understanding of maintaining the topic (green card shows that comment maintained the topic; red card shows that comment stopped conversation or went off topic).

Multiple modalities

- Choose a topic, and then ask students to draw two to four pictures or to cut out magazine pictures of something they'd like to say about the topic.
- Divide the class into small groups of two to four students, and ask them to talk about the topic using their pictures to remind them of what they want to say.
- Give them the red card (off topic) and green card (on topic), and tell them to raise red if anyone in their group says something that is not about the topic and green to show the comment was about the topic.

- Draw or cut out pictures about the topic.
- Engage in conversation using picture cues.
- Raise the appropriate red or green card.

Notes:

Grade K

LANGUAGE AREA:	OBJECTIVE:
Listening and Speaking	Adapt Messages to Different Situations and Listeners

TIER 1 — Adapt Messages

Explain to students that we use different ways of talking for different people or places. For example, we talk differently on the playground than we do in the principal's office, and in the classroom versus in the library. We talk differently to a child than to a grandparent, and we talk differently to our friends than to our teacher.

- Watch and sing the song found on www.youtube.com/watch?v=kG_zSUZv6ZE, and talk about using good manners and being polite to reinforce these different ways of talking.
- Show pictures of different listeners and places.
- Ask students to practice different ways of talking to each other.
- Sing along with the song.
- Practice conveying a certain idea to different audiences or in different places using pictures of different places or people.

TIER 2 — Adapt Messages

Matching

Show pictures of different places such as a library, a playground, or a classroom. For each picture, ask students to say whether it is a place where we should talk quietly or where we can be noisy.

For each picture presented, say whether you can use a quiet or noisy voice in that place.

Role playing/Examples and nonexamples

- Choose a small group of students who appear to understand the concept of talking in different ways in different situations.
- Describe a situation, and ask students to either role play the correct kind of communication or use the incorrect kind of communication.
- Continue practicing using different situations.
- Ask other students to comment on how well the small group did in communicating appropriately.

- Small group: Role play using appropriate and inappropriate communication skills for given situations.
- Remainder of class: Talk about whether verbal and nonverbal communication was appropriate, and give reason(s).

TIER 3   Adapt Messages

Alternative response mode

- Continue the role-playing experience described previously.
- Hold up a smiley face or sad face card to show if the communication is appropriate or inappropriate.
- Give the cards to students, and have them hold up the card that best reflects the communication used.

Hold up the card to show knowledge of appropriate/inappropriate communication.

Visual cues/Modeling

- Use pictures of activities such as playing with a ball with your grandparent versus with a friend, eating dinner at home versus in a restaurant, going to a museum versus a circus, and so forth.
- Give an example of how to talk in a given situation.
- Show a picture, and ask students what they'd say in the situation.

Talk about what you'd say to a particular person or in a particular place.

GRADE K • LISTENING AND SPEAKING   73

LANGUAGE AREA:	OBJECTIVE:
Listening and Speaking	Understand and Use Nonverbal Signals

TIER 1 — Nonverbal Signals

Explain how nonverbal signals such as facial expressions and gestures, help us communicate.

- Select a book that contains good examples of facial expressions and feelings such as *Dinner at the Panda Palace* by Stephanie Calmenson.
- Show the picture on each page where a character enters the restaurant.
- Ask students what they know about that character and how they know it.
- Discuss facial expressions and gestures.
- Describe how each character feels.
- Note the expression on each character's face.

TIER 2 — Nonverbal Signals

Role play

Show a page of the book, and instruct students to act out the same feeling as that shown in the picture.

Use the nonverbal signals to indicate what is happening in the picture.

Different stimuli

Show examples of different emotions using magazine pictures.

Name the emotion in each picture.

| TIER 3 | Nonverbal Signals |

Grade K

Comprehension probe

Review pictures with students and discuss how facial expressions show meaning.

Discuss the meaning of facial expressions shown in the pictures.

Connecting to prior knowledge

- Ask students to recall a time when your teacher was _____ (choose emotion/feeling such as *proud*).

- Ask students how they would look when feeling proud.

- Describe a time when you knew your teacher was proud.
- Show how you look when you're feeling proud.

GRADE K • LISTENING AND SPEAKING   75

LANGUAGE AREA:	OBJECTIVE:
Listening and Speaking	Understand and Use Tone of Voice to Convey Meaning

TIER 1 — Tone of Voice

Explain that the way we say something may be as important as what we say. Further explain that the way we use our voice tells others what we are thinking or feeling. For example, if I say *Where did you get that cookie?* with this tone of voice (use a neutral tone of voice) versus this way (use a voice that conveys a negative tone—as if you're telling them that they weren't supposed to be eating cookies at their desks), you know that I mean something different.

- Practice different tones of voice with other phrases. First, have students say the phrase in a positive way. For example:
    - *Good morning!* (happy)
    - *Who did that?* (neutral)
    - *Get that book.* (polite)
    - *I'll do it!* (eager)
- Next, have students say the same phrases using a negative tone of voice. For example:
    - *Good morning.* (grumpy)
    - *Who did that?* (angry)
    - *Get that book.* (demanding)
    - *I'll do it.* (not willingly)
- Model saying the phrases using two different tones of voice, and ask students to say what is meant with the different voices. For example, say *I'll do it* in an eager voice, or say it as if doing so is a big chore.
- Continue practicing different ways of expressing the same words using different tones of voice.

Say phrases in different tones of voice to convey different meanings.

TIER 2 — Tone of Voice

Visual cues

- Gather examples of different facial expressions using pictures from magazines, Board Maker (*Mayer-Johnson*), or websites (Pics4Learning [http://pics.tech4learning.com] has many pictures that teachers and students can use without charge).
- Create a list of some simple phrases.
- Show students a picture of a facial expression and a phrase.
- Ask students to say each phrase in a way that matches a facial expression in the picture.

Look at the picture and say the phrase in a way that matches the facial expression in the picture.

Negative practice

- Hold up a facial expression card, and say a phrase in a way that does **not** match the expression. For example, use a harsh tone of voice when holding up a smiling face, and say, *I'm so happy*.
- Ask students to say the phrase differently so it matches the facial expression on the card.
- Continue practicing with other phrases and facial expression cards.

Say each phrase in a tone of voice that matches the facial expression in the picture.

TIER 3 — Tone of Voice

Alternative response mode

- Give students a set of pictures of facial expressions.
- Ask students to hold up the picture that matches the phrase being spoken.
- Say phrases to match facial expression pictures by changing tone of voice appropriately.

Hold up the picture that matches the teacher's tone of voice.

Modeling

- Hold up a facial expression card and say a phrase using a tone of voice matching that picture.
- Ask students to say each phrase using the same tone of voice as that of the teacher.
- Repeat with a variety of facial expressions using different tones of voice.

Repeat phrase with same tone of voice as that modeled by the teacher.

GRADE K • LISTENING AND SPEAKING

LANGUAGE AREA:	OBJECTIVE:
Listening and Speaking	Understand and Express Feelings

TIER 1 — Feelings

Help students understand and express feelings, talk about feelings, and explain that it is important to understand our feelings and to know when others are feeling happy or sad.

- Talk about situations that may make someone feel happy and situations that may make someone feel sad.
- Let students demonstrate happy and sad faces. Give several examples of happy and sad events (*birthday party, lost puppy, snowy day*), and ask students to tell and show how this event would make them feel.
- Read *A Baby Sister for Frances* by Russell Hoban and Lillian Hoban. Discuss how Frances felt at the beginning of the story and how she felt at the end.

- Show happy and sad faces.
- Brainstorm examples of events that are happy and sad.
- Identify how Frances felt at different parts of the story.

Note: Be careful about making assumptions about events that may make a student happy or sad, as they may be relative to a student's culture.

 Bonus: Talk about action words we use when we are feeling happy, such as *hum, dance, sing, jump, clap, whistle, giggle, hug,* and *smile*. Talk about action words we use when we are feeling sad, such as *sigh, cry, frown,* and *look away*.

TIER 2	Feelings

Grade K

Advance organizer

- Organize students' ideas with a spider map (see Appendix F).
- In the center of the page, draw a happy face.
- Write students' ideas on slanted lines that connect to the happy face.
- Repeat the activity with a sad face in the center.
- Talk about events that make you feel happy.
- Talk about events that make you feel sad.

Role play/Repeated reading

- Reread the story, pausing frequently.
- Ask students to pretend they are Frances.
- Talk about what happened (a baby sister was born) and how Frances felt.
- Let students pretend to be Frances and paraphrase different parts of the story.

Talk about different parts of the story or how the character felt.

TIER 3	Feelings

Examples and nonexamples

- Give students two events—one that is an example of a happy event (new bike) and one that is an example of a sad event (lost kitten).
- Ask which event makes students feel happy. Ask which event makes students feel sad.

Choose the correct example of the two topics presented by teacher.

Visual dictionary

Show students pictures of events that make people feel happy and sad.

Discuss what is happening and how these events may make people feel.

GRADE K • LISTENING AND SPEAKING   79

Grade K

LANGUAGE AREA: Listening and Speaking

OBJECTIVE: Ask Questions for Repetition/Clarification

TIER 1 — Clarification Questions

Explain to students that we ask questions when more information is needed, setting the stage for students to feel comfortable asking for repetition/clarification as needed using the correct question forms.

- Give incomplete instructions, and prompt students to ask for repetition/clarification.
- Provide students with some reasons why they may need to ask questions. Reasons may include
    - didn't hear what was said;
    - don't understand the words;
    - can't remember everything the teacher said;
    - need more information.
- Play a game similar to Simon Says. Tell students that you will be giving them directions, but sometimes you will forget to tell them something.
- Ask them to follow the directions if they have enough information but to raise their hand and ask a question if they need more information. Here are some examples:
    - *Go to the table and get it for me.*
    - *Put the blue book there.*
    - *Put the book on Billy's desk.*
    - *Give him the pencil.*

Follow directions or ask an appropriate question, such as
- *What should I get from the table?*
- *Where should I put the book?*
- *Who needs a pencil?*

TIER 2 — Clarification Questions

Different stimuli/Auditory cues

Give directions that are missing an important element, and prompt the student with the appropriate *wh*-question word (*what, where, who*).

Use the prompted *wh*-question word to generate the appropriate question.

Check for understanding

Give directions that are missing an important element, and prompt the student with multiple questions.

Provide the following prompt questions:

- *Do you know what to get? What should you ask?*
- *Do you know where to put the book? What should you ask?*
- *Do you know who gets the pencil? What should you ask?*

Ask the appropriate question.

TIER 3 — Clarification Questions

Modeling/Elaboration

Give the direction that is missing an element.

- Prompt the student with an appropriate question.
- Say, *I need to tell you what to get.*
- Tell student to ask, *What should I get?*

Repeat the modeled question.

Concentrated instruction

Give the direction that is missing an element that will require **just one** of the *wh*-question words.

- Ask, *I need to know what…?*
- Ask, *Can you ask me what…?*

Ask a question using *what*.

LANGUAGE AREA:	OBJECTIVE:
Listening and Speaking	Understand and Use Fictional Narratives

TIER 1 — Fictional Narratives

Explain that there are three main parts of a fictional story: beginning, middle, and end.

- Present a large visual representation of a dinosaur, calling it a *Dinastory*, which has three clearly delineated parts. Each part stands for a portion of a story.
- Explain that the head is on top because it is the beginning of the story, the body is the biggest part because the middle is the largest portion of the story, and the tail tapers off to indicate that a story needs an end.
- Read a book with a simple plot structure such as *The Snowy Day* by Ezra Jack Keats and ask students to say which part is the beginning, middle, or end, using the dinosaur as a visual cue. For example:
  - **Beginning:** *A little boy named Peter is excited to play in the snow.*
  - **Middle:** *He plays and plays, and before going inside, he makes a snowball and puts it in his pocket.*
  - **End:** *The next morning, he searches his coat pocket for the snowball and finds only a wet spot in his jacket.*
- Point to the different parts of the dinosaur as the teacher asks you to identify the beginning, middle, and end of the story.
- Tell which part of the story is the beginning, middle, or end.

Bonus: Define *theme* (the main point or moral of story). Help students discuss the overall theme of a story.

TIER 2 — Fictional Narratives

Visual cues/Alternative response mode

- Provide pictures from the story and reread the story.
- Ask students to arrange pictures to show beginning, middle, and end.

Place pictures on the dinosaur representing beginning, middle, and end of the story.

Multiple choice

Read a segment of the story, and ask if that segment is from the beginning, middle, or end of the story.

Choose the correct part of the story where segment was found.

If the student has difficulty, reduce the options to two choices

Choose one of the two options presented.

TIER 3 — Fictional Narratives

Completion/Cloze statements

Reread the book, and have students fill in the end of sentences. For example:

- *The beginning of the book is when _____.*
- *In the middle of the book, Peter _____.*
- *At the end of the book, _____.*

If students have difficulty, provide sentences in a *yes/no* question response format.

Fill in the end of each sentence based on information from the book, or answer *yes/no*.

Concrete materials/Visual cues/Alternative response mode

- Teach the basic concepts of beginning, middle, and end using real objects such as a set of train cars or a caterpillar. (Color-coded blocks also could visually represent the three segments.)
- Connect this train to the image of a story having a beginning, middle, and end.
- Provide three pictures from a story such as *The Snowy Day* by Ezra Jack Keats representing the beginning, middle, and end of the story. For example, use a picture of Peter getting dressed to go outside, a picture of him putting the snowball in his pocket, and a picture of him looking at his empty pocket.

- Place objects/blocks in correct order.
- Place pictures in correct order, and label them as *beginning*, *middle*, and *end*.

Grade K

Grade K

LANGUAGE AREA: Listening and Speaking

OBJECTIVE: Retell a Story or Directions in Correct Order

TIER 1 — Retell Story

Talk about the importance of telling a story or giving directions in the correct order.

- Read a story with repetitive lines—for example, *The Wolf's Chicken Stew* by Kelko Kasza.
- Remind students about the repetitive phrase/sentence, and pause each time the phrase occurs.
- Encourage students to repeat the line each time it occurs.
- Review the plot sequence.
- Give the beginning plot element, and then ask students to take turns telling the next plot event of the story.
- Ask students to use facial expressions that appropriately support the story as they tell the plot element.

Retell the story in the correct order using facial expressions to appropriately convey the storyline.

TIER 2 — Retell Story

Repeated reading/Step-by-step

- Reread the story, but pause after each new story element and ask students to retell just that element.
- Ask students to repeat all critical elements of the story independently in sequence.

- Retell the segment read by the teacher.
- Tell the entire sequence independently after the story is read.

Different stimuli/Auditory cues

- Retell the story using a set of prompts (*first, second, next,* and so forth) to help students recall the story elements.
- Ask students to tell the story in the correct sequence when prompted by the words *first, second, last,* and so forth.

Retell the story sequence in response to the teacher's prompts.

TIER 3 — Retell Story

Visual cues

- Provide copies of pictures from the book representing critical elements of the story.
- Ask student to put the pictures in order representing the sequence of the story elements.

- Using the picture prompts, create the correct sequence of the story.
- Retell the story in the correct sequence.

Advance organizer

- Place pictures of story elements onto a sequence map.
- Direct the student to use sequence map pictures to tell the story in correct order.

Use the sequence map to retell the story in correct sequence.

GRADE K • LISTENING AND SPEAKING 85

LANGUAGE AREA:	OBJECTIVE:
Listening and Speaking	Understand Setting for Stories

TIER 1 — Story Setting

Using previewing and pre-teaching, help students understand that stories occur in a specific place or setting.

- Select a book and describe the setting, explaining what a *setting* is.
- Ask questions about the book, and talk about the location (*Have you been there? Would you like to go to this place or a similar place?*).

Respond to the teacher's questions about the setting.

TIER 2 — Story Setting

Visual cues

- Provide pictured examples from different settings (*kitchen, circus, park, doctor's office*).
- Ask questions about pictured items shown (*Tommy is looking at grass and trees. Where is he?*).

Provide answers to specific questions about the settings.

Different stimuli

- Show students books that they have already read, and ask them to identify the setting.
- Discuss and brainstorm why each item identified is a *setting*.

Identify the correct setting, and participate in a discussion about the concept of settings.

TIER 3 — Story Setting

Visual cues

- Show a picture of a setting such as a park.
- Ask students who is playing, what they are doing, and where the characters are located.

Respond to the teacher's questions about each setting.

Connecting to prior knowledge

Describe a setting in the book and ask students to act out what they do in that setting.

Act out activities for each setting named.

Grade K

LANGUAGE AREA: Listening and Speaking

OBJECTIVE: Understand Characters in Stories

TIER 1 — Story Characters

Using previewing and pre-teaching, help students understand that stories contain characters who can be described.

- Identify and describe the main character in a selected book.
- Ask students to turn to the person next to them and to generate at least two words that describe the classmate.
- Write words on the board.
- Ask students to describe characters from books you read in class.

- Generate words that describe a classmate.
- Generate words that describe characters in books.

TIER 2 — Story Characters

Visual dictionary

Present pictures of characters from books. Ask students to help create a "word wall" by talking about ways to describe each character.

- Ask students to brainstorm descriptive words. Write the words next to each character on the word wall.
- Refer back to the word wall each time a book is read containing one of the characters on the word wall. Add new characters from different books.

Generate words that describe pictures of characters from books.

Matching

- Before reading a book, look at its illustration of characters with students.
- Ask students to find a *silly* person; a *big, happy* animal; a boy who is *worried*.

Point out characters in the book that fit the teacher's descriptions.

88 GRADE K • LISTENING AND SPEAKING

TIER 3 — Story Characters

Role play

- Select a word that describes a storybook character (*silly*).
- Ask students to act out that character.

Act like a storybook character who fits a specific description.

Connecting to prior knowledge

- Ask students to talk about times in which they acted silly.
- Ask students to say the descriptive word in response to a question. For example, *How were you acting? You were acting _____.*
- Repeat activity with additional descriptive words.

- Talk about personal instances in which you've acted in a way fitting a specific descriptive word.
- Repeat the descriptive word, describing specific actions in response to the teacher's prompt.

Grade K

LANGUAGE AREA: Listening and Speaking

OBJECTIVE: Understand Key Concepts in Stories

TIER 1 — Story Concepts

Using previewing and pre-teaching, help students understand that stories have individual concepts that are tied to a key concept.

- Create a "word web" by taking the key concept and placing it at the center of the web.
- Ask students to generate words that are associated with this concept.
- Ask students to talk about their own experiences of other books or stories that are relevant to this story.

- Generate words associated with a key concept.
- Discuss personal experiences and other books/stories related to the concepts portrayed in the story.

TIER 2 — Story Concepts

Multiple choice

- State the key concept of a story to students, and write it on the board.
- Give students two or three words, and ask them to say which word goes with the key concept.
- Repeat this activity five additional times.

Tell the teacher which of the choices provided goes with the key concept.

Memory aid

Ask students questions to review what has been discussed.

Respond to the teacher's questions with appropriate answers relating to the story.

TIER 3 — Story Concepts

Visual cues

- Provide students with pictures illustrating target words that go with the story.
- Ask students to guess a target word based on each picture presented.

Guess target words based on pictures presented.

Imitation

Provide simple definitions for the target words, and ask the student to repeat them.

Repeat definitions for target words.

LANGUAGE AREA:	OBJECTIVE:
Listening and Speaking	Understand and Use Figurative Language: Oral Riddles

TIER 1 — Riddles

Select a book such as *Kindergarten Kids: Riddles, Rebuses, Wiggles, Giggles, and More* by Stephanie Calmenson or *Guess Again* by Lillian Morrison. Before reading the book, explain that students need to listen and solve puzzles to understand riddles.

- Talk about how to listen for cues within riddles by playing a guessing game.
- Use a basic object such as a comb and give students three hints about the object, such as
    - *It can fit in a pocket*
    - *I am often made of plastic*
    - *I help you to make your hair look better*
- Ask students to name what has been described.
- Take individual students aside and give them an object. Ask them to give three hints about that object so that class members can guess what it is.
- Read the book aloud, asking students to guess what each riddle is describing.

- Name objects described by the hints.
- Generate hints about objects.
- Guess answers to the riddles in the book.

TIER 2 — Riddles

Assistive technology

Use a website such as www.storyplace.org/preschool/activities/petsonstory.asp?themeid=13 to practice the skill of understanding riddles. Use the *Pick a Pet Activity* on this website.

Solve the riddle on the website.

Visual dictionary

- Recite the riddle and draw a picture for each descriptive component of the riddle.
- Ask students to raise their hand if they know the answer before the picture is complete. For example:
  - o *I am an animal with no fur.*
  - o *I have four legs.*
  - o *I live in the jungle.*
  - o *I have a large trunk.*
  - o *What am I?*

Name what is being described and drawn.

TIER 3   Riddles

Think aloud/Auditory cues

Tell students that the goal is to create a description of a specific object and name that object. Talk aloud while thinking of the descriptors. For example:

- *I want to describe a pig.*
- *Let me think… a pig is pink, eats a lot, lives on a farm, and likes mud.*

Give the students an animal to describe. Ask students to say the descriptors aloud. If necessary, provide hints such as *Where does it live? What does it do? What does it look like?*

Think aloud to generate a list of characteristics of target objects.

Visual cues/Peer tutoring

- Give students two or three pictures of objects that they will use to create riddles.
- Pair students together.
- Give each pair visual cues to help them describe their object (pictures of shapes of differing sizes to cue size/shape, picture of a house to cue where it lives, picture of hands holding the object to cue how it is used, and so forth).
- Ask students to take turns giving hints and guessing their partner's object.

Give hints about objects and guess partner's objects correctly.

GRADE K • LISTENING AND SPEAKING   **93**

Grade K

LANGUAGE AREA: Listening and Speaking

OBJECTIVE: Understand Humor in Words and Situations

TIER 1 — Humor

Help students to understand when events, pictures, or words do not make sense or are silly by talking about things that are silly, such as

- *wearing your sneakers in the shower*
- *letting your dog do your homework*
- *riding your bike in the house*

Ask students to fill in the blanks, such as in the following sentences.

- *It would be silly to bring a _____ to school.*
- *It would be silly to buy a _____ for your friend's birthday.*
- *It would be silly to eat _____ for dinner.*

Read *The Silly Story of Goldie Locks and the Three Squares* by Grace Maccarone.

- Make a list of silly events in the story. Remember that students may not interpret "silly" in the same way, because of cultural and linguistic differences.
- Ask students to draw a picture of their favorite silly event in the story.

- Fill in the blanks in the teacher's sentences.
- Brainstorm silly events in the story.
- Draw a picture of your favorite silly event in the story. Discuss why it is silly.

TIER 2   Humor

Concrete materials

Show silly pictures, or review the illustrations in the *The Silly Story of Goldie Locks and the Three Squares* by Grace Maccarone.

Discuss reasons why the pictures are silly.

Examples and nonexamples

Ask students to choose the answer that is silly in each of the following phrases:

- *bringing a pencil or a sink to school*
- *giving a chair or a game to your friend*
- *eating corn or a book for dinner*

- Choose the answer that is silly in each phrase presented.
- Brainstorm additional silly things to bring to school, give to a friend, and eat for dinner.

TIER 3   Humor

Different stimuli/Connecting to prior knowledge

- Talk about circus clowns.
- Show pictures of clowns.

Brainstorm a list of silly things that clowns do.

Simplify

- Ask students to make mad faces.
- Next, ask students to make silly faces.
- Talk about how a silly face is funny and may make us laugh.

Look in the mirror and make mad and silly faces.

GRADE K • LISTENING AND SPEAKING   95

Grade K

LANGUAGE AREA: Listening and Speaking

OBJECTIVE: Summarize Stories and Events

TIER 1 — Summarize

Read *Runaway Bunny* by Margaret Wise Brown and provide a summary of the book. Explain that the little bunny uses his imagination and tells his mother that he will become different things if he runs away and that his mother replies to each imaginary thing. The little bunny talks of becoming the following things:

- fish/fisherman
- rock/mountain climber
- crocus/gardener
- sailboat/wind
- trapeze artist/tightrope walker
- boy/mother

Give each student a partner, and assign the roles of bunny and mother. Ask the pair to act out two things that the bunny imagines becoming.

Act out the story and give an oral summary of the plot.

TIER 2 — Summarize

Concrete materials/Repeated instruction

- Instruct students to draw a picture of a favorite object or animal from the story.
- Reread the story.

> - Draw a favorite object or animal from the story.
> - While listening to the story, hold up drawings when your picture is mentioned.
> - Arrange the pictures in order and summarize your part.

Metacognitive thinking stems

- Explain how the bunny's imagination and his mother's replies are related.
- Ask students to complete phrases. For example:
  - *The bunny said he would become a sailboat, and the mother said she would become the wind because the wind would _____.*

Complete the phrases.

TIER 3 — Summarize

Repeated reading/Step-by-step

- Show students the illustrations while rereading the story.
- Stop reading, and talk about how each of the mother's responses is related to the bunny's imagination.

Discuss the story, and summarize each part separately.

Change response length

Discuss the beginning and end of the story.

Summarize the beginning and end of the story.

Grade K

LANGUAGE AREA:	OBJECTIVE:
Listening and Speaking	Understand and Distinguish Fact From Opinion

TIER 1 — Fact and Opinion

Discuss the meaning of facts and opinions. *Facts* are statements that we can prove to be true. *Opinions* are feelings or beliefs about something. For example, *Sarah is 40 inches tall* is a fact. This can be proven by measuring her. Another example is *Sarah is funny*. Not everyone may agree about this statement, so it is an opinion.

- Further explain the difference between fact and opinion using sample sentences.
- Read a book such as *How a House Is Built* by Gail Gibbons that focuses on the difference between fact and opinion.
- Check for comprehension by having students signal with cards for the letter *F* (fact) or *O* (opinion) after each statement in the book is read.
- Make a story chart of the book with sentence strips. Read individual sentences from the story chart, and ask students to listen for facts and opinions. Take a vote on each sentence to decide whether it is a fact or an opinion.
- Cue students that certain words are clues to opinions, such as *I feel* or *I think*. Ask students to meet in pairs. Have students state one fact and one opinion to each other. Ask them to share their statements and say whether they are facts or opinions to the whole group.

- Hold up the correct card to signal fact versus opinion.
- Vote for sentences as either fact or opinion.
- State one fact and one opinion in pairs and in a large group.

TIER 2 — Fact and Opinion

Visual cues/Repeated exposure

- Record results from the discussion on the chart from Tier 1 by underlining facts and opinions in different colors. It may be helpful to color-coordinate the sentence strips and the marker used to underline sentences for both facts and opinions.
- Post the chart and sentence strips in the room.
- Encourage students to continue to listen for facts and opinions and to ask that they be added to the chart.

Tell the teacher when you hear facts or opinions throughout the day.

Auditory cue

Read the sentence strips, emphasizing words that provide clues to the sentence being a fact or an opinion. For example, He **thinks**, I **see**.

Say what words indicate facts or opinions.

TIER 3   Fact and Opinion

Advanced organizer

- Create two spider maps (see Appendix F), one for facts and one for opinions.
- Write the characteristics of each on the spokes around the center circle.
- Discuss the spider map, and then read simple sentences.
- Ask students to use the spider map to determine if the sentence is a fact or an opinion.

Say whether the sentence is a fact or an opinion.

Different stimuli

- Ask students to provide statements about themselves.
- After each statement, ask students to say whether the statement was a fact or an opinion.
- If necessary, prompt students with questions such as the following:

  o *How tall are you?* (fact)

  o *Are you a boy or a girl?* (fact)

  o *Are girls smarter than boys?* (opinion)

  o *What's the best food in the world?* (opinion)

  o *What's the best thing to do after school?* (opinion)

  o *What did you do after school yesterday?* (fact)

Give a statement about oneself, and say whether it is a fact or an opinion.

LANGUAGE AREA: Listening and Speaking

OBJECTIVE: Understand and Use Inferences

TIER 1 — Inferences

Explain that inferences are something you know without being told or something that you can "guess" based on something you see or hear.

- Show pictures to see what students can infer from the information presented. For example, provide a picture of a bicycle lying on the ground with a boy sitting next to it, crying. Ask, *What can you infer?* (He probably fell off his bike) *How do you know? What clues do you have?* (His bike is down. He's crying.)
- When introducing books, start by having students make inferences based on the illustrations.
- Use several pictures to practice making inferences.

Select a book such as *Alligator Baby* by Robert Munsch to teach inferences.

- Show some pictures and ask what is happening (*someone was getting a ticket* or *there was a wedding*).
- Ask students to explain how they knew what was happening.
- Read the story, stopping to see if students can make an inference about each baby that the parents brought home, based on what is known and the clues that are given.
- Play a "guessing" game:
    o Choose a student, and ask her to leave the room. Have the class think of a mystery word.
    o When the student returns, the students give clues/hints to help her guess or infer the mystery word. For the example, to prompt the word *happy*, students may say *I felt this way when I got a new puppy* or *won the race* or *opened my birthday gift and found something I really wanted*.
    o Teach students to prompt with phrases about places, time, colors, textures, body language, action, or situations.
    o Student must guess or infer what the mystery word is (*happy, sad, the beach, the mall, zoo, lunchroom, recess*) by saying *I'm guessing the word/place is…*"

- Make inferences about pictures/events in book and explain why the inference can be made.
- Provide clues to help others make correct guesses or inferences.

TIER 2 — Inferences

Different stimuli

- Review the meaning of *inference*.
- Read one of the *No, David!* books by David Shannon. (Every page contains the words *No, David!* and pictures of activities David was not supposed to be doing. His mother says, *No, David!*).
- Ask students to use the picture cues to guess what David is not supposed to be doing.

Guess what David is not supposed to be doing and why his mother is saying, *No, David!*

Check for understanding

Read aloud books such as *Grandfather Twilight* by Barbara Helen Berger or *Somebody Loves You, Mr. Hatch* by Eileen Spinelli. Before reading, show the pictures in the book and ask what we know about the story without hearing any words.

Explain what we know about the book by looking at the pictures.

TIER 3 — Inferences

Repeated practice

Provide short descriptions of an experience or event, and ask students what will happen next. For example, *Your dog is standing by the door barking. What do you think will happen next?*

Examples of other descriptions can be found on the following website: www.havefunteaching.com/worksheets/reading/inferences/ making-predictions-predict-infer.pdf

Say what happens next.

Matching/Multiple choice

- Create a matching activity by using pictures from a story.
- In one column, place a picture from the story in which something can be inferred.
- In another column, place two or three pictures, including one that represents the correct inference.
- Have students circle the correct picture and say what can be inferred.

Show understanding of inferences by circling the correct picture and saying what you can infer.

GRADE K • LISTENING AND SPEAKING   101

Grade K

LANGUAGE AREA: Phonological Awareness

OBJECTIVE: Identify Initial/Final Sounds in Words

TIER 1 — Initial/Final Sounds

Help students understand that words begin or end with a specific sound.

- Present a letter such as *F*, and explain that the letter makes the *f* sound.
- Ask students to generate words that begin with this sound, first modeling two or three examples (*fish, fun, food*).
- After each example, elongate the initial sound and explain that *ffff—un* begins with the *f* sound; do you hear the *f* sound at the beginning?).
- Ask the group to repeat each student's contribution. As they do so, list each word on the board and underline the initial sound.
- After a number of words starting with the *f* sound are generated, ask the class to read the list on the board.
- Emphasize the first sound of each word.
- Repeat the same instructional sequence for final consonants in words (*beef, safe, leaf, puff*), asking the class what other words end with the target sound.
- Generate words that begin or end with a specific sound.
- Repeat the words generated.

TIER 2 — Initial/Final Sounds

Visual cues/Concentrated instruction

- Present a letter such as *F*, and explain that the letter makes the *f* sound.
- As a word is said (*fun*), present the alphabet letter block representing the corresponding initial sound *f*.
- Pass the letter block around the room to students. Have each student say the target word (*fun*) and generate another word that begins with *f* when the student receives the letter block.
- Repeat activity with 10 additional words.

Say the target word when receiving the letter block, and generate additional words that begin with the target sound.

Visual cues/Concentrated instruction/Matching

- Present a consonant-vowel-consonant (CVC) word, along with two alphabet letters (CVC word—*fun*; alphabet letters—*F* and *N*).
- Explain that the word presented begins with one of the sounds these letters make.
- Ask students to point to/match the word to the sound.
- Repeat activity with 10 additional words.

Point to/match the word said by teacher to the correct initial letter sound.

TIER 3 — Initial/Final Sounds

Repeated practice

- Repeat the second Tier 2 activity with five additional words.

Point to or match the word said by the teacher to the correct initial letter sound.

Visual cues/Concentrated instruction/Imitation

- Present a letter such as *F*, and explain that the letter makes the *f* sound.
- As the CVC word is said (*fun*), present the alphabet letter block representing the corresponding initial sound *f*.
- Pass the letter block around the room. Have each student say the target word and the word's beginning sound (*fun* begins with *f*).

Imitate the target word and initial letter sound.

GRADE K • PHONOLOGICAL AWARENESS   103

LANGUAGE AREA:	OBJECTIVE:
Phonological Awareness	Delete First and Last Syllable of Compound Words

TIER 1 — Delete Syllable

Help students understand that compound words consist of two words, each of which can stand alone when separated.

- Fold a large piece of paper/index card in half or draw a line down its center. Write one part of a two-syllable compound word on each half (*skate…board*), compiling a set of 10 items (*football, popcorn, eyeball, flashlight, weekend, airplane, cowboy, bookshelf, upstairs, bedroom*).

- Say to the class: *Pretend that we are going on a trip to outer space to visit a new planet. On this planet, Martians talk in a secret code—they say only the second part of a word. To understand the Martians' messages, you have to learn their code.*

- Provide two or more examples: *When the Martians want to say cowboy, they say boy, and when they want to say flashlight, they say light.*

- As each example is given, fold and unfold the paper/index card with the compound word written on it.

- Repeat the two examples, this time having the students guess the compound word for each.

- Ask the students to guess how the Martians would say each of the remaining eight compound words.

- Tell the students that they are going to another planet where the space creatures only say the **first** part of their words.

- Repeat the instructional sequence above.

Guess how the Martians would say a word given one part of a compound word.

Note: Linguistic differences may influence a student's performance on this task. Compound words do not exist in certain languages, such as Vietnamese, Mandarin, and Cantonese. Students who speak these languages as their native language may have difficulty with this activity.

TIER 2 — Delete Syllable

Visual cues/Concentrated instruction

Provide students with two or more examples along with pictures: *When the Martians want to say cowboy, they say boy, and when they want to say flashlight, they say light.*

- As the examples are given, fold and unfold the paper/index card with pictures of the compound words depicted on it.
- Repeat the examples, having students guess the word.

Guess how the Martians would say a word given one part of a compound word.

Visual cues/Multiple choice/Concentrated instruction

Provide students with two or more examples along with pictures: *When the Martians want to say cowboy, they say boy, and when they want to say flashlight, they say light.*

- As each example is given, fold and unfold the paper/index card with the picture of the compound word depicted on it.
- Repeat the examples, having students guess the word given *three* choices (one correct; two distracters).

Guess how the Martians would say a word given three choices.

TIER 3 — Delete Syllable

Visual cues/Multiple choice/Concentrated instruction

Provide students with two or more examples with pictures: *When the Martians want to say <u>cowboy</u>, they say <u>boy</u> and when they want to say <u>flashlight</u>, they say <u>light</u>.*

- As each example is given, fold and unfold the paper/index card with the picture of the compound word depicted on it.
- Repeat the examples, having students guess the word given *two* choices (one correct; one distracter).

Out of a set of two choices, point to one choice and say how the Martians would say the word.

Visual cues/Imitation/Concentrated instruction

- Show students a picture of a compound word (*cowboy*).
- Model how the Martians would say the word (*boy*).
- Ask students to say the compound word first blended together (*cowboy*) and then with pauses between the syllables (*cow–boy*).
- As each example is given, fold and unfold the paper/index card with the pictures of the compound word depicted on it.
- Ask students to model how the Martians would say the word *cowboy*.
- Repeat the activity with 10 other compound words.

Model how the Martians would say a word.

Notes:

Grade
K

GRADE K • PHONOLOGICAL AWARENESS   107

LANGUAGE AREA:	OBJECTIVE:
Phonological Awareness	Blend Syllables Into Compound Words

TIER 1 — Blend Syllables

Explain that compound words consist of two separate words blended together.

- Make a list of 5–10 compound words of items that can be purchased at a store (*toothpaste, mouthwash*).

- Say, *We are going shopping to buy some things with special names. The names are special because they have two parts, and each part is its own word.*

- Present the first item on the list (*toothpaste*) and say, *Toothpaste has two parts, and each part has its own word: tooth…paste.*

- Repeat the compound word, placing emphasis on each syllable (*tooth/paste*).

- Say each part of the word with a 1-second pause between the syllables (*tooth… paste*), and then blend the syllables together (*toothpaste*).

- Ask students to repeat the stimulus word as they tap out the number of syllables on their desks.

- Shopping list activity: Ask students to generate other compound words by thinking of items that can be bought at the store that have two words that can be put together to form one word (*pancakes, hotdogs, headphones*). Have students repeat the initial exercise with each word.

- Write the shopping list on the board in chart form to stress the connection among sounds, syllables, and letters.

- Repeat stimulus words after teacher, tapping the number of syllables on your desk.

- Generate compound words by thinking of items that can be bought at the store that have two words that can be put together into one word.

TIER 2 — Blend Syllables

Multiple choice

Present three two-syllable words with a 1-second pause between syllables (one compound word [*toothpaste*]; two words that are not compound words [*turkey, pickle*]).

> Blend together the syllables of each word and choose the one that is the compound word.

Multiple choice

Present two two-syllable words on the board with a 1-second pause between syllables (one compound word [*toothpaste*]; one noncompound word [*turkey*]).

> Blend and choose the noncompound word, and explain why it is not a compound word.

TIER 3 — Blend Syllables

Visual cues/Imitation

- Present two pictures of compound words with a 1-second pause between syllables; then present the words again, this time blended (*toothpaste, pancake*).
- After each word, ask students to point to each picture and repeat the words in both unblended and blended form (*tooth…paste, toothpaste; pan…cake, pancake*).

> Repeat the compound words in both unblended and blended forms while pointing to each picture.

Visual cues/Imitation

- Present pictures along with two different color-coded blocks, each of which represents one syllable in a word (yellow = *tooth*, blue = *paste*).
- Ask students to imitate compound words, first with blocks held apart (unblended) and then with blocks held together (blended) (*tooth…brush, toothbrush*).
- Ask students to slide blocks together while saying the compound words.

> Repeat compound words in both unblended and blended forms while the teacher slides the blocks together and while sliding the blocks together yourself.

Grade K

Grade K

LANGUAGE AREA: Phonological Awareness

OBJECTIVE: Blend Syllables Into Two-Syllable Words

TIER 1 — Blend Two-Syllable Words

Explain that words consist of smaller parts (syllables).

- Show students a puppet, and explain that the puppet talks very, very slowly. So, when the puppet says a word, it only says one part at a time.
- Instruct students to listen carefully so that they can put the parts of the word together and understand the puppet's words.
- Provide two or three examples, saying each syllable 1-second apart (*chick…en, can…dy, ap…ple*), and then blend the parts together to form the whole words (*chicken, candy, apple*).
- Ask students to figure out the puppet's words.

Say the puppet's words in small parts, and then blend the small parts to figure out the puppet's words.

Note: Some languages do not have two-syllable words. Students who speak languages that do not have two-syllable words may have difficulty with this activity.

TIER 2 — Blend Two-Syllable Words

Visual cues/Repeated practice

- Show students two puppets. Have each puppet stand apart and say one syllable of a two-syllable word (Puppet 1 says *can*, and Puppet 2 says *dy*).
- Have puppets hug to blend the word (Puppets say *candy*).
- Ask students to repeat the unblended and blended words while you demonstrate the puppet's movement.
- Repeat the activity with more examples.
- Present each of the words in unblended form, and ask students to blend them.
- Provide a model for students to imitate, if needed.

Say the words in unblended form, and then blend them.

Alternative response mode/Multiple choice/Visual cues

- Present two different pictures of two-syllable words (*apple, candy*).
- Ask students to point to each picture as it is named.
- Present one of the words in unblended form, with syllables 1-second apart. Ask students to point to the picture representing the word said.
- Repeat with five more picture sets.

Point to the two-syllable word said by the teacher.

TIER 3 — Blend Two-Syllable Words

Alternative response mode/Examples and nonexamples

- Provide students with cards of pictures of one- and two-syllable words.
- Read the words aloud, as you sort the pictures into two piles, one representing one-syllable words and the other representing two-syllable words.
- Give the cards to the students and ask them to sort the cards correctly.

Correctly sort the cards into piles of one- and two-syllable words.

Visual cues/Imitation

- Present students with a picture of a two-syllable word.
- Create magnets representing each of the two syllables of the word.
- Place magnets on the board with a big space between them (*can dy*).
- Say the word with a 1-second pause between syllables. Point to each syllable as it is said.
- Slide the magnets together as you blend the syllables to make the whole word (*candy*).
- Ask students to imitate production of words, both unblended and blended.
- Repeat activity with 10 more words.

Repeat the words in both unblended and blended forms.

GRADE K • PHONOLOGICAL AWARENESS 111

LANGUAGE AREA: Phonological Awareness

OBJECTIVE: Segment Sentences Into Words

TIER 1 — Segment Sentences

Help students understand that sentences are composed of separate parts called *words*.

- Select a short poem (*I scream, you scream, we all scream for ice cream*), and write it on the board on a single line.
- Explain that this poem is made up of words, and show the different words by placing a slash mark between each word.
- Ask the class to count the number of words in the poem and clap their hands as each word is pointed out.
- Repeat the poem, pronouncing each word slowly while the class claps out each word.
- Erase the slash marks, and repeat the clapping activity.
- Erase the last part of the poem (*We all scream for ice cream*), and ask students to count the number of words left in the poem.
- Ask student volunteers to come to the board and insert slash marks between the remaining words.
- Count the number of words in the poem, and clap your hands as each word is pointed out.
- Count the number of words left in the poem when the second half of it is erased.
- Insert slash marks between remaining words after the second half is erased.

Bonus: Students can segment the names of their classmates into syllables, counting the number of parts of the names (*Steven = ste/ven*) = 2.

TIER 2 — Segment Sentences

Concentrated instruction

Begin with simple sentences (*I like pizza*), and repeat the instructional sequence of Tier 1.

- Count the number of words in the sentence given, and clap your hands as each word is pointed out.
- Count the number of words left in the sentence when the latter part of it is erased.
- Insert slash marks between remaining words after the latter part is erased.

Visual cues/Concentrated instruction

Begin with simple sentences (*I like pizza*), with each word of the sentence color coded.

- Count the number of words in the sentence given, and clap your hands as each word is pointed out.
- Count the number of words left in the sentence when the latter part of it is erased.

TIER 3 — Segment Sentences

Visual cues

- Give each of three student volunteers a card with one of the words of a sentence (*I like pizza*) written on it.
- Have students stand close together as you run your hand left to right to produce the sentence *I like pizza*.
- Have student volunteers say their word in rapid succession in the correct order to produce the sentence *I like pizza*.
- Have students stand farther apart from one another.
- Ask students in the class to identify each word and to count the number of words in the sentence.

Identify each word, and count the number of words in the sentence.

Forced-Choice Questions

- Review the concept of a sentence being made up of words.
- Read simple sentences.
- After reading each sentence, give two numbers, and ask student to tell which number shows how many words were in the sentence.

Provide the correct number of words in sentences.

LANGUAGE AREA:	OBJECTIVE:
Print Knowledge	Understand Concept of Letter/Alphabet

TIER 1 — Letter/Alphabet Concept

Help students understand that letters make sounds.

- Present the uppercase letter *B*, and name the letter.
- Ask students to name the letter.
- Explain that letters also make sounds. Give examples such as *The letter B makes the b sound*. Have students repeat.
- Ask students to name the letter that makes the *b* sound.
- Repeat sequence with three or more uppercase letters *(S, F, M)*.
- Give students a stack of pictures that begin with two different letters *(B and T)*, and have them sort pictures according to the beginning letter.

- Name the letter that makes the sound presented by the teacher.
- Sort pictures according to the beginning letter.

TIER 2 — Letter/Alphabet Concept

Different Stimuli

- Give each student a copy of a story and a letter card.
- Ask students to circle all of the words containing that letter in the story, saying the sound the letter makes as they circle it.

Circle words and name the sound presented by the teacher.

Repeated practice

Conduct the Tier 2 activity using five or more additional examples of letter names and associated sounds.

Name the letter that makes the sound presented by the teacher.

TIER 3 — Letter/Alphabet Concept

Concentrated instruction/Visual cues

Conduct the activity from Tier 1 using a set of two letters.

Name the letter that makes the sound presented by the teacher.

Visual cues

- Provide students with sponge letters and paint, and ask students to make the letters with the materials provided.
- Tell students to name letters they have made.

Select sponge letters, make painted letters, and name each letter.

LANGUAGE AREA: Print Knowledge

OBJECTIVE: Understand Concept of Word

TIER 1 — Word Concept

Help students understand that printed words have spaces between them.

- Read a storybook such as *I Went Walking* by Sue Williams. Select a book that has simple, short sentences with one sentence on each page.
- Write a sentence on the board that describes the main character.
- Call students' attention to the spaces between the words, and explain why they are there: Words *"stand for something else," and the spaces tell us that each word has a meaning of its own.*
- Give some examples of the concrete words in the sentence.
- Show students a sentence in the book, and ask them to count the number of words in the sentences by focusing on the spaces between the words.

Point to and count the number of spaces as the teacher highlights the spaces on the board.

TIER 2 — Word Concept

Visual cues

Ask students to place colored cards between words and to count the number of words aloud.

Insert colored cards between words, and then count the number of words aloud.

Repeated practice/Elaboration

Repeat the concept, and provide more examples of sentences.

Point to spaces between words for each example, and then count the number of words aloud.

TIER 3 — Word Concept

Imitation

- Count the number of spaces between words.
- Ask students to repeat as you count the number of spaces and words.

Repeat what the teacher says as he counts the number of spaces and words.

Simplify

- Introduce sentences with fewer words (two to three words).
- Count the number of spaces between words.
- Ask students to repeat as the number of spaces and words is counted.

Repeat what the teacher says as he counts the number of spaces and words.

| Grade K | LANGUAGE AREA: Print Knowledge | OBJECTIVE: Understand Concept of Sentence |

TIER 1 — Sentence Concept

Explain that sentences are made up of words.

- Show students three wooden word blocks that depict three familiar words and a fourth block with a black circle on it denoting a period.
- While explaining the "building block" concept, move the three blocks together to make a simple three-word sentence (*It is big*), and then add the period at the end, explaining that the period shows us the end of a sentence.
- Repeat several times, and ask students to help move blocks together.
- Repeat with two more simple sentences, using familiar sight-word vocabulary.
- Explain that sentences are made up of different numbers of words, and show students a sentence that has four words, then five words, and repeat the activity.
- Present some nonsentences such as *the new car, it big,* or *raining.*
- Discuss that these are not sentences because they are not complete thoughts; they are missing something.
- Brainstorm the kinds of words that are missing.
- Move blocks together as the teacher says the words of the sentence, and put the "period" block at the end.
- Brainstorm the kinds of words that are missing in nonsentence examples.

TIER 2 — **Sentence Concept**

Visual cues

- Hang up a clothesline with clothespins, and give students a basket containing three word cards and a "period" card.
- Explain that the words on the three cards make up a sentence.
- Model how to hang up the words on the clothesline with the clothespins.
- Write a sentence on the board. Have students take cards from the basket, hang them on the clothesline to make the sentence, and then "read" the sentence.
- Refill the basket with more three-word card sets, and repeat the activity.

- Say sentences as the teacher hangs up the cards.
- Take cards from the basket, hang them up to make the sentence, and then "read" the sentence.

Examples and nonexamples/Repeated practice

- Provide an example of a three-word sentence (*I like toys; Today is sunny*), and ask students if what was presented is a sentence.
- Provide an example of a nonsentence (*like toys I*), and ask students if what was presented is a sentence. Discuss why the example is not a sentence, and rearrange the words to make it a sentence.
- Repeat the activity three times, and then introduce another two sets of sentences/nonsentences.

Indicate if the set of words presented forms a sentence.

TIER 3 — Sentence Concept

Visual cues/Completion/Cloze statements

- Present three-word sentences and nonsentences on different-colored cards (red, blue, and yellow), and explain that the color shows whether the word is the first, second, or last word of the sentence.
- Ask students to complete the following sentence: *This (is/is not) a sentence.* Discuss the reasons for their answers.

- Complete the sentence frames.
- Explain answers.

Matching/Visual cues

- Place three colored cards in a row in front of students, reminding them that each color stands for the first, second, or last word of a sentence.
- Give students word cards, and ask them to place each word under the correct color to make a sentence.
- Repeat each three-word set two times, and then present two additional sets.

Match the word cards to the correct color, and then "read" the sentences.

Notes:

Grade K

GRADE K • PRINT KNOWLEDGE 121

Grade K

LANGUAGE AREA: Print Knowledge

OBJECTIVE: Understand and Track Conventions of Print

TIER 1 — Conventions of Print

Help students understand that, in English, print is read from left to right and top to bottom.

- During a shared book reading activity with a familiar storybook, run your finger along the text line to show that text is read from left to right.
- Ask students to use their pointer fingers to make "air drawings," moving from left to right in the air.
- Repeat this sequence for a few more pages, and then invite individual student volunteers to point to a page as you read the text.
- Read a page of text and, while tracking the sentence with a pointer finger, say, *I just read the words at the bottom of the page. Where should I begin on the next page? At the top of the page? So, we begin to read at the top of the page and read all the way to the bottom of the page.*
- Alternately ask left-to-right and top-to-bottom questions.
- Make "air drawings" of print directionality.
- Take turns pointing left to right on book pages as the teacher continues to read the book.
- Repeat the air drawings to demonstrate top versus bottom.

| TIER 2 | Conventions of Print |

Repeated practice

Repeat activity for an additional 10 pages of the book.

- Make air drawings of print directionality.
- Take turns pointing left to right on book pages as the teacher continues to read the book.
- Repeat the air drawings to demonstrate top versus bottom.

Visual cues

- Present four different icons on the board to serve as cues for directionality (▲ = top; ▼ = bottom; ♣ = left; and ☺ = right). Explain the meaning of each icon.
- As you read from a book, point to a place in the book and ask students to point to the icon representing the spot you are reading from. For example, when reading the title have students point to the icon representing where the title occurs (▲ = top).

Point to the appropriate icon.

| TIER 3 | Conventions of Print |

Imitation

- State the directionality while pointing to it.
- Make air drawings, and ask students to copy those actions (left to right; top to bottom).

Imitate the teacher's air drawings.

Visual cues

- Draw four long, horizontal lines on the board to demonstrate the print. Put the icons in the appropriate locations.
- Remind students about what the icons mean, and explain that the lines represent how we read (from left to right and from top to bottom).
- Ask students to point to the beginning, the ending, the top, and the bottom.
- Repeat the directionality words (*left to right*; *top to bottom*)

- Point to the appropriate icon.
- Say the appropriate convention of print.

GRADE K • PRINT KNOWLEDGE   123

LANGUAGE AREA:	OBJECTIVE:
Print Knowledge	Recognize Environmental Print

TIER 1 — Environmental Print

Help students understand that print carries meaning.

- Bring in five common signs or logos (pictures of street signs, restaurant logos), and write the name of each on large index cards. Display the logos, and have students point to them as they are named.
- Explain what each sign/logo means, and ask students to talk about what comes into their minds when they see each of these.
- Write the words under each sign/logo to show that they tell us something about the meaning of each.
- Ask students to take turns explaining each sign/logo, helping them put their thoughts into words.
- Remove index cards, shuffle them, hold one up, and ask students to match the written label to the sign/logo, discussing why the word goes with a given sign/logo.
- Ask students to generate examples of other signs/logos that are their favorites.

- Point to each sign/logo as the teacher names it.
- Take turns explaining what each sign/logo means.
- Match written words to signs/logos.
- Generate names of other favorite signs/logos.

124 GRADE K • PRINT KNOWLEDGE

TIER 2 — Environmental Print

Change response length/Repeated practice

Conduct the Tier 1 activity with three signs/logos and repeat each at least five times.

- Point to each sign/logo as the teacher names it.
- Take turns explaining what each sign/logo means.
- Match written words to signs/logos.
- Generate names of other favorite signs/logos.

Completion/Cloze statements

Conduct the Tier 1 activity, asking students to complete a sentence with a single word or phrase (rather than an explanation). For example:

- *This sign means _____.*
- *This sign tells us _____.*

Complete the sentence presented by the teacher.

TIER 3 — Environmental Print

Alternative response mode/Multiple choice

Conduct the Tier 1 activity; then, name or describe a sign/logo and ask students to point to the correct one from a set of three.

Point to each sign/logo after the teacher names or describes it.

Matching/Visual cues

- Present three signs/logos and three words for each.
- Ask students to place the appropriate sign/logo under the name of each word.

Match words with the appropriate sign/logo.

Grade K

LANGUAGE AREA: Print Knowledge

OBJECTIVE: Match Spoken to Written Words

TIER 1 — Match Spoken to Written Words

Help students understand that print carries meaning.

- Present five pictures of CVC words that differ only in the first consonant (*can, fan, man, pan,* and *ran*). Write the words on chart paper or cards.
- Read each word aloud. Ask students to point to the corresponding picture as each word is said with exaggerated pronunciation.
- Shuffle the cards, and hold up one card at a time. Ask students to identify the word that matches the picture.
- Repeat the activity with words that differ in final consonant (*cave, cane, cake, cage,* and *cape*).

Point to the appropriate picture card, and say the corresponding word with exaggerated pronunciation.

TIER 2 — Match Spoken to Written Words

Concentrated instruction

Conduct the Tier 1 activity with only three words.

Point to the appropriate picture card, and say the corresponding word with exaggerated pronunciation.

Visual cues

Highlight the first sound in each stimulus word, and conduct the Tier 1 activity.

Point to the appropriate picture card, and say the corresponding word with exaggerated pronunciation.

TIER 3 — Match Spoken to Written Words

Concentrated instruction

- Present two picture cards at a time and two words that differ only in the initial sound.
- Ask students to point to the word that is said.
- Use exaggerated pronunciation on the initial sound, and ask students to repeat the word in a similar manner.

Point to the word said by the teacher, and repeat it with exaggerated pronunciation on the first sound.

Repeated practice

Conduct the activity, and triple the number of times each word is presented.

Point to the word said by the teacher, and repeat it with exaggerated pronunciation on the first sound.

Grade K

LANGUAGE AREA: Print Knowledge

OBJECTIVE: Participate in Shared Book Reading

TIER 1 — Shared Book Reading

Help students actively participate throughout book-reading activities.

- Read a book with a well-developed plot structure that has a clear beginning, middle, and end.
- Throughout the book reading, engage students using the **CROWD** strategy. **CROWD** is a set of five question types/prompts that are asked throughout book reading—each targets a different area:
    - **C** = Comprehension questions. Target: Particular linguistic structures (Q: *What did the bunny do?* A: *He hopped and skipped*).

      Note: The past-tense form does not exist in some languages, so some students may have more difficulty with this part of the lesson.

    - **R** = Recall questions. Target: Story content (Q: *Do you remember how the story ended?*).
    - **O** = Open-ended questions. Target: Increased amount of talk and amount of detail (Q: *What is happening on this page?*).
    - **W** = Wh-questions. Target: New vocabulary (Q: *Goldilocks tasted the porridge. What is porridge?*).
    - **D** = Distance questions. Target: Linking of book event to students' own experiences (Q: *Does your family eat porridge?*).
- As the book is read, pause and ask students **CROWD** questions appropriate to the storyline. Encourage many contributions.

Reply to **CROWD** questions.

TIER 2 — Shared Book Reading

Concentrated instruction

Ask only C, R, and O questions.

Provide responses to C, R, and O questions posed by the teacher.

Visual cues

Display the appropriate page of the book as a question is posed.

Provide responses to C, R, and O questions posed by the teacher.

TIER 3 — Shared Book Reading

Concentrated instruction

Ask only C and O questions.

Answer C and O questions posed by the teacher.

Alternative response mode

Ask concrete questions about what is happening on each page.

Point to or provide verbal or nonverbal *yes/no* answers in response to the teacher's questions.

Grade K

LANGUAGE AREA:	OBJECTIVE:
Print Knowledge	Understand Features of Print

TIER 1 — Features of Print

Explain that features of print have meaning.

- Introduce a familiar storybook, and use the following passage as part of an interactive reading experience:

  *Let's look at the **front** of the book. This is called the **cover** of the book. The name of the book is right here (point to title). A Place Called Kindergarten is the **title.** The person who wrote the book is called the **author**. Her name is right here (point to author's name), Jessica Harper. There is another name here (point to illustrator's name). G. Brian Karas is the **illustrator,** the person who drew the pictures. The **first** word on this page is **A**. The **next** word is **place.***

- Introduce at least two more books.
- Have students play the *I Spy* game using the following phrasing:
    - I spy a book whose author is _____.
    - I spy a book whose illustrator is _____.
    - I spy a book whose title begins with the word _____.

- Respond to questions asking you to name the author, title, illustrator, first word, and next word (*Where do I begin reading? Where do I read next?*).
- Play the *I Spy* game.

TIER 2	Features of Print

Multiple choice

- Show three different book parts while naming one part.
- Ask students to select the appropriate part and to say it aloud.

Select the correct part of the book and name it.

Multiple choice/Visual cues

- Write book parts on different cards.
- Identify a specific part of a book and ask students to select the part presented from a choice of two.

Name each book part that the teacher presents, and select the correct book part from a choice of two.

TIER 3	Features of Print

Imitation

- Review and name each book part.
- Ask students to repeat the name of each book part.

Repeat the name of each book part.

Modeling

Review and name each book part.

Watch and listen as the teacher names the different book parts.

GRADE K • PRINT KNOWLEDGE   131

References

Assessments

Boehm, A. E. (2000). *Boehm Test of Basic Concepts, Third Edition.* San Antonio, TX: Pearson Assessments.

Bracken, B. A. (1998). *Bracken Basic Concept Scale—Revised.* San Antonio, TX: Pearson Assessments.

Wiig, E. H. (2004). *Wiig Assessment of Basic Concepts.* Greenville, SC: Super Duper Publications.

Resources

Books

Asserín asserán: Folklore infantil. [*Asserín asserán: Children's folklore*]. San Francisco, CA: Donars Productions/Iaconi Book Imports.

Berger, B. H. (1984). *Grandfather twilight.* New York, NY: Philomel Books.

Brett, J. (1989). *The mitten.* New York, NY: Putnam Juvenile.

Brown, M. W. (1942). *Runaway bunny (C. Hurd, Illus.).* New York, NY: HarperCollins.

Calmenson, S. (1995). *Dinner at the panda palace* (N.B. Wescott, Illus.). New York, NY: HarperCollins.

Calmenson, S. (2005). *Kindergarten kids: Riddles, rebuses, wiggles, giggles, and more.* (M. Sweet, Illus.). New York, NY: HarperCollins.

Carle, E. (1987). *Do you want to be my friend?* New York, NY: HarperCollins.

Cohen, C. L. (2000). *How many fish?* (S.D. Schindler, Illus.). New York, NY: HarperCollins.

Dantzer-Rosenthal, M. D. (1986). *Some things are different, some things are the same* (M. Nerlove, Illus.). Park Ridge, IL: Albert Whitman.

Flora, S. B. (2005). *Listen, look, and do! Over 120 activities to strengthen visual and auditory discrimination and memory skills.* Minneapolis, MN: Key Education.

Frank, G. W. (1986). *Follow me!: Listen and do activities.* East Moline, IL: LinguiSystems.

Gibbons, G. (1996). *How a house is built.* New York, NY: Holiday House.

Harper J. (2006). *A place called kindergarten* (G. B. Karas, Illus.). New York, NY: Penguin Group.

Hoban, R. (1993). *A baby sister for Frances* (L. Hoban, Illus.). New York, NY: HarperCollins.

Hoban, T. (1985). *A children's zoo.* New York, NY: Greenwillow Books.

Kasza, K. (1987). *The wolf's chicken stew.* New York, NY: Putnam Juvenile.

Keats, E. J. (1962). *The snowy day.* New York, NY: Viking.

Maccarone, G. (1996). *The silly story of Goldie Locks and the three squares* (A. Kennedy, Illus.). New York, NY: Scholastic.

Martin, B., Jr.(1996). *Brown Bear, Brown Bear, what do you see?* (E. Carle, Illus.). New York, NY: Henry Holt. (Original work published 1983)

Morris, J. E., (2005). *May I please have a cookie?* New York, NY: Scholastic.

Morrison, L. (2006). *Guess again! Riddle poems.* (C.Hale, Illus.). Little Rock, AR: August House.

Munsch, R. (2002). *Alligator baby.* (M. Martchenko, Illus.). New York, NY: Cartwheel.

Numeroff, L. J. (1998). *If you give a pig a pancake* (F. Bond, Illus.). New York, NY: HarperCollins.

Sendak, M. (1963). *Where the wild things are.* New York, NY: HarperCollins.

Shannon, D. (1998). *No, David!* New York, NY: Blue Sky Press.

Slobodkina, E. (1999). *Caps for sale: A tale of a peddler, some monkeys and their monkey business.* New York, NY: HarperCollins. (Original work published 1940)

Spinelli, E. (1991). *Somebody loves you, Mr. Hatch.* (P. Yalowitz, Illus.). New York, NY: Simon & Schuster Children's.

Williams, S. (1996). *I went walking* (J. Vivas, Illus.). New York, NY: Red Wagon Books, Harcourt.

Vowels, T. (2002). *Listening skills for young children.* Westminster, CA: Teacher Created Resources.

Grade 1

RTI in Action:
Oral Language Activities for Grade 1 Classrooms

BASIC CONCEPTS

Understand and Use Basic Concepts.....................136

VOCABULARY

Understand and Use Nouns......................................140
Understand and Use Action Words......................142
Understand and Use Adjectives............................144
Understand and Use Pronouns..............................146
Understand and Use New
  Vocabulary Words...148
Categorize Words and Ideas..................................150
Understand Classification.......................................154
Recognize Comparisons and Contrasts..............156
Understand and Produce
  Word Definitions...158
Understand Cause and
  Effect Relationships..160
Understand and Use Synonyms............................162
Understand and Use Antonyms............................164
Understand and Use Similes..................................166
Understand and Use Homophones......................168

LISTENING AND SPEAKING

Respond to Multistep Directions..........................170
Understand and Use Different
  Types of Sentences...172
Use Complete Sentences.......................................174
Speak for Different Purposes: Describe...............176
Speak for Different Purposes:
  Ask Questions..178
Speak for Different Purposes: Persuade..............180
Participate in Conversations:
  Change and End Topics......................................182

Adapt Messages to Different
  Situations and Listeners.....................................184
Understand and Use Nonverbal Signals...............186
Understand and Use Tone of Voice to
  Convey Meaning..188
Understand and Express Feelings.........................190
Ask Questions for Repetition/
  Clarification...192
Understand and Use Logical
  Order of Events...194
Understand and Use Fictional Narratives.............196
Retell a Story or Directions in
  Correct Order..200
Understand and Use Figurative
  Language: Idioms..202
Understand Humor in
  Words and Situations...206
Summarize Stories and Events..............................208
Paraphrase Stories..210
Understand and Distinguish
  Fact From Opinion..212
Share Opinions..214
Understand and Use Inferences............................216

PHONOLOGICAL AWARENESS

Identify Initial/Final Sounds in Words..................218
Delete First and Last Syllable of
  Compound Words..220
Blend Phonemes Into Words.................................224

PRINT KNOWLEDGE

Understand Features of Print.................................226
Understand Concept of Paragraph.......................228

Teacher Instruction: Black text on white background   **Student Response:** Black text on shaded background

Grade 1

LANGUAGE AREA:
Basic Concepts

OBJECTIVE:
Understand and Use
Basic Concepts

TIER 1 — Basic Concepts

Help students understand and use basic concepts such as spatial relationships, time, and quantity.

Snack time: Give students different amounts of snack food. Talk about who has *more*, *less*, and *equal* amounts of food.

Lining up: Give directions using basic concept words:
- *Line up by **every other** row.*
- *Stand in the **front/back** of the line.*
- *Stand **between** _____ and _____.*
- *Before you stand **beside** (student), clap your hands.*
- *Find _____ (name student). **Skip** a student and stand **behind** the next student.*

Writing: Talk about letters that go **above** and **below** the lines.

Reading: Find words, sentences, and paragraphs **in the center** and **in the corner** of the page.

Science: Talk about animals that fly *above* and live *below* the water.

Vocabulary: Use body part vocabulary to reinforce basic concept words:
- *What is in the **middle** of your face?*
- *What do you have **pairs** of?*
- *What is **above** and **below** your nose?*
- *What is on the **left** and **right** sides of your head?*
- *What is at the **end** of your hand?*
- *What is in the **middle** of your leg?*
- *Do we have **more** toes or **more** ears?*
- *What part of you is **narrow**?*

136   GRADE 1 • BASIC CONCEPTS

Calendar activities: Review calendar concepts daily:

Ask students questions such as the following each day:

- *How many days are **before** the weekend?*
- *How many days are in this month? Are there **more, less,** or **equal** to last month?*
- *Name all the days of the week **except** Saturday.*
- *Is it the **beginning, middle,** or **end** of the month?*
- ***Skip** a day and tell me what day it is.*
- *We are _____ (give activity) the day **after** tomorrow; what day will that be?*
- *When is your birthday—in a **few** days or in **many** days?*
- *What month comes **next**? What month came **before** this month?*
- *Tell something we would **never** do in _____ (name of month). Tell something we **always** do in _____.*
- *What days are **between** today and the weekend?*
- *Choose an activity that will happen today. Talk about what we will do **before** this activity and what will happen **after** this activity.*
- *What day **separates** Tuesday and Thursday?*

These are additional basic concepts to use for practice with students in first grade:

- first/last
- longer/shorter
- part/whole
- thin/thick
- wide/narrow
- yesterday/today/tomorrow
- closer/farther
- similarities/differences

Respond to the teacher's questions.

Grade 1

TIER 2 — Basic Concepts

Repeated exposure

- Administer an inventory of basic concepts or do a structured observation to determine student mastery. Administer a screening such as the *Boehm Test of Basic Concepts, Third Edition*; *Bracken Basic Concept Scale—Revised*; or *Wiig Assessment of Basic Concepts*.
- For the concept the student has not mastered, determine which ones may be interfering with the ability to follow the general education curriculum without support.
- Throughout the day, provide models and opportunities for the student to practice using targeted concepts.

Practice using basic concepts.

Negative practice

Give students statements with basic concept words used incorrectly. For example:

- *My knee is **closer** to my nose than my mouth is.*
- *My legs are **shorter** than my fingers.*
- *A pencil is **thicker** than a can.*
- *My nose is at the **end** of my face.*

Correct the sentences by replacing the incorrect basic concept words with correct ones.

TIER 3 — Basic Concepts

Concrete materials

Use manipulatives or actions to illustrate basic concept words.

- *Lean **forward**.*
- *Put your pencil **over** the table.*
- *Put objects in order from **smallest** to **largest**.*

Follow the directions using the objects.

Visual dictionary/Alternative response mode

Show pictures and ask students to find a person or object that is **last**, **tallest**, **in between**, **the same as**, **in the corner**, and so forth.

Point to the person or object.

Notes:

Grade 1

LANGUAGE AREA:	OBJECTIVE:
Vocabulary	Understand and Use Nouns

TIER 1 — Nouns

Explain that a *noun* is the name of a person, place, animal, or thing.

Use animal vocabulary to teach nouns. Write person, place, animal, or thing as headings on the board or paper. Guide students to brainstorm a list of

- animals—place the words under the category *animal* (*bear, bird,* or *cat*);
- animal homes—place the words under the category *place* (*cave, nest,* or *house*);
- animal caretakers—place the words under the category *person* (*zookeeper, mother,* or *child*);
- animal objects—place the words under the category *thing* (*water dish, ball,* or *leaves*).

Ask students to name a type of noun that is missing from the list.

- Name a person: lion, zoo, _____.
- Name an animal: _____, farm, farmer.
- Name a place: chicken, _____, farmer.
- Name a thing: dog, home, _____.

Provide the name of a person, place, animal, or thing.

TIER 2 — Nouns

Simplify

- Talk about places where animals live, such as a cave, house or jungle.
- Ask students to list animals and people associated with each place.

Brainstorm a list of animals that live in each place and talk about the people who take care of them.

Concrete materials

- Provide drawing materials to students.
- Ask students to draw a picture of their favorite animal.
- Write the noun headings *person*, *place*, *animal*, and *thing* on the picture.
- Ask students to circle the correct heading (*animal*).
- Repeat with other drawings.

Draw a picture and circle the correct heading.

TIER 3 — Nouns

Independent practice

- Gather old magazines or drawing materials and place them in the art center in the classroom.
- Ask students to find nouns—persons, places, animals, and things.

Find or draw pictures of nouns.

Visual dictionary

- Display a picture of a farm. *Farm* is the name of a place.
- Explain that *animal* is a noun.
- Talk about the person who might take care of the animal.
- Repeat the activity with a picture of a zoo or pet shop.

Find additional nouns in the picture.

Grade 1

GRADE 1 • VOCABULARY   141

LANGUAGE AREA: Vocabulary

OBJECTIVE: Understand and Use Action Words

TIER 1 — Action Words

Present tense: Explain to students that an action word or verb is something that we can *do*. Have a discussion about actions students can do.

- Write *I can _____* on a large visual display and ask students to fill in the blank with an action word that portrays something they have learned to do.
    - I can swim.
    - I can run.
    - I can ride my bike.
- Write the action words on note cards and place the cards in a bag.

Draw a card and pantomime the action word. Ask your classmates: *What am I doing?* Classmates guess the action word.

Past tense: Explain to students that some action words tell about things that we have *already done*. Talk about what you did before you came to school.

- I ate breakfast.
- I brushed my hair.
- I got dressed.
- I walked.

Write the action words on note cards and place the cards in a bag.

Draw a card and pantomime the action word. Ask your classmates: *What did I do?* Classmates guess the action word.

Future tense: Explain to students that some action words tell about what we *will do* in the future. Write *I will _____* on a large visual display and ask students to fill in the blank with things that they will do after they get home from school, on the weekend, or on a special holiday.

Write the action words on note cards and place the cards in a bag.

Draw a card and pantomime the action word. Ask your classmates, *What will I do?* Classmates guess the action word.

TIER 2	Action Words

Concentrated instruction/Visual cues

- Focus on verbs for a specific category.
- Ask the students to tell you action words for that category.
- Make a list of the words the students brainstorm on the board. For example, name action you do
  - on the playground
  - in a store
  - at the beach
  - in art or gym class
- Teach each word and ask students to finish the sentences.
  - *Today I ...* (*hop, talk, color*).
  - *Yesterday I ...* (*hopped, talked, colored*).
  - *Tomorrow I ...* (*will hop, will talk, will color*).

- Brainstorm a list of action words for each place.
- Finish the sentences using action words.

TIER 3	Action Words

Visual dictionary

Show students pictures to illustrate actions.

Express the action word in the picture.

Different stimuli

Read *To Root, to Toot, to Parachute: What Is a Verb?* by Brian P. Cleary and Jenya Prosmitsky.

- Read the text, saying the action words louder and longer.
- Stop after each page and pick an action word in the story and ask the students: *Can you _____?*

Respond to questions with action words. Say, *I can _____.*

GRADE 1 • VOCABULARY   143

LANGUAGE AREA: Vocabulary

OBJECTIVE: Understand and Use Adjectives

TIER 1 — Adjectives

Talk about adjectives as words that tell about size, color, shape, and what something smells like, feels like, or tastes like. Talk about how we use many adjectives to describe the food we eat. Present foods with different tastes and textures:

- *apples*
- *raisins*
- *pretzels*

Brainstorm words with students that describe the size, shape, and feel of each food sample.

Choose one food. Describe how it looks, feels, smells, and tastes.

TIER 2 — Adjectives

Visual cues

- Write *size, color, shape, smell, feels like,* and *tastes like* on the top of a piece of paper.
- Give students one of the sample foods.

List words that fit in each category that describe the food.

Forced-choice questions

Give students choices:

- Are apples red or white?
- Are raisins large or small?
- Are pretzels sweet or salty?

Choose the correct adjective to describe the food samples.

144 GRADE 1 • VOCABULARY

TIER 3 — Adjectives

Completion/Cloze statements

Ask students to complete your statement with an adjective.

- *Raisins feel _____.*
- *The shape of the raisin is _____.*
- *The raisin tastes _____.*

Fill in the sentence with an adjective.

Different stimuli

- Read *Hairy, Scary, Ordinary? What Is an Adjective?* by Brian P. Cleary and Jenya Prosmitsky.
- Raise your voice when you come to an adjective.

Raise your hand when you hear an adjective.

| Grade 1 | LANGUAGE AREA: Vocabulary | OBJECTIVE: Understand and Use Pronouns |

TIER 1 — Pronouns

Talk about pronouns being words that replace nouns. Explain that there are different kinds of pronouns.

- Read a story together and find the singular, plural, and possessive pronouns.
- Discuss what nouns the pronoun is used for and place the word on a sticky note.
- Discuss how pronouns make the story shorter and the writing clearer and more interesting.

- Put the sticky notes over the pronouns and reread the story, substituting the nouns for the pronouns.
- Contribute to the discussion about how and why pronouns are used in writing.

TIER 2 — Pronouns

Different stimuli

- Give examples of singular, plural, and possessive pronouns.
- Make a chart and state the definition of a pronoun at the top. Divide the chart into three parts (*singular*, *plural*, and *possessive*).
- Read *I and You and Don't Forget Who: What Is a Pronoun?* by Brian P. Cleary.
- Ask students to identify the pronouns and write them in the correct area of the chart.

Raise your hand when you hear a pronoun, and write it on the chart.

Visual dictionary/Visual cues

- Show the student action pictures.
- Say and write two or three sentences about the picture without using pronouns.
- Underline the words that could be replaced with pronouns. For example:
  o *Michael is riding* <u>Michael's</u> *bike.* <u>Michael's</u> *bike is blue.*
  o *The dog is eating a bone.* <u>The</u> <u>dog</u> *likes the bone.* <u>The</u> <u>bone</u> *is bigger than* <u>the</u> <u>dog</u> *is.*

Replace the underlined words with a pronoun.

146 GRADE 1 • VOCABULARY

TIER 3 — Pronouns

Forced-choice questions

Use a pronoun worksheet. Ask students to complete the worksheet using the correct pronoun:

- **He/him** is my brother.
- **Her/she** wants to come to the park.
- **I/me** went skating yesterday.
- Mary gave the ball to **him/he**.
- **She/her** house is white.

Choose the correct pronoun.

Negative practice

Give the student incorrect examples of pronoun use.

- **Him** goes to the store.
- **Me** is happy today.
- **She's** dress is red and white.
- **Them** have a big pool.

Repeat the sentence correctly.

Grade 1	LANGUAGE AREA: Vocabulary	OBJECTIVE: Understand and Use New Vocabulary Words

TIER 1 — New Vocabulary Words

Talk about how important it is to learn new words to express ideas.

Write a paragraph on the board that describes material in a unit covered in class (such as holidays). In this paragraph, include three to five overused words that students often rely on (such as *good, happy, sad, nice,* and *make*).

- Read the paragraph aloud, underlining, with the teacher's help, the overused words.
- Generate new words for each overused word.

Overused word		New word
happy	⟶	glad
mad	⟶	angry
nice	⟶	polite
make	⟶	create

- Substitute the new words and then reread the paragraph.

TIER 2 — New Vocabulary Words

Multiple choice/Concentrated instruction

Provide students with the original word and three additional words (one synonym and two nonsynonyms). Ask students, *Is another word for (original word) (Choice 1-nonsynonym), (Choice 2-synonym), or (Choice 3-nonsynonym)?*

For example, Is (happy) another word for (disappointed), (glad), or (sad)? Is make another word for (fix), (create), or (touch)?

Focus on two or three overused words. Provide students with the original word and three additional words (one synonym and two nonsynonyms). Ask students, *Is another word for (original word) (Choice 1-nonsynonym), (Choice 2-nonsynonym), or (Choice 3-synonym)?*

For example, Is another word for (mad) (happy), (excited), or (angry)?

Provide teacher with correct word choice.

148   GRADE 1 • VOCABULARY

Turn and talk

- Ask students to work in pairs to review the meaning of the target word.

- Direct each pair to make a list of words associated with the target word.

- Have students use a sentence with the new word.

- Talk with a partner about everything you know about the target word.
- Discuss other words that go with the target word.
- Create sentences with the new word.

TIER 3   New Vocabulary Words

Forced-choice questions/Repeated practice

Provide students with the original word and two additional words (one synonym and one nonsynonym). Ask students, *Is another word for (original word) (Choice 1-synonym) or (Choice 2-nonsynonym)?*

Provide students with the original word and two additional words (one synonym and one nonsynonym). Ask students, *Is another word for (original word) (Choice 1-synonym) or (Choice 2-nonsynonym)? Repeat each item three times.*

Provide the teacher with the correct word choice.

Elaboration

- Review the target vocabulary word by placing it in context. Prompt students to discuss:

  o *Who uses or is connected to the target word?*

  o *Where is this word used?*

  o *What does it do or what does it look like?*

  o *What are other words that go with the target word?*

- Provide cues as necessary to help students respond to the questions and then to use the target word in a sentence.

Answer the questions and then use the word in a sentence correctly.

Grade		
1	**LANGUAGE AREA:** Vocabulary	**OBJECTIVE:** Categorize Words and Ideas

TIER 1 — Categorize

Talk about the relationship between words and ideas and how words can be sorted into groups based on similar characteristics.

- Review a semantic category (*birds*) and common items in a category (*robin* and *bluebird*). Provide a brief definition (*Birds are animals that have wings and feathers and lay eggs*).

- Provide concrete examples of items that do and do not belong in the *bird* category (*hawk, ostrich, penguin, owl,* and *cockatoo* vs. *elephant, horse, kangaroo, rhinoceros,* and *ape*).

- Introduce more subtle examples of items that do not belong in the category (*lizard, bee, monkey, fly, bat*). Place pictures of these items on the board.

- Ask students why each is not an example of a bird.

Explain why the pictured items are not birds.

150   GRADE 1 • VOCABULARY

TIER 2   Categorize

Multiple choice/Visual cues

- Present sets of four pictures (three birds and one nonbird)

- Present sets of four pictures (one bird and three nonbirds)

Select the picture of the bird.

Repeated practice

- Provide students with a list of words or pictures that can be categorized in different ways, such as

  o four-letter words

  o words beginning with a certain sound

  o things that grow

  o things that are used by a teacher

  o things that are round

- Ask students to take the same group of words or pictures and organize them according to one of the categories.

- Ask students to reorganize the words or pictures in a different category. Direct them to talk about why they placed the words or items in the category.

Organize the words or pictures in different categories and tell why you placed them in that category.

| TIER 3 | Categorize |

Peer tutoring

- Pair one student who has mastered the concept of categorizing with a student who is having difficulty.
- Give each pair two to three sets of objects (pennies, blue blocks, short pencils, red crayons) and ask students to practice sorting them.
- Give each pair a set of pictures of birds. Instruct each pair to first decide if each picture is a bird or other animal.
- Ask each student to take a turn sorting the pictures, with the other student being the "coach," providing corrections as needed.

Sort the objects and pictures into the correct groups.

Modeling

- Provide students with a variety of objects such as coins, colored blocks, pencils, and crayons.
- Model sorting each group of items into specific categories (pennies, blue blocks, short pencils, red crayons).
- Direct students to sort items in the same categories as modeled.
- Next, provide pictures of a variety of animals.
- Model categorizing pictures choosing animals that fly, swim, or walk.
- Direct students to categorize the animals as modeled.

Categorize the objects and pictures into correct groups.

Notes:

Grade 1

LANGUAGE AREA: Vocabulary

OBJECTIVE: Understand Classification

TIER 1 — Classify

Explain how things are alike and can be grouped together in a specific category.

- Display a poster of the grocery store or food circulars from the newspaper.
- Discuss how the aisles are arranged by groups or categories in a supermarket.
- Say: *Pretend you are going on a shopping trip. Brainstorm items you would see in the fruit aisle, vegetable aisle, dairy case, meat case, paper goods aisle, cleaning supplies aisle, and snack aisle.*

Draw or write your own shopping list. Read your list to the class.

Ask a student to express where items on another student's list would be found by stating what groups or category this product is in.

Provide the group or category for different items.

TIER 2 — Classify

Visual cues/Repeated practice

- Display pictures of things we buy at the supermarket. The colorful inserts in a newspaper are useful for this activity. You also can use clip art to find pictures of items in a supermarket.
- Ask students to find a picture of an item that fits in a particular category: *Find a kind of fruit. What is another kind of fruit that you can buy at the supermarket?*

Find the word that fits in the category and brainstorm additional words.

Visual dictionary

- Provide a newspaper supermarket insert.
- Ask students to place items in groups.

- Cut the pictures out of the newspaper and arrange them in groups.
- Talk about why they go together and the name of the group.

154 GRADE 1 • VOCABULARY

TIER 3 — Classify

Restricted-choice questions

Give the student *yes/no* questions about categories:

- *Is an apple a kind of fruit?*
- *Is a bear a kind of animal?*
- *Is a car a vehicle?*
- *Is a scooter a kind of furniture?*

Answer *yes* or *no*. Provide other words that fit into each category.

Double dose of instruction/Visual cues

Review the concepts of *same* and *different*. Explain how we put words into groups based on things that are the same. Give examples of categories:

- *Things we eat are called food.*
- *Things we wear are called clothes.*
- *Things that make music are called instruments.*

Give the student pictures of food, clothes, animals, and instruments in random order.

- Group pictures into categories.
- Say or draw additional members of each group.

Grade 1

LANGUAGE AREA: Vocabulary

OBJECTIVE: Recognize Comparisons and Contrasts

TIER 1 — Compare and Contrast

Describe ways that things are alike or different.

- Explain to students that early settlers in this country told a story about a man named Johnny Appleseed who roamed the wilderness and planted apple trees. He is credited with spreading apple trees throughout the country.
- Place five to six different kinds of apples in front of the classroom. Talk about how all of these apples are alike:
  - *They grow on trees.*
  - *They are all fruit.*
  - *They have seeds inside.*
  - *They are food we eat.*
- Show two apples and ask how they are different.

Choose two apples and give two ways they are different.

 Bonus: Ask students to pick an apple and describe it without telling the other students which one they chose (*The apple is green and has a short stem*).

TIER 2   Compare and Contrast

Visual cues

Present a visual organizer such as a Venn diagram (see Append x G) and record students' answers in the organizer.

Choose two apples and brainstorm how they are alike and how they are different as the teacher writes responses on a Venn diagram.

Auditory cues

Choose two apples and ask the student questions:

- *Are these two apples the same color?*
- *Are these two apples the same size?*
- *Do they both have stems?*

Talk about how the apples are alike and how they are different.

TIER 3   Compare and Contrast

Different stimuli

- Give student common class objects to examine, such as stapler, paper, pencil, marker, ruler, textbook, and workbook.

- Ask students to tell how these objects are the same and how they are different.

Examine common classroom objects and compare and contrast them.

Simplify

Focus on comparing skills only. Show objects and only talk about how they are the same.

Talk about how two apples are alike.

GRADE 1 • VOCABULARY   157

LANGUAGE AREA:	OBJECTIVE:
Vocabulary	Understand and Produce Word Definitions

TIER 1 — Word Definitions

Discuss how we define words to describe their meaning.

- On a piece of paper, write a concrete noun (such as *volcano*) from a text or curricular material.
- Draw lines to make three columns underneath the word from left to right: Ask the class:
    - *What is it?* (category)
    - *What is it like/What does it do?* (properties)
    - *What are some examples?* (provide illustrations)
- Brainstorm answers for each question and write them in the appropriate column. For *volcano*, an answer to *What is it?* could be *mountain*. Responses to *What is it like/What does it do?* could be *has a hole*, *erupts*, or *has hot lava*.
- Say the whole definition while pointing to the appropriate columns.
- Ask the class to say the definition for the concrete noun.
- Ask individual students to generate definitions while viewing the information on the chart.
- Read a paragraph from the students' text/unit to place the word in context.

Brainstorm the items for each column and say the definition of the target word.

 Bonus: Ask students to give the names of volcanoes: *Etna, Mauna Loa,* or *Kilauea.*

TIER 2 — Word Definitions

Concentrated instruction

Conduct the Tier 1 activity with a two-column chart (*What is it?* and *What is it like?*).

Brainstorm the items for each of the two columns and say the definition of the target word.

Visual cues

Conduct the Tier 1 activity while showing picture(s) representing the target word from text/curricular materials.

Brainstorm the items for each of the two columns while looking at the picture, and say the definition of the target word.

TIER 3 — Word Definitions

Visual cues/Completion/Cloze statements

Conduct the Tier 1 activity while showing picture(s) representing the target word from text/curricular materials.

Ask students to complete sentences for each of the items:

- *A volcano is a _____.*
- *It has _____.*
- *Examples of volcanoes are _____.*

Complete sentences presented by the teacher while looking at the pictures of the target word.

Visual cues/Alternative response mode

- Conduct the Tier 1 activity while showing picture(s) representing the target word from text/curricular materials.
- Ask students to point to the part of the picture that represents the appropriate portion of the definition. For example, say
  - *Show me: A volcano is a mountain.*
  - *Show me: A volcano has a hole.*
  - *Show me: A volcano has hot lava.*

Point to the correct part of the picture as the teacher says a portion of the definition.

LANGUAGE AREA:	OBJECTIVE:
Vocabulary	Understand Cause and Effect Relationships

TIER 1 — Cause and Effect

Explicitly teach cause and effect prior to reading a book such as *If You Give a Mouse a Cookie* or *If You Give a Moose a Muffin* by Laura Joffe Numeroff; *Why Mosquitoes Buzz in People's Ears: A West African Tale* by Verna Aardema; or *Who Sank the Boat?* by Pamela Allen.

Demonstrate cause and effect using an activity such as making popcorn in the classroom.

- Ask what causes the kernels to pop (cooking or heat). The heat (cause) leads to the popping (effect).
- Tie the concept of cause and effect back to the books.
- On the board, draw a popcorn kernel with an arrow to popped popcorn.
- Draw the first event in the book and an arrow, and ask *What happens when (describe event)? What is the effect?*

Respond to the teacher's questions regarding cause and effect as appropriate.

 Bonus: Use this opportunity to teach a new word (*kernel*), homophone (*colonel*), and idiom (*kernel of truth*).

TIER 2	Cause and Effect

Modeling/Completion/Cloze statements

Provide additional examples of cause and effect, in the format *if/then*:

- *If I turn off the light switch, then the light will go out.*
- *If I drink the cup of water, then the cup will be empty.*

Ask students to provide their own examples of cause and effect. Students also can be asked to complete the *if/then* sentences.

Generate examples of cause and effect.

Visual cues

Present a colored card for the word/concept *if* and a card of a different color for the word/concept *then*, and repeat the Tier 1 activity.

Generate examples of cause and effect.

TIER 3	Cause and Effect

Role play

- Present activities of interest to students such as batting a ball or mixing paint to get new colors.
- Use these activities to act out (via gesture or pantomime) cause and effect. While acting out each activity, talk about cause-and-effect relationships: *If I hit the ball with the bat, what happens to the ball?*

Act out the cause-and-effect activities.

Completion/Cloze questions

Use a sentence completion task and provide a picture, gesture, or verbal prompt when needed. For example, *If I hit the ball with the bat, what happens to the ball?*

Provide the correct response to complete each sentence.

Bonus: Use opportunities throughout the day to demonstrate examples of cause and effect (*It is raining, so we _____.*).

<table>
<tr><td>**Grade 1**</td><td>LANGUAGE AREA:
Vocabulary</td><td>OBJECTIVE:
Understand and Use Synonyms</td></tr>
</table>

TIER 1 — Synonyms

Explain that synonyms are different words that mean the same thing.

- Demonstrate a happy face and a glad face. Explain that *happy* and *glad* are different words, but they have the same meaning. Introduce the term *synonym*.

- Continue giving concrete examples of synonyms:
  - *over/above*
  - *good/fine*
  - *separated/apart*
  - *shut/close*
  - *center/middle*
  - *neat/tidy*
  - *near/close*
  - *difficult/hard*
  - *fight/argue*

- Read the book *Crazy Hair Day* by Barney Saltzberg; while reading, pause and ask students to provide synonyms for words in the story.

Replace words in story with synonyms.

TIER 2 — Synonyms

Examples and nonexamples

Write the words *wrong, present,* and *speak* on the board. Give examples and nonexamples of synonyms for these words.

Choose the correct examples of synonyms for each word.

Matching

Make two columns on the board, listing the words *wrong, speak, present,* and *hill* on the right side and synonyms for these words in random order on the left side. Ask students to match the words.

Match the synonym pairs.

162   GRADE 1 • VOCABULARY

TIER 3	Synonyms

Role play

Ask student volunteers to pantomime *Crazy Hair Day* by Barney Saltzberg as you read the original story. Next, ask student volunteers to substitute the synonym words.

Discuss how the actions were the same in both versions and talk about the synonym pairs.

Repeated practice/Adjust pace

Repeat the Tier 1 lesson above at a slower pace. Give the student additional time to respond.

Discuss how the actions were the same in both versions and talk about the synonym pairs.

Grade
1

GRADE 1 • VOCABULARY   163

Grade 1

LANGUAGE AREA: Vocabulary

OBJECTIVE: Understand and Use Antonyms

TIER 1 — Antonyms

Talk about antonyms being pairs of words with opposite meanings.

Write a word that has a familiar antonym on a sticky note and place it on the back of a student volunteer without showing him the word.

Name the antonym for the word that is on the student's back. The student volunteer guesses the word on his back.

Write the two words on the board and repeat the activity.

 Bonus: Discuss the opposite of high-frequency words: *big/little*, *in/on*, and *hot/cold*.

TIER 2 — Antonyms

Different stimuli

Read *The Greatest Gymnast of All* by Stuart J. Murphy. This book illustrates 16 antonym pairs about the gymnast's activities. Ask students to draw a picture of their favorite antonym pair.

Illustrate your favorite antonym pair in the story.

Matching

List each antonym from the book on an index card. Mix up the cards. Ask students to match pairs of antonyms.

Match the antonym pairs.

TIER 3	Antonyms

Negative practice

Give examples of antonyms that are incorrect:

- **Hot** is the antonym of **soft**.
- **Sit** is the antonym of **heavy**.
- **Open** is the opposite of **door**.

Correct the opposite sentences.

Restricted-choice questions

Ask yes/no questions:

- Is hot an antonym for man?
- Is sit an antonym of stand?
- Is boy an antonym of girl?

Answer yes or no.

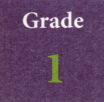

LANGUAGE AREA: Vocabulary

OBJECTIVE: Understand and Use Similes

TIER 1 — Similes

Explain how similes help you see pictures in your mind. Similes are used to compare two unlike things using phrases that begin with *like* or *as*.

Give examples:

- *The tree was as tall as a giant.*
- *The children in the classroom were busy like a beaver making a dam.*

Read a book about seasons, such as *Four Seasons Make a Year* by Anne Rockwell. Brainstorm examples of similes for each season.

- *Spring flowers smell like candy.*
- *Winter is as cold as ice.*
- *The leaves in the fall are as colorful as a rainbow.*
- *Summer clothes are as light as a feather.*

Create and illustrate a simile for each season.

TIER 2 — Similes

Completion/Cloze statements

Give simile examples. Ask students to provide additional words that will complete the simile:

- *Winter is as cold as ice or a _____.*
- *Summer heat is hot like an oven or a _____.*
- *Snow is as white as a marshmallow or a _____.*
- *Fall leaves are crunchy like a potato chip or a _____.*

Fill in the blank and repeat the simile with your word.

Different stimuli

- Read *Crazy Like a Fox: A Simile Story* by Loreen Leedy.
- Instruct students to listen for similes and to raise a hand when one is used.

Raise your hand when you hear a simile.

TIER 3 — Similes

Forced-choice questions

Give students the first part of a simile and ask them to choose between two words:

- *Winter is as cold as ice or as cold as a stove.*
- *Snow is as white as an apple or a marshmallow.*
- *Autumn leaves are as crunchy as a potato chip or pudding*

Choose the correct word and repeat the simile.

Visual cues

Look at the illustrations in a book about seasons from the Tier 1 activity and brainstorm a list of words that go with each season:

- *Autumn: leaves, jackets, Halloween*
- *Winter: snow, ice, cold, mittens, snowman*
- *Summer: hot, beach, vacation*
- *Spring: flowers, grass, baseball*

Give students visual cues. Ask them to create similes using the list of words.

Choose a word from the list and create a simile.

Grade 1

LANGUAGE AREA:
Vocabulary

OBJECTIVE:
Understand and Use Homophones

TIER 1 — Homophones

Explain to students that homophones are two or more words that sound the same but have different meanings and different spellings. Give students examples that can be easily demonstrated:

- *I* and *eye*
- *tail* and *tale*
- *son* and *sun*
- *by* and *buy*
- *won* and *one*

Read *Dear Deer: A Book of Homophones* by Gene Barretta. Aunt Ant has just moved to the zoo and, using homophones, she describes the quirky animal behaviors.

- Make a list of the homophones in the story.
- Give examples of sentences that contain a pair of homophones:
  o The monkey <u>ate</u> <u>eight</u> bananas.
  o The <u>knight</u> rode his horse in the <u>night</u>.
  o The <u>hare</u> has white <u>hair</u>.

Say and illustrate a sentence that contains a homophone pair.

168   GRADE 1 • VOCABULARY

TIER 2	Homophones

Matching

Ask students to match lists of homophones with their definitions. For example, ask, *It is someone who lives in my house and also something that shines in the sky. Which homophone pair am I talking about?*

Match the definitions to the homophone word pairs.

Visual dictionary

Ask students to create their own book of homophones.

- Draw two pictures that illustrate the meanings of the homophone pair.
- Write the words under your pictures.
- Share your drawings and explain the meanings of the words with your classmates.

TIER 3	Homophones

Completion/Cloze statements

Ask students to fill in the blanks and express the homophone pairs.

- *The wind _____. (blew in the blue sky)*
- *I will _____ you on Saturday. (see you at the sea)*
- *I want _____ for dinner. (meat when we meet)*

Fill in the blanks with a pair of homophones.

Word bank/Repeated practice

Create a class word bank. Encourage students to find homophones as they go about their daily activities.

- Write your homophone pairs on the class chart.
- At the end of each week, discuss the additions to your class chart.

GRADE 1 • VOCABULARY 169

Grade 1

LANGUAGE AREA: Listening and Speaking

OBJECTIVE: Respond to Multistep Directions

TIER 1 — Multistep Directions

Explain the importance of remembering what is said and of following directions. Give specific, simple, two-step directions. Increase length and complexity gradually. First graders are expected to complete two- and three-step directions successfully.

- *First, walk to the door; next, skip back to your chair.*
- *First, stand beside your desk; next, hop to the window.*
- *First, put the blue ball under your chair; next, touch the bookshelf; last, bring me a book.*
- *First, pick up your pencil; next, put it on my desk; last, stand beside the window.*

Worksheets (www.tlsbooks.com/followdirectionsshapes.pdf), activity books such as *Listen, Look, and Do* or *Listening Skills for Young Children* (O'Block Books), and websites (www.gameclassroom.com) may provide some good ideas for practicing directions.

Errors with following directions can be attributed to weaknesses in listening, understanding basic concepts or other vocabulary, understanding the complexity of language, attention, memory, sequencing, and possibly hearing loss. When children make errors, attempt to evaluate where the breakdown occurs. Be vigilant about keeping your directions simple during training stages. Do the following to set up the activity for success:

- Get student's attention before giving a direction.
- Use an appropriate and varied tone of voice.
- Speak slowly and clearly.
- To increase complexity, use words like *before*, *after*, *first*, and *finally*. Make sure that students understand concepts in isolation before embedding them in directions.
- Check for understanding throughout the activity.
- Encourage students to ask questions.

Follow the directions.

TIER 2 — Multistep Directions

Assistive technology

- Use a website such as www.internet4classrooms.com (click on Grade Level Help and then 1st Grade Skills–Current Standards–Language Arts) or www.education.com and follow the directions.
- Start at the easiest level and move to progressively more difficult levels.
- Ask students to perform the directions.

Follow the directions on the website.

Simplify/Peer tutoring

- Give two-step directions to student pairs. Ask each student to follow one of the directions.
- Repeat the direction and ask students to follow the direction they did not follow the first time.
- Repeat the direction a third time and ask both students to follow the two-step direction.

Follow the directions.

TIER 3 — Multistep Directions

Alternative response mode

Ask students to work in pairs. Ask one student to follow a two- or three-step direction. Ask the second student to report if the direction was correctly followed.

Observe and decide if the direction was followed correctly.

Simplify/Mental imagery

- Give a two-step direction. Ask students to close their eyes and visualize themselves following the direction.
- Next, repeat the direction, pausing between steps.
- Allow students to follow the first step before saying the second step of the direction.
- Next, give a two-step direction and encourage students to visualize before following both steps.

Visualize and follow directions.

Grade 1

LANGUAGE AREA: Listening and Speaking

OBJECTIVE: Understand and Use Different Types of Sentences

TIER 1 — Different Types of Sentences

Explain the differences between questions and statements.

- Use a familiar story or *Stop That Bus,* which can be found online at www.tampareads.com/books-ol/stopbus/intro.htm, to make a list of questions and statements.
- Show how questions end with a question mark and statements end with a period.
- Give examples of questions and statements and ask students to identify whether it is a question or statement.

Tell if the sentence read was a question or statement.

- Explain how commands demand something be done and exclamations show excitement about something.
- Demonstrate voice changes as you read, and write these different kinds of sentences.
- Show how commands end with a period and exclamations end with an exclamation point.

Tell if the sentence is a question, statement, exclamation, or command.

| TIER 2 | Different Types of Sentences |

Independent practice

Give students a copy of the story. Instruct them to independently circle question sentences and underline statement sentences.

Underline or circle sentences to show understanding of the differences between the two kinds of sentences.

Matching

- Give students four cards with a label of a type of sentence on each card (*statement, question, exclamation,* and *command*).
- Give students a set of sentence strips.
- Tell them to place each sentence strip under the correct card, showing what kind of sentence it is.

Correctly sort the sentence strip into the correct category.

| TIER 3 | Different Types of Sentences |

Visual cues/Repeated practice

- Give students four cards, indicating the four different kinds of sentences. Cards can have the following symbols or words: ? (question), . (statement), ! (exclamation), and *YOU* (command).
- Read independent sentences or sentences from a familiar story. Pause after each sentence.

Hold up the card showing what kind of sentence you heard.

- Provide feedback. Explain why a student's choice was correct or incorrect.
- Repeat those sentences that were evaluated incorrectly later in the lesson for review and more practice.

Examples and nonexamples

- Review explanation of one sentence type and give 5–10 examples.
- Next, give students examples and nonexamples of the targeted sentence type.

Listen to the example and identify the target sentence type.

GRADE 1 • LISTENING AND SPEAKING   173

LANGUAGE AREA: Listening and Speaking

OBJECTIVE: Use Complete Sentences

TIER 1 — Complete Sentences

During a lesson about friendship, explain that a sentence expresses a complete thought about a subject and what that subject is or does. Before reading *Frog and Toad All Year* by Arnold Lobel, explain that Frog and Toad are good friends who do many things together. As you read the story, ask students to think about things that good friends do together.

- Explain that complete sentences must contain a subject (what you are talking about) and an action word (what's happening).
- Ask students to ask questions about their friends using complete sentences:
    - *What is your friend's name?*
    - *Where does your friend live?*
    - *Why do you like your friend?*
    - *What does your friend always do?*
    - *What do you and your friend like to do together?*

Answer the question in a complete sentence. Next, say a complete sentence about a friend.

TIER 2	Complete Sentences

Completion/Cloze statements

Give student the following sentence fragments:

- *My friend's name is _____.*
- *My friend lives in _____.*
- *My friend has a _____.*
- *My friend and I like _____.*

Repeat the sentence starter and complete the sentence.

Multiple choice/Examples and nonexamples

Ask students to identify the complete sentence from two choices: *My friend* or *My friend has a dog.* Provide additional examples and nonexamples.

Repeat the complete sentence.

TIER 3	Complete Sentences

Visual cues/Different stimuli

- Put pictures of nouns and verbs in two piles. Demonstrate how you can say a complete sentence by using a card from each pile.
- Ask students to choose a card from each pile and ask them to create a complete sentence with cards.

Choose a card from each pile and say a complete sentence.

Concrete materials/Simplify

Reread the story. Brainstorm a list of activities that Frog and Toad did together and activities the student likes to do with his friends.

Illustrate an activity from the list. Say a complete sentence about your picture.

GRADE 1 • LISTENING AND SPEAKING   175

LANGUAGE AREA:	OBJECTIVE:
Listening and Speaking	Speak for Different Purposes: Describe

TIER 1 — Describe

Discuss how words tell how something feels, tastes, looks, smells, or sounds.

- Ask students to close their eyes and think about a soft kitten, a loud siren, a sour lemon, and a blue sky. Emphasize the describing words.
- Choose a student volunteer to stand in front of the classroom.

Brainstorm a list of words that describe your classmate's physical features and clothing: *black shoes, long curly hair,* and *blue eyes.*

Ask students to sit in a circle. Give one student a ball. Instruct students to describe a classmate they will roll the ball to.

Describe the student you will roll the ball to. Say *I will roll the ball to*

- *a boy with a red shirt*
- *a girl who has curly hair*
- *a teacher with black shoes*

TIER 2 — Describe

Completion/Cloze statements

Present the first part of sentences for students to complete with a describing word.

Complete the sentences with a describing word.

Visual cues

Ask students to draw a colorful self-portrait. Illustrate eye, hair, and clothing colors, and designs.

Share your drawing and describe yourself.

TIER 3	Describe

Paraphrasing

Choose one student to stand in front of the group. Describe facial and physical characteristics by asking questions:

- *What color are (name) eyes?*
- *What word describes (name) eyes?*

Answer the questions with a describing word.

Advance organizer

Make an attribute web listing words that describe the student.

Brainstorm words that describe your eye color, hair color and length, clothing colors, and designs.

Grade
1

Grade 1

LANGUAGE AREA: Listening and Speaking

OBJECTIVE: Speak for Different Purposes: Ask Questions

TIER 1 — Ask Questions

Discuss how question words help us gain information. Question words include *who, what, where, when, why,* and *how.*

- Display a large poster or picture of a circus and talk to the students about what they know from looking at the picture.
    - *Many people are watching the circus.*
    - *People are happy.*
    - *The clown is riding in a small car.*

- Continue brainstorming a list of things you know when looking at the picture.
- Next, brainstorm a list of things you do not know when looking at the picture.
    - *What time does the circus start?*
    - *How many peanuts does the elephant eat each day?*
    - *Who bought the ticket?*

Make believe that the different people and animals in the picture can talk, and assign students to be different characters in the picture.

Ask the people and animals questions to gain information that you don't know.

Use the story *Have You Seen My Cat?* by Eric Carle to help students ask questions. Copy pictures of the various cats that the boy sees in the story. Choose one picture and hide it. Have students generate questions to guess the hidden cat.

- *Is it a long haired cat?*
- *Does it live in the jungle?*
- *Where does it come from?*
- *What noises does it make?*
- *What does it like to eat?*

Ask questions to find out which cat is hidden.

 Bonus: Whenever something special is about to happen in your classroom (field trip, celebration, or visitor), give the students a statement and ask them to ask questions to find out more information. Encourage the students to ask *what, when, why, who,* and *where* questions to gather information about the event.

TIER 2 — Ask Questions

Visual cues

- Refer to the picture of the circus in the Tier 1 activity.
- Print question words on index cards: *who*, *where*, *what*, *when*, *why*, and *how*.

Pick a card and ask a specific question about the animal or person in the picture.

Simplify

- Tell students the information they need to find out.
- Show pictures of three cats from the story and describe one of them. For example, *This is the biggest cat. It has stripes and lives in the jungle. Ask me about the size of the cat I'm thinking about.*

Ask a specific question.

TIER 3 — Ask Questions

Connecting to prior knowledge

Build background knowledge about the lesson by looking at additional pictures or books about the circus or cats.

- Brainstorm a list of animals, people, and special tricks that you would see at a circus.
- Talk about what you know and want to know about the circus.
- Put your want-to-know list in the form of questions.
- After the lesson, talk about what you learned.
- Ask the teacher questions about the circus or cats.

Concentrated instruction

Focus on two types of questions until the student has mastered understanding and expression of these types across the curriculum.

Ask different types of questions.

 Bonus: Instruct students to ask questions that would help them learn more about their classmates. Draw a spider map (see Appendix F) with an inner circle and lines extending outward. In the center circle, write the phrase *getting to know you*. Write down questions on lines radiating out from the circle. Have students pair up and ask questions to get to know each other better.

Grade 1

GRADE 1 • LISTENING AND SPEAKING   179

| Grade 1 | LANGUAGE AREA: Listening and Speaking | OBJECTIVE: Speak for Different Purposes: Persuade |

Grade 1

TIER 1 — Persuade

Explain that sometimes we try to persuade someone to think, feel, or act in a certain way. One way to persuade someone is to give good reasons.

- Demonstrate how pictures and words in an advertisement persuade us to buy a product. Ask questions:
  - o *What do the words say about the product?*
  - o *What does the picture tell you about the product?*
  - o *Why would you want to buy this product?*

- Underline the words in an advertisement that persuade someone to buy this product. Talk about why you would or would not want to buy the product.
- Talk about your favorite book and why it is your favorite. Make an advertisement that will persuade a classmate to read it. Explain your advertisement to the class.

TIER 2 — Persuade

Completion/Cloze statements

Give students sentence starters:

- *I like this book because _____.*
- *My favorite part was _____.*
- *The character I like the best was _____.*
- *I learned about _____.*
- *This book is my favorite because _____.*

Fill in the sentence blanks.

Simplify

Select a popular book and talk about why you would want a student to read it. Provide assistance and feedback to the students as they brainstorm additional reasons why someone should read this book. Ask students to draw a picture and talk about why this is your favorite book.

Draw a picture of your favorite part and explain why it is your favorite.

180   GRADE 1 • LISTENING AND SPEAKING

TIER 3 — Persuade

Previewing

- Preview examples of advertisements that persuade us to buy a product.
- Direct students to underline words that tell about the product and persuade us to buy it.

- Underline the words that tell about the product in the advertisements.
- Think of additional words that tell about the product that would persuade someone to buy it.

Role play/Different stimuli

- Explain that in order to persuade someone to think, feel, or act in a certain way, you must give them good reasons.
- Ask the student to explain how she could persuade a parent or caregiver to take her to a special place, buy a new toy, and so forth.

Take the role of the parent or child and use reasons to persuade.

Grade 1

Grade 1

LANGUAGE AREA: Listening and Speaking

OBJECTIVE: Participate in Conversations: Change and End Topics

TIER 1 — Change and End Topics

Talk about how conversations are used to share our thoughts and ideas with one another. We keep conversations going by asking questions or sharing thoughts and ideas about the same topic. Use objects, pictures, or one of the following websites for conversational starter ideas:

- www.speakingofspeech.com/uploads/Group_Conversation.pdf
- http://iteslj.org/questions
- www.straightdopeforparents.org (under the Get Informed tab, click on Prevent; select Talk to Your Kids, and click on Conversation Starters – Elementary and Middle School.pdf)
- www.dailyesl.com
- www.canteach.ca/elementary/prompts.html
- www.cindysautisticsupport.com/socialskills/conversationpictures.pdf

Explain that there are good ways to change the topic of conversation or talk about something different. You may use phrases such as:

- *Do you also know that*
- *I forgot to tell you*
- *I am so excited that I want to tell you about*
- *Excuse me*
- *Is it okay if I talk about*
- *I'd like to say something about*
- *Did you hear about*
- *My mom/dad/friend said that*
- *Let's talk about*
- *I don't want to talk about that now*
- *I have something else to tell you*
- *Before I forget, can I tell you*
- *I'd like to change the topic/subject*
- *Sorry to change the subject but*
- *Oh, by the way*
- *I don't mean to change the topic, but*

Arrange students into small groups. Write topics of conversation on cards for the groups to view (see the websites listed above for conversational topics).

Student 1 turns over a card and starts a conversation. When you say, *Change*, Student 2 turns over a new card. Student 2 talks about the new topic after using an appropriate conversation topic change phrase.

Introduce new conversation topics using an appropriate topic change phrase.

182 GRADE 1 • LISTENING AND SPEAKING

TIER 2	Change and End Topics

Multiple modalities

Design several simple game boards and distribute to small groups along with game pieces for each student.

- Arrange students into groups of two to four and give each group a conversational starter phrase to discuss.
- Each time a student appropriately changes the topic, he moves ahead one space trying to get to the finish line first.
- If a student doesn't change the topic appropriately, he moves back one space.
- Float among groups to ensure that students are changing topics.

Engage in conversation and appropriately change topics.

Visual cues

Display question words to help students ask questions to extend a conversation.

Change topic of conversation appropriately when you move to different topics.

TIER 3	Change and End Topics

Alternative response mode/Examples and nonexamples

- Give each student a green and red card.
- Begin talking and give examples and nonexamples of how to change a conversation appropriately.

Raise the green card when you hear an appropriate topic change statement and the red card when the topic change statement was inappropriate.

Multiple modalities

Introduce a topic. Ask students to draw two to four pictures or cut out pictures of something they'd like to say about the topic.

- Discuss the topic introduced by teacher.
- Using pictures, change the topic appropriately.
- Listen to group members and raise a red card if the topic was not changed appropriately.

GRADE 1 • LISTENING AND SPEAKING   183

Grade 1

LANGUAGE AREA: Listening and Speaking

OBJECTIVE: Adapt Messages to Different Situations and Listeners

TIER 1 — Adapt Messages

- Help students change messages depending on the situation and listener.
- Read the book *I Want to Play* by Elizabeth Crary. The book describes different things children can say when they want to join a group to play.
- Talk about what the characters say to one another, what works in getting what you want, and how each person feels.
- Use Reader's Theater (www.teachingheart.net/readerstheater.htm) to help students adapt messages.

Tell about different ways we can talk to one another.

TIER 2 — Adapt Messages

Double dose of instruction

- Read the book *How to Lose All Your Friends* by Nancy Carlson. Using humor, the book describes bullies, tattletales, and grouches, and shows that you can lose friends if you don't talk appropriately.
- As you read the book, pause and ask students to say how the story character could have been nicer.

Describe what can be said to be nicer and make friends.

Examples and nonexamples

- Reread the book from Tier 1.
- Choose pairs of students to act out scenes from the book as it is read.
- Ask students to act it out again but changing to act nicely and say things to make friends.

Act out the inappropriate communication and the appropriate communication.

184 GRADE 1 • LISTENING AND SPEAKING

TIER 3 — Adapt Messages

Turn and talk

Describe different social situations to students. As you describe each one, ask students to turn to a partner and talk about what they would say in each situation. You may want to use pictures that represent these activities. Scenes you may want to discuss include

- asking to join a game on the playground
- asking to sit with someone on the school bus or in the lunchroom
- asking a friend to visit your house
- choosing a partner for a game or school activity

Talk in pairs about what to say in each situation.

Grade 1

Repeated exposure

- Throughout the day, point out examples of students using the correct communication.
- When you hear examples of inappropriate (*unkind, too loud,* or *impolite*) communication, ask students to repeat what they are saying in a more appropriate or nicer way.

Communicate in a way that is appropriate for the situation and listener.

LANGUAGE AREA:	OBJECTIVE:
Listening and Speaking	Understand and Use Nonverbal Signals

TIER 1 — Nonverbal Signals

Explain how nonverbal signals such as facial expressions and gestures help us communicate.

- Read a book that contains many examples of facial expressions and feelings, such as *Dinner at the Panda Palace* by Stephanie Calmenson. Ask students
    - *What do you know about a specific character?*
    - *How do you know this?*

Describe how each character feels based on facial expressions and gestures.

TIER 2 — Nonverbal Signals

Examples and nonexamples

Read the same sentence two times using appropriate or inappropriate facial expression or gesture.

Choose the reading that reflected the appropriate facial expression or gesture.

Advance organizer

- Draw a spider map and write the feeling word in the center (see Appendix F). Write emotion/feeling cue words on the lines that emanate from the center and discuss each one separately. Emotion/feeling cues include
    - *happy*
    - *sad*
    - *surprised*
    - *angry*
- Ask students to use the spider map as a cue to read a sentence with the appropriate emotion/feeling and a facial expression that matches the emotion/feeling.

Demonstrate the appropriate emotion/feeling and facial expression while reading a sentence provided by the teacher, using the spider map cues.

TIER 3	Nonverbal Signals

Modeling

Choose an emotion and model what you might say, how you might move, and how you might look, and what gestures you might use if you were feeling this way.

Repeat what the teacher has modeled.

Connecting to prior knowledge

- Ask students to recall a time when they were proud and show how they looked.
- Discuss facial expressions and gestures.
- Repeat with other emotions.

Talk about how you used different nonverbal signals to show your feelings.

Alternative response mode

- Prepare a set of cards showing four faces displaying different expressions such as happy, sad, surprised, and angry, with the words *facial expression*.
- Model the facial expressions in random order.

Hold up the card that matches the teacher's model.

Grade
1

GRADE 1 • LISTENING AND SPEAKING   187

LANGUAGE AREA: Listening and Speaking

OBJECTIVE: Understand and Use Tone of Voice to Convey Meaning

TIER 1 — Tone of Voice

Explain that using a different tone of voice can convey a different meaning.

- Repeat common phrases such as *It's great* or *How are you?* or *Where did you go?* using a different tone of voice.
- Ask students to indicate the meaning conveyed by tone of voice.
- Talk about what meaning was conveyed each time the phrase was said.
- Practice saying common phrases using a different tone of voice.

Give student pairs a set of common phrases.

- *I'm fine.*
- *Are you sick?*
- *You look tired.*
- *You're cool.*
- *Let's get to work.*
- *I'm feeling great.*
- *Nice!*
- *I'm talking to you.*
- *Who is your friend?*
- *That's mine.*

Take turns saying the phrase in different ways and describing the meaning conveyed.

TIER 2 — Tone of Voice

Role play

Give students a phrase and tell them what emotion to use to convey the meaning. If necessary, demonstrate the emotion and ask what feeling is being conveyed.

Say the phrase with the appropriate tone of voice.

Visual cues

Act out or use a gesture to convey different meanings of phrases.

Describe the meaning of the phrase.

TIER 3 — Tone of Voice

Assistive technology/Repeated practice

- Go to the website www.storylineonline.net and click on *Sebastian's Roller Skates* by Joan De Deu Prats and Francesc Rovira.
- As the actor reads the story aloud, pause and ask students to talk about the meaning conveyed by the actor's tone of voice.
- Pause whenever Sebastian talks and have students practice talking as he does, and then talk as he wants to talk.
- Discuss how the meaning is different depending on tone of voice.

- **Listen to the story as it is read aloud and talk about the meaning conveyed by the actor's tone of voice.**
- **Try talking like Sebastian talks and how he wants to talk.**
- **Discuss how tone of voice affects meaning.**

Visual cues

- Provide students with pictures of people displaying different emotions such as happy, sad, angry, and scared.
- Say a phrase and ask students to point to the picture that shows the emotion conveyed by the tone of voice.
- Repeat with several other phrases.

Point to the picture of a person displaying the emotion conveyed by the tone of voice.

Grade 1 • Listening and Speaking

Grade 1

LANGUAGE AREA: Listening and Speaking

OBJECTIVE: Understand and Express Feelings

Grade 1

TIER 1 — Feelings

Discuss how talking helps us know how others are feeling and express our own feelings.

- Talk about happy feelings. Tell a short story: *Tommy's mom told him that they were going to the zoo on Saturday.*

- Ask *How do you think Tommy felt? Why was he happy?* Continue telling two or three short stories about characters who felt happy, sad, surprised, or angry.

- Read or summarize *The Three Bears* by Byron Barton. Ask students to complete sentence starters:

    o *Baby Bear was happy when _____.*

    o *Baby Bear was sad when _____.*

    o *Baby Bear was surprised when _____.*

    o *Baby Bear was angry when _____.*

    o *Baby Bear was scared when _____.*

- Change *Baby Bear* to *I* and ask the students to complete the sentence starters.

Complete the sentence starters.

TIER 2 — Feelings

Examples and nonexamples

Give examples and nonexamples of situations that would cause a student to feel happy, sad, surprised, angry, or scared.

Choose the situation that goes with the feeling.

Multiple choice

Give examples of events and ask the students to choose the word that describes how they would feel: *If you got a new bike, would you feel scared, happy, or mad?*

Choose a feeling that goes with an event.

190   GRADE 1 • LISTENING AND SPEAKING

TIER 3	Feelings

Concentrated instruction

Pick one feeling word and ask student to draw a picture of an event that would make her feel this way.

Discuss your drawing and feelings.

Alternative response mode

Show students pictures that show people who are happy, sad, angry, or surprised. Ask students to point to the person who is feeling _____.

Point to the picture that demonstrates the feeling.

Grade
1

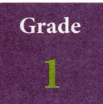

Grade 1

LANGUAGE AREA:	OBJECTIVE:
Listening and Speaking	Ask Questions for Repetition/Clarification

TIER 1 — Clarification Questions

Explain to students that we ask questions when we need more information.

- Provide students with some reasons why they may need to ask questions. Reasons may include
    - didn't hear what was said;
    - don't understand the words;
    - can't remember everything the teacher said;
    - need more information.
- Give incomplete step-by-step directions to draw a specific picture (*Draw a big one in the center*).
- Instruct students to raise their hand and ask for clarification if the direction is not clear (*What will I draw in the center?*).
- Provide clarification (*Draw a big circle in the center*).

Listen to directions and ask for repetition or clarification when needed.

TIER 2	Clarification Questions

Different stimuli/Elaboration

Give directions that are missing an important element and prompt the student with the appropriate question word (*what, where, who*):

- *Do you know what to draw? What should you ask?*
- *Do you know where to draw the circle? What should you ask?*
- *Do you know what color to use? What should you ask?*

Use the prompted question word to generate the appropriate question.

Modeling/Elaboration

Give directions that are missing an important element. Prompt the student with an appropriate question. Say, *I need to tell you what to get.* Tell student to ask *What should I get?*

Repeat the modeled question.

TIER 3	Clarification Questions

Concentrated instruction

Give directions that are missing an important element that will require **just one** of the *wh*-question words:

- Say, *I need to know what _____?*
- Say, *can you tell me what _____?*

Ask a question using *what*.

Visual cues

- Use the activity in Tier 1—giving directions to draw something on a page.

- Use three separate cue cards—one illustrating multiple colors, one illustrating multiple shapes, and one illustrating multiple locations.

- Explain that you will give a direction, and the card you are holding will give a clue about the missing direction.

Ask the appropriate question after the teacher prompts with one of the cue cards.

GRADE 1 • LISTENING AND SPEAKING   193

Grade 1

LANGUAGE AREA: Listening and Speaking

OBJECTIVE: Understand and Use Logical Order of Events

TIER 1 — Logical Order of Events

Discuss how important it is to be able to understand and tell about the correct order of events.

- Ask the student to draw a rainbow.
- Show several rainbows and talk about which colors the student chose first, next, and last. Arrange students in pairs, facing each other, keeping their rainbows out of view.
- Give Student A a blank rainbow.
- Tell Student B to give Student A directions on how to draw a rainbow.
- Student B: Give directions to Student A on how to make an exact replica of your rainbow. Student A: Draw a rainbow using Student B's instructions.
- Compare the rainbows to see if the colors are in the right order.

TIER 2 — Logical Order of Events

Visual cues

Give the student a picture of a blank rainbow, listing a number in each section of the rainbow.

Use the numbers to give instructions for coloring in the right order (such as *1 is red, 2 is orange*).

Visual cues

Ask the student to color a rainbow using different colors in random order. Give the student a set of color words, each on a separate card.

Lay out the color word cards in the order in which they appear in your rainbow. Give verbal directions to the other student.

TIER 3	Logical Order of Events

Concrete materials/Visual cues

- Provide a colored rainbow and a blank rainbow.
- Place the crayons from left to right in the order in which they appear in the rainbow.
- Give directions for coloring each section.

Color the rainbow in the correct color sequence.

Imitation

- Display a colored rainbow and give each student a blank rainbow.
- Model how to give the directions.

Repeat and follow the direction.

Grade
1

LANGUAGE AREA: Listening and Speaking

OBJECTIVE: Understand and Use Fictional Narratives

TIER 1 — Fictional Narratives

Provide definitions for story elements to help students understand narrative structure.

Story grammar elements

1. **Setting:** When and where the story occurs
2. **Main Characters:** Who the story is about, the main characters
3. **Problem or Conflict:** The focal point of the story
4. **Events/Attempts/Actions:** Attempts by the main characters to resolve the problem or conflict
5. **Resolution/Solution/Conclusion:** How successfully the characters resolve the problem or conflict

Using a simple, familiar story make a story map (see Appendix H) to introduce the concept of story grammar. Remind students that most stories have a beginning that includes the time of the story and where it takes place (**setting**), and introduces the **main character**(s). Then, a **problem or conflict** sets the story in motion, which is followed by **events/attempts/actions** to reach the goal or **resolve** the conflict. Finally, the story ends with a **resolution/solution/conclusion**.

Model the way to complete a story map by writing in the components of each part of the story. If students are prereaders, do this activity with pictures.

Questions to guide discussion

1. **Setting:** *Where does the story occur? When does the story occur?*
2. **Main Characters:** *Who are the main characters?*
3. **Problem or Conflict:** *What major problem do the main characters face? What do these characters hope to achieve?*
4. **Events/Attempts/Actions:** *What do the main characters do?*
5. **Resolution/Solution/Conclusion:** *Do the characters solve the problem? How?*

Use pictures or sentence strips from the story discussion to develop a story map independently or in a small group.

Give students pictures or sentence strips from another story.

Develop a story map independently or in small groups.

Bonus: Define theme as the main point or moral of the story. Help students to discuss the overall theme of the story.

TIER 2 — Fictional Narratives

Double dose of instruction/Repeated practice

- Reread a familiar story and redefine each story element using examples from the story.
- Display pictures of the five story elements out of sequence.

Place the pictures in the correct sequence.

Elaboration

- Define the story elements of a familiar story in greater detail.
- Give several examples using pictures or sentence strips and a blank story map.
- While retelling the story, place the pictures or sentences on specific areas of the story map.
- Remove the pictures or sentence strips from the story map.

Recreate the story map using this same story.

TIER 3 — Fictional Narratives

Concentrated instruction/Change response length

Define and place only three elements of a familiar story on a story map. Create a story.

- **Problem or Conflict:** Sue was not allowed to eat cookies before dinner.
- **Events/Attempts/Actions:** One afternoon, she sneaked into the kitchen to get a cookie out of the cookie jar.
- **Resolution/Solution/Conclusion:** As she grabbed it, it fell on the floor and broke right when her mother walked into the room.

Place the pictures or sentence strips on the simplified story map.

Advance organizer

Put a story guide on the board and review all the parts of a story by asking probing questions to help students understand the story elements. Provide blank story guides as a checklist to help students self-monitor the development of new stories.

Story Guide

1. **Setting**
   - When does the story take place?
   - Where does the story take place?

2. **Main Characters**
   - Who is the story about?

3. **Problem or Conflict**
   - What problem do the main characters face?

4. **Events/Attempts/Actions**
   - What do the main characters do?

5. **Resolution/Solution/Conclusion**
   - How is the problem solved?
   - What happens at the end of the story?

- Answer the questions in the guide.
- Use the answers from the guide to recreate the story.
- Compare your completed guide to the story to ensure that you recalled all of the critical elements of the story.
- Use the story guide to create new stories.

Notes:

Grade
1

GRADE 1 • LISTENING AND SPEAKING   199

Grade 1

LANGUAGE AREA: Listening and Speaking

OBJECTIVE: Retell a Story or Directions in Correct Order

TIER 1 — Retell Story

Talk about sequencing and listening for what happens first, second, third, and last in a story.

- Use a book, such as *Arthur's Reading Race* by Marc Brown or *The Tiny Seed* by Eric Carle.
- Provide students with a blank story map (see Appendix H).

- Write the words or draw pictures in the correct order to help you record the story on a story map and retell the story in the correct sequence.
- In *Arthur's Reading Race*, list each place Arthur and his sister traveled to read words. Also list what words they read at each place (*zoo, street, park, bank,* and *ice cream shop*).
- In *The Tiny Seed*, list the sequence of how seeds change and grow into plants.

TIER 2 — Retell Story

Alternative response mode

Reread the story and ask students to write down the sequence of the story as it is read.

- Write the words or draw pictures in the correct order to help you record the story on a story map and retell the story in the correct sequence.
- In *Arthur's Reading Race*, write the words as they are read by the characters.
- In *The Tiny Seed*, draw pictures of each variation of the seed.

Repeated reading/Imitation

Reread the story, pausing after each new segment of the sequence. Ask students to repeat that critical element.

- In *Arthur's Reading Race*, repeat each new word and location.
- In *The Tiny Seed,* repeat the name of the new variation of the seed.

| TIER 3 | Retell Story |

Visual cues

After reading the story, give students pictures of each segment of the story.

Use pictures to retell the story in correct order.

Multiple choice

After retelling the story, ask students to retell the story by giving three choices for each new segment.

Choose the correct choice when given three choices for each segment of the story.

	LANGUAGE AREA:	OBJECTIVE:
Grade 1	Listening and Speaking	Understand and Use Figurative Language: Idioms

TIER 1 — Idioms

Explain that idioms are expressions that mean something different than the actual words.

- Give examples of common idioms that students might hear or find in books:

  - butterflies in my stomach
  - back to back
  - raining cats and dogs
  - eat like a horse
  - don't have a cow
  - top dog
  - all thumbs
  - in a pickle
  - go bananas
  - open a can of worms
  - green thumb
  - chill out
  - fish out of water
  - I'm all ears
  - don't cry wolf
  - in the doghouse
  - let the cat out of the bag
  - cat got your tongue?
  - as sick as a dog
  - bite off more than you can chew
  - fits like a glove
  - get the ball rolling
  - in hot water
  - on the right track

- Present pictures of the literal meaning and the figurative meaning of a sample idiom.
- Assign each student a different idiom. Have student draw two pictures representing the literal and figurative meaning of the idiom.

- Draw pictures showing the literal and figurative meaning of the idiom.
- Present pictures to the class and explain the meaning of assigned idiom.

 Bonus: Make a *Classroom Idiom Chart* and reward students when they are able to add a new idiom to the list.

202 GRADE 1 • LISTENING AND SPEAKING

These are some websites and books with more information about idioms:

Websites:
- www.idiomconnection.com (idioms list)
- www.worldalmanacforkids.com
- www.funbrain.com/funbrain/idioms (Paint by Idioms game)

Books:
- *Idioms for Everyday Use – Student Book* by Milada Broukal
- *Raining Cats and Dogs: A Collection of Irresistible Idioms and Illustrations to Tickle the Funny Bones of Young People* by Will Moses
- *It's Raining Cats and Dogs: Making Sense of Animal Phrases* by Jackie Franza.

TIER 2 — Idioms

Assistive technology/Repeated practice

- Use the website www.funbrain.com/funbrain/idioms, which is a paint-by-number game to practice idioms, or the website www.idiomconnection.com, which is an idioms list with a quiz at the end of each category of idioms.
- Choose idioms from each of these programs and sit with the student to read the item and explain the meaning.
- Go to www.speakingofspeech.com and click on Language Materials Exchange; then select Language and click on Vocabulary – Semantics.
- Choose the figurative language flashcards and illustrated idiom symbols for more practice materials.

Choose correct answers showing understanding of the meaning of the idiom.

Matching

- Review the concept of idiom. Give more examples for practice.
- Provide a worksheet for using various idioms.
- Ask students to match the literal meaning in the first column with the actual meaning in the second column.

Draw a line to match the literal meaning to the actual meaning of the idiom.

TIER 3 — Idioms

Role play

Teach a set of idioms.

> Act out each figurative and literal meaning of the idiom.

Repeated exposure/Alternative response mode

- Choose a set of five idioms and develop opportunities throughout the school day to model and reteach each idiom.
- Ask the student to use each one in context. For example, *Let's catch our breath* could be used each time you end an activity and prepare for the next activity.

> As you go about your daily classroom activities, raise your hand when you hear an idiom.

Notes:

Grade 1

GRADE 1 • LISTENING AND SPEAKING   205

LANGUAGE AREA:	OBJECTIVE:
Listening and Speaking	Understand Humor in Words and Situations

TIER 1 — Humor

Talk about silly things and how they make us laugh:

- *A bike with square wheels*
- *A cold sun*
- *A monkey who didn't eat bananas*

Brainstorm a list of animal attributes:

- *Elephant – trunk*
- *Giraffe – long neck*
- *Mouse – small body*
- *Dog – eats bones*
- *Shark – has sharp teeth*

Mix and match different animals and attributes. Draw a picture of a silly animal.

TIER 2 — Humor

Different stimuli

- Read *The Silly Story of Goldie Locks and the Three Squares* by Grace Maccarone.
- Make a list of silly events in the story.

Draw a picture of your favorite silly event in the story. Discuss why it is silly.

Simplify

Ask the student to make a list of actions and write a silly sentence that does not go with a specified noun. For example, list actions that do not go with *dog*: *fly*, *dresses*, *cleans*, or *studies spelling words*.

- Make a list of actions that do not go with *dog*.
- Put the action word in a silly sentence about a dog.
- Continue with other nouns.

TIER 3	Humor

Connecting to prior knowledge

Talk about a circus clown. Show pictures of clowns.

Brainstorm a list of silly things that clowns do.

Visual dictionary

Show simple comic strips that focus on absurdities and silly situations.

Identify what could or couldn't happen and why it is funny.

Grade 1

| Grade 1 | LANGUAGE AREA: Listening and Speaking | OBJECTIVE: Summarize Stories and Events |

TIER 1 — Summarize

Discuss how important it is to be able to summarize information so you can share ideas, experiences, and events with others.

- Read *The Day Jimmy's Boa Ate the Wash* by Trinka Hakes Noble. Ask students to talk about what was important in the story.
- Bring in a clothes basket and make a supply of white paper T-shirts.
- Brainstorm a list of the events that happened in the beginning, middle, and end of the story.

- Draw an event from the beginning, middle, or end of the story on your T-shirt and place it in the clothes basket.
- Student volunteers pick a T-shirt from the basket and take turns arranging the chosen T-shirts in sequential story order.
- After all the T-shirts have been picked, summarize what happened in the story.

TIER 2 — Summarize

Advance organizer

Look at the illustrations together and talk about what happened at the beginning, middle, and end of the story.

- Fill in the sequence map with your own illustrations.
- Summarize the events of the story.

Visual cues

Use written prompts: *beginning*, *middle*, and *end*.

Summarize one event from the beginning, middle, and end of the story.

208   GRADE 1 • LISTENING AND SPEAKING

| TIER 3 | Summarize |

Repeated reading

Reread the story slowly, pausing after each event.

Summarize the events in the story.

Repeated practice/Different stimuli

Ask students throughout the day to summarize directions, announcements, or curriculum content they have just heard:

- *What did the principal say we would be doing after lunch today?*
- *How do we find out how to spell a difficult word?*
- *What did we learn in science today?*

Summarize the important information you have just heard.

Grade

1

Grade 1

LANGUAGE AREA: Listening and Speaking

OBJECTIVE: Paraphrase Stories

TIER 1 — Paraphrase

Discuss how important it is to retell a story in your own words. Give the examples of telling someone about a movie you saw.

- Read *The First Snowfall* by Anne Rockwell.

- Ask students to restate the important parts of the story in their own words. *In this book, a little girl tells the story of the first snowfall from the time she sees the first snowflake.*

- Ask students to act out the story.

Paraphrase what happened in the story as other students act out the story.

TIER 2 — Paraphrase

Connecting to prior knowledge

Talk about a snowy day. Discuss how you felt or would feel and what you did or would like to do in the snow.

Tell your story in your own words.

Concrete materials/Simplify

Lead a discussion about a student's favorite part of the story.

Draw a picture of your favorite part of the story and paraphrase what happened.

| TIER 3 | Paraphrase |

Advance organizers

Talk about what happened first, next, and last in the story.

Draw pictures of each event in order. Paraphrase the events of the story.

Mental imagery/Adjust pace

Discuss each event separately in the story and ask students to form a mental image of what is happening.

Paraphrase each event.

Grade 1

LANGUAGE AREA:
Listening and Speaking

OBJECTIVE:
Understand and Distinguish Fact From Opinion

TIER 1 — Fact and Opinion

Discuss the meaning of facts and opinions. *Facts* are statements that can be proven to be true. *Opinions* are feelings or beliefs about something. For example, *Sarah is 40 inches tall* is a fact. This can be proven by measuring her. Another example is *Sarah is funny.* Not everyone may agree with this statement, so it is an opinion.

- Further explain the difference between fact and opinion using sample sentences.

- Read a book such as *How a House Is Built* by Gail Gibbons that focuses on the difference between fact and opinion. Explain that when a sentence begins with *I feel* or *I think,* it is a clue that you are hearing or reading an opinion, not a fact.

- Write *Fact* and *Opinion* on two different cards.
- Listen to the story and hold up the card that explains a specific statement in the book.

- Make a story chart with sentence strips about the story.

- Read individual sentences, asking students to listen for facts and opinions.

- Take a vote on each sentence to decide if it is fact or opinion.

- Ask students to meet in pairs. Have each pair state one fact and one opinion to each other.

- Ask them to share their statements and tell if they are fact or opinion to the whole group.

- Hold up the correct card to signal fact versus opinion.
- Vote for the sentence as either fact or opinion.
- State one fact and one opinion in pairs and in the large group.

| TIER 2 | Fact and Opinion |

Visual cues

- Make a story chart with sentence strips about the story.
- Read individual sentences asking students to listen for facts and opinions.
- Take a vote on each sentence to decide if it is fact or opinion.

Decide if the statement is a fact or opinion.

Auditory cues

Read the sentence strips, emphasizing words that provide clues that a statement is a fact or an opinion: *He thinks …* or *I see …*

Listen for clue words and decide if the sentence is a fact or opinion.

| TIER 3 | Fact and Opinion |

Different stimuli

Make a statement about a familiar topic:

- *I think boys are smarter than girls.*
- *Spaghetti is the best food in the world.*
- *Mary has one brother.*
- *The best thing to do after school is ride your bike.*
- *In February, we will celebrate Valentine's Day.*

Decide if each statement is an opinion or fact.

Repeated practice

Conduct the Tier 1 activity at least three times.

Decide if each statement is an opinion or fact.

GRADE 1 • LISTENING AND SPEAKING 213

Grade 1	LANGUAGE AREA: Listening and Speaking	OBJECTIVE: Share Opinions

TIER 1 — Share Opinions

Explain that an opinion is an idea, thought, or feeling someone has about a topic.

Talk about your favorite book and why it is your favorite. Talk about how others may or may not feel the same way. It is your opinion or how you feel about this book. Ask the following questions:

- *How long should children be allowed to watch television each day?*
- *What animal makes the best pet?*
- *Does your teacher give too much homework?*
- *What is the best thing to do on a rainy day?*

Express your opinion about the topic being discussed.

TIER 2 — Share Opinions

Completion/Cloze statements

Provide a declarative sentence with one blank:

- *I think a _____ is the best pet.*
- *I couldn't live without my _____.*
- *If it is raining, I like to _____.*

Fill in the sentence blanks.

Elaboration

Ask different students to express their opinion about familiar things or events (homework, TV shows, or holidays).

Express your opinion and discuss similarities and differences among your classmates.

214   GRADE 1 • LISTENING AND SPEAKING

TIER 3	Share Opinions

Metacognitive thinking stems

- Explain to students how we express opinions based on how we are feeling.

- Give students the phrase *I'm feeling* _____.

- Ask an opinion question.

Listen to the question. Complete the thinking stem *I'm feeling* _____.

Turn and talk

- Give students opportunities to practice expressing their opinions to others.

- Explain the rules of turn and talk.

- Ask an opinion question.

Express your opinion to your partner.

Grade
1

GRADE 1 • LISTENING AND SPEAKING   215

| Grade 1 | LANGUAGE AREA: Listening and Speaking | OBJECTIVE: Understand and Use Inferences |

Grade 1

TIER 1 — Inferences

Explain that inferences are something you know without being told or something that you can "guess" based on something you see or hear.

- Give examples of inferences
  - *I baked cookies and left them on the table when I walked outside. When I came back there were cookie crumbs on the dog's bed. What happened?*
  - *A boy walked outside. A few minutes later he came inside dripping wet. What happened?*
- Use the book *Animals Should Definitely Not Wear Clothing* by Judi Barrett to practice inferences. Read the story without showing the pictures and ask students to answer *Why shouldn't (animal name) wear clothing?*
  - *Snake would lose it.*
  - *Porcupine would shred it.*
  - *Billy goat would eat it for lunch.*
  - *Walrus would get it all wet.*
- Continue through the book, talking about how students were able to answer the question. Discuss how making inferences is like uncovering the secrets the author is trying to share with us.

See also www.mandygregory.com/Inferencing_mini_lessons.htm for a lesson plan using several other children's stories to teach inferences.

Respond to questions about inferences.

TIER 2 — Inferences

Assistive technology

Use this website to help students practice making inferences: www.bbc.co.uk/schools/magickey/adventures/floppy.shtml

Choose the right answer to reflect understanding of the inference.

Different stimuli

- Review the meaning of *inference*.

- Read one of the *No, David!* books by David Shannon. On every page there are pictures of activities David is not supposed to be doing, while his mother says, *No, David!*

- Ask students to use the picture cues to guess what David s not supposed to be doing.

Guess what David is not supposed to be doing and why his mother is saying, *No, David!*

TIER 3   Inferences

Repeated practice

Provide short descriptions of an experience or event, and ask students what will happen next. For example, *Your dog is standing by the door barking. What do you think will happen next?*

Examples of other descriptions can be found on the following website: www.havefunteaching.com (click on Worksheets and then Reading; select Inferences and then the Inference Worksheet, You Make the Call).

Write about what happens next and read it back to the teacher.

Matching/Multiple choice

- Create a matching activity by using pictures from a story.

- In one column, place a picture from the story from which something can be inferred.

- In another column, place two or three pictures, including one that represents the correct inference.

- Have students circle the right picture and tell what can be inferred.

Show understanding of inference by circling the correct picture and saying what you can infer.

Grade 1

LANGUAGE AREA: Phonological Awareness

OBJECTIVE: Identify Initial/Final Sounds in Words

TIER 1 | Initial/Final Sounds

Discuss how words begin or end with a specific sound.

- Present a letter such as *S*, and explain that the letter makes the *s* sound.
- Ask students to generate words that begin with this sound, first modeling two or three examples, elongating the initial sound along with an explanation of each example (*sssss—un begins with the s sound; do you hear the s sound at the beginning?*).
- Ask students to repeat each other's contributions, listing each word on the board and underlining the initial sound.
- After a number of *s* words are generated, ask the class to read the list on the board, emphasizing the first sound of each word.
- Repeat the same instructional sequence for final consonants in words (*bus, juice, horse, mice,* and *mess*), asking the class what other words end with the sound indicated.

Generate words that begin or end with a specific sound.

218   GRADE 1 • PHONOLOGICAL AWARENESS

TIER 2 — Initial/Final Sounds

Visual cues/Concentrated instruction

Discuss how words begin with a specific sound.

- Present a letter such as *S* and explain that the letter makes the *s* sound.
- As a word is said (*sun*), present the alphabet letter block representing the corresponding initial sound *s*.
- Pass the letter block around the room to students. Have each student say the target word (*sun*) and generate another word that begins with *s* when the student receives the letter block.
- Repeat the activity with 10 additional words.

Say the target word when receiving the letter block, and generate additional words that begin with the target sound.

Visual cues/Concentrated instruction/Matching

- Present a consonant-vowel-consonant (CVC) word, along with two alphabet letters (for the word *sun*, use alphabet letters *S* and *N*).
- Explain that the word presented begins with one of the sounds these letters make.
- Ask students to point to/match the word to the sound.
- Repeat the activity with 10 additional words.

Point to/match the word said by the teacher with the correct initial letter sound.

TIER 3 — Initial/Final Sounds

Repeated practice

Repeat the second Tier 2 activity with five additional words.

Point to or match the word said by the teacher with the correct initial letter sound.

Visual cues/Concentrated instruction/Imitation

Discuss how words begin with a specific sound:

- Present a letter such as *S*, and explain that the letter makes the *s* sound.
- As the CVC word is said (*sun*), present the alphabet letter block representing the corresponding initial sound *s*.
- Pass the letter block around the room. Have each student say the target word and the word's beginning sound (*sun begins with s*).

Imitate the target word and initial letter sound.

Grade 1

| Grade 1 | LANGUAGE AREA: Phonological Awareness | OBJECTIVE: Delete First and Last Syllable of Compound Words |

Grade 1

TIER 1 — Delete Syllable

Explain that compound words consist of two words that can stand alone when separated.

- Fold a large piece of paper or an index card in half or draw a line down its center. Write one part of a two-syllable compound word on each half (*skate ... board*), compiling a set of 10 such items (*baseball, airport, goldfish, fireman, haircut, driveway, cupcake, homework, snowboard,* and *earthquake*).

- Say to the class: *Pretend that we are going on a trip to outer space to visit a new planet. On the planet, Martians talk in a secret code—they say only the second part of a word. To understand the Martians' messages, you have to learn their code.*

- Provide two or more examples: When the Martians want to say <u>baseball</u>, they say <u>ball</u>, and when they want to say <u>airport</u>, they say <u>port</u>.

- As each example is given, fold and unfold the paper/index card with the compound words written on it.

- Repeat the two examples, this time having the students guess the compound word for each.

- Ask the students to guess how the Martians would say each of the remaining eight compound words.

- Tell the students that they are going to another planet where the space creatures only say the **first** part of their words.

- Repeat the instructional sequence above.

Guess how the Martians would say a word given one part of a compound word.

Note: Linguistic differences may influence a student's performance on this task. Compound words do not exist in certain languages, such as Vietnamese, Mandarin, and Cantonese. Students who speak these languages as their native language may have difficulty with this activity.

220   GRADE 1 • PHONOLOGICAL AWARENESS

TIER 2 — Delete Syllable

Visual cues/Concentrated instruction

Provide students with two or more examples along with pictures: When the Martians want to say _baseball_, they say _ball_, and when they want to say _airport_, they say _port_.

- As the examples are given, fold and unfold the paper/index card with pictures of the compound words depicted on it.
- Repeat the examples, having the students guess the word.

Guess how the Martians would say a word given one part of a compound word.

Visual cues/Multiple choice/Concentrated instruction

Provide students with two or more examples along with pictures: When the Martians want to say _baseball_, they say _ball_, and when they want to say _airport_, they say _port_.

- As each example is given, fold and unfold the paper/index card with pictures of the compound words depicted on it.
- Repeat the examples, having the students guess the word given three choices (one correct; two distracters).

Guess how the Martians would say a word given three choices.

Grade
1

GRADE 1 • PHONOLOGICAL AWARENESS   221

TIER 3 — Delete Syllable

Visual cues/Multiple choice/Concentrated instruction

Provide students with two or more examples along with pictures: When the Martians want to say _baseball_, they say _ball_, and when they want to say _airport_, they say _port_.

- As each example is given, fold and unfold the paper/index card with pictures of the compound words depicted on it.
- Repeat the examples, having students guess the word given two choices (one correct; one distracter).

Out of a set of two choices, point to one choice and say how the Martians would say the word.

Visual cues/Imitation/Concentrated instruction

- Show students a picture of a compound word (_baseball_).
- Model how the Martians would say the word (_ball_).
- Ask students to say the compound word first blended together (_baseball_) and then with pauses between the syllables (_base–ball_).
- As each example is given, fold and unfold the paper/index card with pictures of the compound word depicted on it.
- Ask students to model how the Martians would say the word _baseball_.
- Repeat the activity with 10 other compound words.

Model how the Martians would say a word.

Notes:

Grade 1

GRADE 1 • PHONOLOGICAL AWARENESS   223

| Grade 1 | LANGUAGE AREA: | OBJECTIVE: |
| | Phonological Awareness | Blend Phonemes Into Words |

TIER 1 — Blend Phonemes

Explain to students that a word is composed of sounds blended together.

- Gather three large blocks of different colors to represent sounds/letters of 10 CVC words that begin with continuant sounds (*sun, fan, head, nose, fish, thumb, mouse, soap, ship,* and *van*).

- Tell students that they are going to make a sound train by putting together blocks. Each block makes a different sound.

- Place the blocks on the table set apart from one another. Model the blending activity by saying the sound of each block with a 1-second pause between each sound (*s...u...n*). Point to each colored block as the sound is said.

- Show the class how to make blocks form a *train* by slowly blending the sounds together into the word *sun*, pushing the blocks together as the sounds are merged.

- Repeat the demonstration having students say the isolated sounds and blend them together to form the whole word. Repeat with remaining nine CVC words.

Say isolated sounds and blend them together to say a whole word.

Note: Linguistic differences may influence a student's performance on this task.

TIER 2 — Blend Phonemes

Visual cues

Repeat the Tier 1 activity with colored magnets, each representing one sound (*s-u-n*).

Say the isolated sounds and blend them to say a whole word as the teacher slides the magnets together.

Visual cues/Concentrated instruction

Reduce the number of stimulus items to five and increase the number of trials per item.

Say isolated sounds and blend them to say a whole word as the teacher slides the magnets together.

224   GRADE 1 • PHONOLOGICAL AWARENESS

TIER 3	Blend Phonemes

Visual cues/Imitation

- Show a picture of an item.
- Ask students to imitate isolated sounds in a word and then blend them to form a whole word.
- Repeat the activity for five additional items.

Imitate the teacher's word production of sounds isolated and then blended to form a whole word.

Visual cues

- Show a picture of an item.
- Say the first sound of the word (s-s-s-s) with a prolonged duration and have students finish the word (un) as you point to the item.
- Repeat activity for five additional items.

When you are shown a picture and the first sound of a word, complete production of the word.

Grade
1

GRADE 1 • PHONOLOGICAL AWARENESS   225

| Grade 1 | LANGUAGE AREA: Print Knowledge | OBJECTIVE: Understand Features of Print |

TIER 1 — Features of Print

Explain that features of text have meaning.

- Introduce a familiar textbook and highlight the following:
  - o **Table of contents:** Gives a brief description of all of the topics in the book and the page numbers where they can be found.
  - o **Chapter titles/headings:** Tells what that section is about.
  - o **Illustrations:** Another word for pictures. Illustrations often have a caption or words that tell about the picture.
- Ask questions to elicit the name of each part.
- Play the *I Spy* game for each book part.
- Repeat activity with two other books.

- Respond to questions.
- Play the *I Spy* game.

TIER 2 — Features of Print

Multiple choice

- Show three different book parts while naming one part.
- Ask students to select the appropriate part and say it aloud.

Select the correct part of the book and name it.

Multiple choice/Visual cues

- Write book parts on different cards.
- Identify a specific part of a book and ask students to select the part presented from a choice of two.

Name each book part the teacher presents, and select the correct book part from a choice of two.

| TIER 3 | Features of Print |

Imitation

- Review and name each book part.
- Ask students to repeat the name of each book part.

Repeat the name of each book part.

Modeling

Review and name each book part.

Watch and listen as the teacher names the different book parts.

Grade
1

Grade 1

LANGUAGE AREA: Print Knowledge

OBJECTIVE: Understand Concept of Paragraph

TIER 1 — Paragraph

Explain that sentences are made up of words and stories are made up of paragraphs.

- Write a short composition called *A Very Special Person … Me* on the board: *I'm very special. I can jump rope and ride a bike. I have two brothers and a funny dog named Scotty. All of these things make me special.*

- Explain that this story is a called a *paragraph*. Define the term *paragraph* (a group of sentences about the same topic) and explain that paragraphs have a beginning, middle, and end:

    o **Beginning:** *A statement is made* (**topic sentence:** *I'm very special*).

    o **Middle:** *The statement is explained* (**supporting details:** *why?*).

    o **End:** *The thought is ended* (**concluding sentence:** *what the topic sentence is about*).

- Place the key words next to each sentence in the composition.

- Ask students to help the teacher brainstorm another composition on the same topic, while the teacher writes it on the board.

- Ask students to identify which key terms go with each sentence and help students explain why.

- Identify the key terms (*topic sentence*, *supporting details*, and *concluding sentence*) that go with each sentence of the composition.

- Help the teacher brainstorm another story about the same topic and identify which key terms go with each sentence of the paragraph.

228   GRADE 1 • PRINT KNOWLEDGE

TIER 2 — Paragraph

Restricted-choice questions/Elaboration

- Read each sentence aloud and ask students: *Is this sentence the topic sentence? Supporting detail? Concluding sentence?*
- Explain each key term and link the terms to the concepts *beginning, middle,* and *end.*
- Ask students which key term is the beginning, middle, and end.

- Provide *yes/no* answers or *thumbs up/thumbs down* responses to the questions.
- Identify which key term is another name for the beginning, middle, and end of a paragraph.

Matching/Visual cues

- Use three cards with a key term written on each, along with a symbol to represent the key term (▸ = topic statement/beginning; ■ = supporting detail/ middle, ◂ = concluding sentence/end).
- As you read each sentence in the paragraph, instruct students to place the correct card next to each sentence.

Match each card with its corresponding sentence in the paragraph.

TIER 3 — Paragraph

Repeated practice

- Ask students to tell their own short story.
- As the story is told, write it where the student can see it.
- Use the key term cards and place them next to that section of the story.
- Take the cards away and ask students to put them in the right place again.

Place the key terms next to the appropriate sections of the story.

Elaboration/Imitation

- After reading the whole paragraph, read each sentence, identify the corresponding key term, and give several examples of each term.
- Repeat this instruction two more times.
- Instruct students to say the name of the key term after you.

Say the name of the key term after the teacher.

References

Assessments

Boehm, A. E. (2000). *Boehm Test of Basic Concepts, Third Edition*. San Antonio, TX: Pearson Assessments.

Bracken, B. A. (1998). *Bracken Basic Concept Scale—Revised*. San Antonio, TX: Pearson Assessments.

Wiig, E. H. (2004). *Wiig Assessment of Basic Concepts*. Greenville, SC: Super Duper Publications.

Resources

Books

Aardema, V. (1992). *Why mosquitoes buzz in people's ears: A West African tale* (L. Dillon & D. Dillon, Illus.). New York, NY: Puffin.

Allen, P. (1996). *Who sank the boat?* New York, NY: Putnam Juvenile.

Barrett, J. (1998). *Animals should definitely not wear clothing* (R. Barrett, Illus.). New York, NY: Simon & Schuster.

Barretta, G. (2007). *Dear, deer, a book of homophones*. New York, NY: Henry Holt.

Barton, B. (1997). *The three bears*. New York, NY: HarperCollins. (Original work published 1991)

Broukal, M. (2001). *Idioms for everyday use—student book: The basic text for learning and communicating with English idioms*. Chicago, IL: National Textbook.

Brown, M. (1996). *Arthur's reading race*. New York, NY: Random House.

Calmenson, S. (1995). *Dinner at the panda palace* (N. B. Wescott, Illus.). New York, NY: HarperCollins.

Carle, E. (1997). *Have you seen my cat?* New York, NY: Simon & Schuster.

Carle, E. (1991). *The tiny seed*. New York, NY: Simon & Schuster.

Carlson, C. (1997). *How to lose all your friends*. New York, NY: Puffin.

Cleary, B. P. (2004). *I and you and don't forget who: What is a pronoun?* (B. Gable, Illus.). Minneapolis, MN: Millbrook Press.

Cleary, B. P. (2000). *Hairy, scary, ordinary: What is an adjective?* (J. Prosmitsky, Illus.). Minneapolis, MN: Millbrook Press.

Cleary, B. P. (2001). *To root, to toot, to parachute: What is a verb?* (J. Prosmitsky, Illus.). Minneapolis, MN: Millbrook Press.

Crary, E. (1996). *I want to play* (M. Megale, Illus.). Seattle, WA: Parenting Press.

De Deu Prats, J. (2005). *Sebastian's roller skates* (F. Rovira, Illus.). San Diego, CA: Kane Miller.

Flora, S. B. (2005). *Listen, look, and do! Over 120 activities to strengthen visual and auditory discrimination and memory skills.* Minneapolis, MN: Key Education.

Franza, J. (2006). *It's raining cats and dogs: Making sense of animal phrases* (S. Gray, Illus.). Irvine, CA: BowTie Press.

Gibbons, G. (1996). *How a house is built.* New York, NY: Holiday House.

Heller, R. (1981). *Chickens aren't the only ones.* New York, NY: Grosset and Dunlap.

Janssen, S. (Ed.). (2009). *The world almanac for kids.* New York, NY: The World Almanac.

Leedy, L. (2008). *Crazy like a fox: A simile story.* New York, NY. Holiday House.

Lobel, A. (1984). *Frog and Toad all year.* New York, NY: HarperCollins.

Maccarone, G. (1996). *The silly story of Goldie Locks and the three squares* (A. Kennedy, Illus.). New York, NY: Scholastic.

Moses, W. (2008). *Raining cats and dogs: A collection of irresistible idioms and illustrations to tickle the funny bones of young people.* New York, NY: Philomel.

Murphy, S. J. (1998). *The greatest gymnast of all* (C. Jabar, Illus.). New York, NY: HarperCollins.

Noble, T. H. (1991). *The day Jimmy's boa ate the wash* (S. Kellogg, Illus.). New York, NY: Puffin.

Numeroff, L. J. (1985). *If you give a mouse a cookie* (F. Bond, Illus.). New York, NY: HarperCollins.

Numeroff, L. J. (1991). *If you give a moose a muffin* (F. Bond, Illus.). New York, NY: HarperCollins.

Rockwell A. (2004). *Four seasons make a year* (M. Halsey, Illus.. New York, NY: Walker Books for Young Readers.

Rockwell, A., & Rockwell, H. (1992) *The first snowfall.* New York, NY: Simon & Schuster.

Saltzberg, B. (2008). *Crazy hair day.* Cambridge, MA: Candlewick.

Shannon, D. (1998). *No, David!* New York, NY: Blue Sky Press.

Grade 2

RTI in Action:
Oral Language Activities for Grade 2 Classrooms

BASIC CONCEPTS

Understand and Use Basic Concepts.................... 234

VOCABULARY

Understand and Use Nouns.................................. 236
Understand and Use Action Words..................... 238
Understand and Use Pronouns............................ 240
Understand and Use Adjectives 242
Understand and Use New
  Vocabulary Words 244
Categorize Words and Ideas................................246
Understand Classification 248
Recognize Comparisons and Contrasts 250
Understand and Produce
  Word Definitions 252
Understand Cause and
  Effect Relationships..................................... 254
Understand and Use Synonyms........................... 258
Understand and Use Antonyms 262
Understand and Use Similes............................... 266
Understand and Use Homophones 268
Use Words With Greater
  Depth of Meaning..270
Understand and Use Multiple
  Meaning Words..274

LISTENING AND SPEAKING

Respond to Multistep Directions...........................276
Understand and Use Different
  Types of Sentences....................................... 280
Use Complete Sentences 284
Speak for Different Purposes: Describe.............. 286
Speak for Different Purposes:
  Ask Questions... 288

Speak for Different Purposes: Persuade.............. 290
Participate in Conversation:
  Change and End Topics.................................292
Adapt Messages to Different
  Situations and Listeners............................... 298
Understand Nonverbal Signals:
  Personal Space 300
Understand and Use Tone of Voice to
  Convey Meaning.. 302
Understand and Express Feelings 304
Ask Questions for Repetition/
  Clarification 306
Understand and Use Logical
  Order of Events 310
Understand and Use Fictional Narratives............. 312
Retell a Story or Directions in
  Correct Order.. 316
Understand and Use Figurative
  Language: Metaphors.....................................318
Understand and Use Humor in
  Words and Situations.................................... 322
Summarize Stories and Events 324
Paraphrase Stories 326
Understand and Distinguish
  Fact From Opinion...328
Share Opinions...332
Understand and Use Inferences 334

PHONOLOGICAL AWARENESS

Blend Phonemes Into Words 336
Substitute Sounds in Words.................................338

PRINT KNOWLEDGE

Understand Concept of Paragraph....................... 340

Teacher Instruction: Black text on white background   **Student Response:** Black text on shaded background

Grade 2

LANGUAGE AREA:
Basic Concepts

OBJECTIVE:
Understand and Use Basic Concepts

TIER 1 — Basic Concepts

Help students understand and use basic concepts such as spatial relationships, time, quantity, and attributes.

Math: Give students different amounts of paper clips. Ask students and classmates:

- *Is Student A's amount of paper clips **greater** than Student B's?*
- *Is Student B's amount **less** than Student A's?*
- *What happens if we give Student A paper clips **in addition to** what he has?*
- *What happens if we **subtract** paper clips from Student B?*
- *Who will have an **increased** amount?*
- *Who will have a **decreased** amount?*

Reading: Find the **first** or **last** word, sentence, or paragraph.

Science: Ask questions such as

- *What is the **distance** from your desk to the door?*
- *What is the **distance** from our classroom to the cafeteria?*
- *Which is **farther**? Which is **nearer**?*
- *How are these two (object names) **alike**? How do they **differ**?*
- *Which of these two (object names) is **heavier**? Which is **lighter**?*
- *What kinds of objects **sink**? What kinds of objects **float**?*
- *Talk about the **characteristics** of different plants and animals.*

Social Studies: Name something or someone from

- the ***past***
- the ***present***
- the ***future***

Respond to the teacher's questions/directions.

234   GRADE 2 • BASIC CONCEPTS

| TIER 2 | Basic Concepts |

Repeated exposure

- Administer an inventory of basic concepts or do a structured observation to determine student mastery.

- Administer a screening such as the *Boehm Test of Basic Concepts, Third Edition*; *Bracken Basic Concept Scale—Revised*; or *Wiig Assessment of Basic Concepts*.

- For the concepts the student has not mastered, determine which ones may be interfering with the ability to follow the general education curriculum without support.

- Throughout the day, provide models and opportunities for the student to practice using targeted concepts.

Practice using basic concepts.

Negative practice

Give students statements with basic concept words used incorrectly. For example:

- *The feather is **heavier** than the rock.*
- *My nose is **farther** from my ear than my foot.*
- *Ten sticks are **greater** than twenty sticks.*
- *Twenty sticks are **less** than ten sticks.*

Correct the sentences by replacing the incorrect basic concept words with correct ones.

| TIER 3 | Basic Concepts |

Concrete materials

Use manipulatives or actions to illustrate basic concept words.

- *Put your book **farther** from the desk.*
- *Put your book **nearer** to the table.*

Follow the directions using the objects.

Visual dictionary/Alternative response mode

Show pictures and ask students to find a person or object that is **heavier**, **lighter**, **nearer**, **farther**, and so forth.

Point to the person or object.

GRADE 2 • BASIC CONCEPTS 235

| Grade 2 | LANGUAGE AREA: Vocabulary | OBJECTIVE: Understand and Use Nouns |

TIER 1 — Nouns

Explain that a *noun* is the name of a person, place, animal, or thing. Talk about proper versus common nouns and singular versus plural nouns and regular versus irregular nouns. Give several examples. (These are variable across languages.)

- **Common nouns** (Name general items)
    - boy
    - school
    - kitten
    - book
- **Proper nouns** (Specific names)
    - Mt. Lebanon Elementary School
    - Gifford's Ice Cream Shop
    - United States
    - Simon
- **Regular singular–plural nouns** (Add s for plural form)
    - girl–girls
    - creature–creatures
    - tiger–tigers
    - backpack–backpacks
- **Irregular singular–plural nouns** (Have different plural form)
    - cactus–cacti
    - hypothesis–hypotheses
    - child–children
    - fish–fish
    - foot–feet
    - tooth–teeth

- Write the words to a popular song or ask the music teacher for lyrics from a song the students are learning in music class. Read or sing each line.

- Ask students to underline nouns and list different types of nouns. Indicate that proper nouns require capitalization.

- Underline words that are nouns.
- Make a list of the common nouns, proper nouns, singular nouns, and plural nouns in the song.

TIER 2   Nouns

Visual cues

- Divide a piece of paper into four sections: *person, place, animal,* or *thing.*
- Revisit each song line and ask students to place the nouns in the correct section.
- Review the list and create a second paper with sections for common, proper, singular, and plural nouns.
- Point out common, proper, singular, and plural nouns.
- Ask students to place the words in the correct sections.

List nouns under the correct section.

Simplify

Give the student only two lines from a familiar song. Tell students the specific number of nouns to find and underline.

Find and underline the nouns.

TIER 3   Nouns

Different stimuli

Instruct students to listen for nouns as you read *A Mink, a Fink, a Skating Rink: What Is a Noun?* by Brian P. Cleary.

- Divide a piece of paper into four sections: *person, place, animal,* or *thing.*
- Listen to the story and fill in the categories with nouns from the story.

Negative practice

Write the words to a familiar song and underline words that are not nouns.

Correct the teacher's mistakes and find the nouns.

GRADE 2 • VOCABULARY   237

Grade 2

LANGUAGE AREA:
Vocabulary

OBJECTIVE:
Understand and Use
Action Words

TIER 1 — Action Words

Explain that an action word or verb is something that we can do, already did, or will do.

- Talk about movies and make a list of class favorites. Explain the words *scene, actor,* and *actress.*

- Ask students to think about the actions of their favorite characters in the movies.

- Tell students that the class is going to be actors and actresses in a scene from an action movie.

- Explain that when you say, *Lights, Camera, Action,* the students will perform an action word. When you say, *Cut!,* the movie will stop.

- Designate a setting for the movie (park, beach, school, or zoo) and ask students to brainstorm all the actions that might take place there. Write *I will _____* and ask several students to tell you what action they are planning to do in the movie.

- Announce, *Lights, Camera, Action.* As students perform their actions, select several students and ask, *What are you doing?* Next, say, *Cut!* and make all actions stop. Ask, *What did you do in the movie?*

Say the action word and start or stop the action as directed.

TIER 2	Action Words

Mental imagery

Give students the name of a familiar place and instruct them to form a mental image of themselves in that place.

- Make a list of actions that happen in that place.
- Pantomime the actions.

Alternative response mode

- Pretend to make a movie about a familiar event that happens often (getting ready for bed).
- First, make a list of actions that students would do before going to bed.
- Next, ask students to pick an action from the list.
- Say, *Lights, Camera, Action* and ask them to demonstrate the action.
- Next, say, *Cut!* Ask, *What did you do?*

Understand and use the action word.

TIER 3	Action Words

Repeated practice

Throughout the day, ask students, *What are you doing? What will we do next?* Model the action words often in different activities.

Answer the teacher's question with an action word.

Visual dictionary

Show students pictures of a place (park, store, or beach).

Brainstorm a list of actions that can be done in this place.

Grade
2

GRADE 2 • VOCABULARY   239

Grade 2	LANGUAGE AREA: Vocabulary	OBJECTIVE: Understand and Use Pronouns

TIER 1 Pronouns

Define pronouns and types of pronouns. Give examples.

- Brainstorm a list of singular and plural subjective pronouns (*I, he, she, we, they*) and singular and plural possessive pronouns (*mine, yours, his, hers, its, ours, yours, theirs*).

- Say a sentence and ask students to tell you the pronoun that can take the place of the noun in the sentence.

  o *Jack and Jack's friend rode their bikes down the street. Which word can we replace with a pronoun? (they)*

  o *Mary left Mary's sweater at school. Which word can be replaced with a pronoun? (her)*

  o *Manuel likes to visit Manuel's aunt on Sundays. Which word could be replaced with a pronoun? (his)*

Replace the noun with a pronoun in each sentence.

- Give students a blank bingo card and instruct them to choose pronouns and write them in the blank spaces on their cards.

- Continue saying sentences and ask students to tell you the pronoun that can take the place of the noun in the sentence and to cover up the pronoun on their bingo card.

Cover the pronoun on your bingo card.

240   GRADE 2 • VOCABULARY

TIER 2	Pronouns

Modeling

When the student uses a pronoun incorrectly, repeat or paraphrase the student's utterance saying the correct pronoun louder and longer. For example:

- Student: *Him is going home early.*
- Teacher: *Yes, HE is going to the dentist.*

Different stimuli

Display simple comic strips with the captions deleted.

Use appropriate pronouns.

TIER 3	Pronouns

Assistive technology

- Use a picture book and demonstrate how to tell a story about the pictures.
- Ask students to tell a story and record or videotape their story.
- Play the recording and listen for correct pronoun usage.

Practice using pronouns correctly as you tell a story.

Step-by-step

- Brainstorm a list of singular and plural pronouns.
- Provide students with written sentences in which they need to change from a proper noun to a singular or plural pronoun.

Use the list as a reference and change the proper nouns to appropriate singular or plural pronouns.

Grade 2

LANGUAGE AREA: Vocabulary

OBJECTIVE: Understand and Use Adjectives

TIER 1 — Adjectives

Talk about adjectives as words that tell about size, color, shape, and what something smells like, feels like, or tastes like. Tell students that adjectives make what we say, read, and write more interesting.

- Ask students to use adjectives to describe a tree.
- Ask students to list other words that can be described in the same way.
- Brainstorm a list of words that describe the color, shape, size, and texture of a tree.
- Make a list of other objects that can be described using each adjective.

TIER 2 — Adjectives

Concrete materials

- Give each student in the group a marshmallow to examine.
- Write *smells like, feels like, tastes like, color, size,* and *shape* on a piece of paper.
- Ask students to use adjectives to describe the marshmallow.

Examine the marshmallow and fill in words that describe the marshmallow.

Examples and nonexamples

- Select the correct adjective to describe the marshmallow:
    - *Is it red or white?*
    - *Does it feel smooth or rough?*
    - *Is it large, small, or medium sized?*
    - *Does it taste delicious or bad?*
    - *Does it smell sweet or sour?*
- Ask students to list other words that can be described in the same way.
- Choose the correct adjective.
- Brainstorm a list of other objects that can be described using this adjective.

TIER 3 · Adjectives

Advance organizer

- Choose an adjective that describes a car.
- Place the describing adjective in the center of a graphic organizer such as a spider map (see Appendix F).
- On the lines that radiate from the center, ask students to list other things that can also be described using this adjective.

Brainstorm a list of words that can be described using the adjective.

Visual dictionary/Alternative response mode

- Place five or six pictures of common objects in front of the student.
- Say an adjective to describe one of the pictures.

Choose the picture of the object that is described by the adjective.

| Grade 2 | LANGUAGE AREA: Vocabulary | OBJECTIVE: Understand and Use New Vocabulary Words |

TIER 1 — New Vocabulary Words

Help students learn new words using current vocabulary knowledge. Introduce students to lists of three to five words such as baseball, football, and soccer ball or fork, chopsticks, and spoon. Other suggested word lists are paintings (abstract, landscapes, still-lifes) or music (folk, rock 'n' roll, show tunes, opera, country).

- Start a discussion of how these words are the same and different (*How is a fork like a spoon? How are they different?*).

- Ask students to select two of these words and write a sentence showing their correct and incorrect use.

- Choose two of the words. Write sentences that show their correct use and sentences that show their incorrect use.

- Place all of the sentences in a pile and take turns reading them aloud.

- Vote on correct/incorrect usage and explain why.

TIER 2 — New Vocabulary Words

Concentrated instruction/Modeling

- Repeat the Tier 1 activity.

- Model how the words are used and what they mean.

- Ask students to select two of the three words and write sentences that show their correct use.

Choose two of the three words and write sentences that show their correct use.

Elaboration

- Repeat the Tier 1 activity.

- Define each of these words and give multiple examples of how these words are used.

Define words and give examples of how they are used.

| TIER 3 | New Vocabulary Words |

Simplify/Alternative response mode

- Repeat the Tier 1 activity.

- Present sentence pairs with one showing correct use and one showing incorrect use.

- Ask students to choose the correct sentence.

- Point to the sentence with the correct use of the word.

- After the teacher confirms that the choice is correct, read the sentence aloud.

Negative practice

- Repeat the Tier 1 activity.

- Present sentences in which the term is used correctly and incorrectly and ask students to provide the correct response.

- Read the sentence aloud after the student makes the correct choice.

Say whether the term is used correctly or incorrectly in each sentence and provide the correct response.

Grade
2

Grade 2	LANGUAGE AREA: Vocabulary	OBJECTIVE: Categorize Words and Ideas

TIER 1 — Categorize

Introduce two categories (*rock* and *mineral*) from students' science text or unit and write them on the board. Provide simple definitions for each (*rock: a large piece of stone; mineral: a natural material usually found in the ground*).

Provide examples of each category (*marble, granite,* and *slate* vs. *copper, aluminum,* and *diamond*).

- Present 8–10 cards, each containing a picture and word for students to sort into *rock* versus *mineral*.
- Divide students into groups and ask each group to present word sort results and explain the reasons for the sorts.
- Repeat the same activity with *sink* and *float* (*sink: to fall to the bottom; float: to rest on top of water or air*).

As a group, sort words into categories and then explain your reasons for sorting.

TIER 2 — Categorize

Repeated practice

Repeat the Tier 1 activity three times, providing feedback as the student responds.

Sort words into categories and say the names of the categories.

Mental imagery

- Present a picture of a rock and a picture of a mineral.
- Ask students to close their eyes and think about how each would look.
- Ask students to open their eyes and remember their mental pictures as they are asked to identify whether a picture is a rock or mineral.

- Form a mental picture of a rock and a mineral.
- Identify whether a picture is a rock or mineral based on these mental pictures.

246   GRADE 2 • VOCABULARY

| **TIER 3** | Categorize |

Visual cues/Restricted-choice questions

- Present eight cards, each with a picture and an icon on the top right-hand corner of the card (rock = ♦; mineral = ▨).

- After each of the eight pictures is presented, ask students, *Is this a rock?*

- Repeat the activity with, *Is this a mineral?*

Look at the cards and say whether each is a rock or a mineral.

Completion/Cloze statements

- Repeat definitions of rock and mineral showing icons (rock = ♦; mineral = ▨).

- Present each card to the students along with a fill-in-the-blank statement: *This picture is an example of a _____ (rock or mineral).*

- Repeat definitions as necessary.

Complete each sentence with the appropriate word.

Grade
2

Grade 2

LANGUAGE AREA: Vocabulary

OBJECTIVE: Understand Classification

TIER 1 — Classify

Teach students about classifying by designing a lesson about occupations. Begin by explaining that other words that refer to occupations are *job* and *work*.

- Ask students what they already know about kinds of occupations. Make a list of occupations. To expand students' notion of what work is, read the book *Work* by Ann Morris. This book gives a survey of all kinds of work around the world.
- Discuss the similarities between the jobs you have listed.
    - Teacher: *Why do a painter and a firefighter go together?*
    - Student: *They both use ladders.*
- Sort workers into groups of workers whose jobs have similar characteristics.
- Ask other students to guess why you grouped these workers together and add additional jobs that fit into your group.

TIER 2 — Classify

Alternative response mode

Show students pictures of workers. Ask students to point to jobs that are done inside or outside, workers who take care of people, or workers whose jobs are similar in other ways.

Point to pictures that correspond to the categories that the teacher names.

Simplify

Brainstorm a list of jobs that are performed inside and jobs that are performed outside.

- Choose one job on the list.
- Draw pictures of the tools you may need to do this job.
- Brainstorm additional jobs that use these tools.

TIER 3	Classify

Double dose of instruction/Visual cues

Review the concepts of *same* and *different*. Explain how we put words into groups based on things that are the same. Give examples of categories.

- *Things we ride in or on are called vehicles.*
- *Things that we use in the living spaces of our house are called furniture.*
- *Things we eat that are made from milk are called dairy foods.*

Give students pictures of vehicles, furniture, and dairy foods in random order.

- Group pictures into categories.
- Say or draw additional members of each group.

Examples and nonexamples

Ask the student to choose the word that doesn't belong.

- *Which job is usually not done outside—firefighter or librarian?*
- *Which worker does not use water to do his/her job—landscaper or toll collector?*
- *Which worker does not work with animals—cashier or zoo keeper?*

Choose the word that doesn't belong.

Grade
2

GRADE 2 • VOCABULARY   249

Grade 2

LANGUAGE AREA: Vocabulary

OBJECTIVE: Recognize Comparisons and Contrasts

TIER 1 — Compare and Contrast

Talk about how we often compare and contrast things to better understand them and to explain new things to others.

- Read *Little Polar Bear* by Hans De Beer. Lars, the little polar bear, sleeps so soundly he doesn't hear the ice cracking and floats away to sea. He is carried to the tropics where he meets Henry, the hippopotamus. The author and illustrator contrast the polar bear's world of ice and snow and the beautiful sights of a tropical world.

- Ask students to compare and contrast the different worlds in the book.

- Ask students to make comparisons and contrasts with these worlds and where they live.

- Compare and contrast the two different worlds.

- Compare and contrast the North Pole and the tropics with the place where you live.

Bonus: Ask students to make comparisons about where they want to live and why using opposite pairs (*city, country; hot climate, cold climate*).

TIER 2	Compare and Contrast

Advance organizer

Look at the illustrations and make a Venn diagram (see Appendix G) comparing and contrasting the North Pole and the tropics.

Brainstorm things that are the same and different about the North Pole and the tropics using the Venn diagram.

Visual cues

- Give students directions to brainstorm a list of things they know about the place where they live.
- Ask students to look at the illustrations in the *Little Polar Bear* or other book about the tropics.
- Ask them to compare each item on the list with the pictures and decide if it is the same or different.

Make a list of things that are the same about the tropics and your town and things that are different.

TIER 3	Compare and Contrast

Concrete materials

Instruct students to draw a picture of their towns. Compare and contrast the pictures with the illustrations in the *Little Polar Bear* book.

Draw a picture of your town and talk about how your town is the same as and different from the towns described in the book.

Concentrated instruction

Focus only on comparing.

Make a list of things in the North Pole or the tropics that are the same in the places where you live.

Grade 2

GRADE 2 • VOCABULARY   251

| Grade 2 | LANGUAGE AREA: Vocabulary | OBJECTIVE: Understand and Produce Word Definitions |

TIER 1 — Word Definitions

Talk about how important it is to be able to define a word and understand the meaning of new words.

- Introduce a definitions map (see Appendix I) and draw it on the board.
- Place a concrete noun from text or curricular materials in the center circle and provide appropriate descriptors.
- Talk about the critical attributes of the definition.
- Ask students to use the filled-in map to formulate a definition for the concrete noun.
- Read a paragraph from the students' text or curricular materials to place the word in context.
- Repeat with abstract nouns, verbs, and adjectives also from the students' text or curricular materials.

Use the filled-in map to formulate definitions for the word in the center of the map.

TIER 2 — Word Definitions

Different stimuli

- Review ways to teach new vocabulary at http://people.bu.edu/jpettigr/Artilces_and_Presentations/Vocabulary.htm.
- Use these strategies to help students define new target vocabulary from the curriculum.

Give definitions of new words.

Matching

Write nouns from the curriculum in a column on the left. Place definitions in random order on the right.

Match words and their definitions.

| **TIER 3** | Word Definitions |

Auditory cues

Play a category game using target vocabulary. Call out a category such as words that describe feelings, places, or appearance and ask students to say as many words as possible that fit in that category.

List words for each category.

Auditory Cues

Use words from the student's text or curricular materials and state an incomplete definition.

Decide what word or words are missing and complete the statement or question by filling in the blanks.

| Grade 2 | LANGUAGE AREA: | OBJECTIVE: |
| | Vocabulary | Understand Cause and Effect Relationships |

TIER 1 — Cause and Effect

Explain that every action has a reaction and that we call that *cause and effect*. Provide a few examples:

- *I had a hole in my pocket so I lost my money.*
- *My hair grew long so I got a haircut.*

Brainstorm events that might happen in school. Examples:

- dropping a tray in the cafeteria
- being late with a school paper
- getting a good grade on a test
- hearing the fire alarm

As students generate ideas, list them on the board/chart paper.

- To the left of each event, brainstorm three things that might cause this event (*a wet floor might cause a student to slip and drop his tray*).
- Then, to the right of the event, brainstorm three effects of the event (*the effect of dropping the tray might be that the student carrying the tray got his pants dirty*).
- Discuss each event and its cause and effects, explaining that it is like a chain in which each link is connected to the other links.
- Select some of the event sequences and ask students to explain the cause and effects.
- Ask students to give reasons why the action could have caused the reaction.

Brainstorm events and explain the cause and event sequences.

254   GRADE 2 • VOCABULARY

| TIER 2 | Cause and Effect |

Concentrated instruction

Explain again that every action has a reaction and that we call that *cause and effect*. Provide a few examples:

- *It was hot outside, so my ice cream melted quickly.*
- *My dog was dirty, so we gave him a bath.*
- *I outgrew my shoes, so I got a new pair.*
- *The baby was crying, so we gave her a bottle.*
- *I skinned my knee, so I got a bandage.*

Brainstorm events that might happen in school. Examples:

- falling down on the playground
- forgetting your lunch
- losing your homework
- missing the bus
- helping a friend

As students generate ideas, list them on the board/chart paper.

- To the left of each event, brainstorm two things that might cause this event (*running too fast may cause a student to fall on the playground*).
- Then, to the right of the event, brainstorm two effects of the event (*the effect of a student falling down might be that she dropped her books*).
- Discuss each event and its cause and effects, explaining that it is like a chain in which each link is connected to the other links.
- Select some of the event sequences and ask students to explain the cause and effects.
- Ask students to give reasons why the action could have caused the reaction.

Brainstorm events and explain the cause and effect sequences.

Visual cues

Provide pictures of events from magazines or a familiar book.

Explain the cause and effect sequence.

GRADE 2 • VOCABULARY   255

| TIER 3 | Cause and Effect |

Multiple choice/Matching

Repeat the Tier 1 activity.

- Cover or remove the list and present one of the events with three choices for the answer.
- Ask students to select the correct answer from the set of three.

- Brainstorm events and explain their causes and effects.
- Explain why a certain action could cause a particular reaction.
- Select the correct answer from the three choices.

Forced-choice questions

Repeat the Tier 1 activity.

Ask students to select the correct answer from the two choices.

Brainstorm events and select the correct answer from the two choices.

Notes: _____

Grade 2

GRADE 2 • VOCABULARY 257

Grade 2	LANGUAGE AREA: Vocabulary	OBJECTIVE: Understand and Use Synonyms

Grade 2

TIER 1   Synonyms

Talk about synonyms being words that have the same meaning. See the Synonym Pairs Table on the next page for examples.

- Use a story that the class is reading to identify words that have synonyms.
- Have students name the synonyms for words in the book.
- Choose one or two synonym pairs each day while you talk to your students. Use both words to illustrate how the meaning does not change. _Choose_ the crayons *you need to draw a picture.* _Select_ *your colors from the class crayon bin.*
- Reward (homework pass, sticker, pencil) students if they catch you using a synonym pair.

Listen for synonyms throughout the school day and add the synonym pairs to a classroom chart.

TIER 2   Synonyms

Word bank

Brainstorm a synonym word bank. Give students a word that has a synonym in the word bank.

- *glad (happy)*
- *right (correct)*
- *quiet (silent)*

Find the synonym in the word bank.

Negative practice

Give students examples of two sentences that have different meanings.

- *I have a belly ache. I have a knee ache. (stomach)*
- *I am sad. I am glad. (unhappy)*

Replace the underlined word in the second sentence with the correct synonym for the underlined word in the first sentence.

258   GRADE 2 • VOCABULARY

Synonym Pairs Table

A/B

able/capable	agree/consent	all/entire	almost/approximately
always/continuously	answer/reply	ask/inquire	back/rear
before/previously	behavior/conduct	blaze/fire	break/shatter

C

careful/considerate	carry/tote	cat/kitty	center/middle
change/alter	chase/follow	cheerful/sunny	child/youngster
choose/select	clear/transparent	copy/duplicate	

D/E

do/complete	done/finish	eager/keen	end/conclusion
enjoy/appreciate	entire/whole	erase/delete	error/mistake

F/G/H

false/untrue	fast/rapid	finish/complete	first/initial
funny/laughable	gather/collect	gentle/mild	get/acquire
giant/huge	give/contribute	glad/happy	go/proceed
great/outstanding	group/cluster	happy/content	help/assist
hollow/empty	hopeful/optimistic	house/home	

I/J/K

imagine/suppose	immediately/instantly	improve/enhance	increase/expand
job/chore	jump/spring	keep/retain	kid/youth

L/M/N

large/immense	last/final	late/tardy	laugh/chuckle
leave/depart	lift/hoist	look/gaze	lost/missing
make/create	many/numerous	market/store	mellow/calm
mistake/error	more/additional	need/desire	new/fresh
nice/agreeable	noisy/loud	now/immediately	

O/P/Q/R

obey/comply	often/frequently	only/unique	opinion/belief
past/prior	pick/choose	place/location	prior/earlier
question/quiz	quiet/silent	raise/elevate	relate/describe
remark/comment	rest/relax	right/exact	rule/law
run/dash	rush/hurry		

S/T/U/V/W/X/Y/Z

same/exact	save/conserve	scatter/spread	shiny/bright
sick/ill	silly/giddy	skill/expertise	sloppy/untidy
smile/grin	soon/shortly	sorry/regretful	suggestions/ideas
teach/educate	tell/say	thankful/grateful	too/additionally
total/entire	try/attempt	under/below	unsure/doubtful
use/apply	view/examine	wait/linger	walk/stroll
want/desire	watch/look	well/correctly	windy/blustery
work/job	worry/concern	wrong/incorrect	

| TIER 3 | Synonyms |

Examples and nonexamples/Role play

Give students two sentences with synonym pairs used correctly and incorrectly. If students have difficulty understanding whether the sentences mean the same thing, ask them to act them out.

Decide if the two sentences mean the same thing.

Connecting to prior knowledge/Concrete materials

Say or write two or three related sentences that contain overused words instead of synonyms such as *happy* instead of *glad*.

Be sure that students understand the concepts of *same* and *different*.

- Replace the overused words with synonyms.
- Repeat the sentences.

Notes:

Grade 2

GRADE 2 • VOCABULARY 261

| Grade 2 | LANGUAGE AREA: Vocabulary | OBJECTIVE: Understand and Use Antonyms |

TIER 1 — Antonyms

Talk about antonyms being pairs of words with opposite meanings. See the Antonym Pairs Table on the next page for examples.

- Read a book about Johnny Appleseed such as *Johnny Appleseed* by Steven Kellogg; *Johnny Appleseed* by Reeve Lindberg; *Johnny Appleseed* by Gini Holland and Kim Palmer; or *The Story of Johnny Appleseed* by Aliki.

- Talk about how Johnny Appleseed traveled around the United States planting apple trees.

- Display a map. Ask students to find a place on the map that Johnny Appleseed may have visited that is the opposite of

    o   north

    o   east

    o   top of the country

    o   right side of the country

    o   a cold place

    o   a place with mountains

    o   a state above our state

    o   a state that is near an ocean

Find the opposite places on the map and state the opposite pairs.

Antonym Pairs Table

A/B/C

after/before	all/none	always/never	ashamed/proud
asleep/awake	behind/in front	best/worst	bitter/sweet
black/white	blunt/sharp	buy/sell	city/country
clever/foolish	closed/open	combine/separate	crooked/straight

D/E/F

day/night	dead/alive	deep/shallow	dirty/clean
dull/sharp	easy/difficult	empty/full	exciting/dull
exit/entrance	expensive/cheap	fat/skinny	few/many
find/lose	front/back	foolish/wise	full/empty

G/H/I

girl/boy	give/take	go/stay	grin/frown
happy/sad	hard/soft	healthy/sick	heavy/light
hollow/solid	husband/wife	imaginary/real	include/exclude

J/K/L

joy/grief	kind/mean	king/queen	lead/follow
left/right	length/width	loose/tight	lower/raise

M/N/O

mix/sort	moist/dry	morning/night	necessary/useless
no one/everybody	obey/disobey	outer/inner	outside/inside

P/Q/R

part/whole	permit/forbid	polite/rude	poor/rich
positive/negative	question/answer	quick/slow	quiet/noisy
receive/send	reckless/cautious	right/wrong	rough/smooth

S/T/U/V/W/X/Y/Z

send/receive	sink/float	soften/harden	strengthen/weaken
sudden/gradual	sweet/sour	swift/slow	tame/wild
tardy/early	thaw/freeze	thick/thin	true/false
unbreakable/fragile	vacant/occupied	wake/sleep	war/peace
warm/cool	whisper/yell	winter/summer	worthless/valuable

TIER 2 — Antonyms

Completion/Cloze Statements

Give the student clues:

- *Philadelphia is north and Florida is _____.*
- *New York is east and California is _____.*
- *Maine is a cold place in the winter and Florida is a _____ place.*
- *New Jersey is _____ the ocean and Illinois is _____ from the ocean.*
- *_____ is above our state and _____ is _____ our state.*

Fill in the blanks with the appropriate antonyms.

Previewing

- Before the lesson, talk about antonyms.

- Brainstorm a list of antonyms.

- Underline specific words in a sentence and ask students to change the sentence meaning by replacing the words in bold with their antonyms.

  - *In the **summer**, Florida is very **cold**.*
  - *We traveled **east** on the interstate and soon were in the **country**.*
  - *Johnny Appleseed planted **a few** apple trees.*

Replace words in bold with antonyms.

TIER 3 — Antonyms

Different stimuli/Visual dictionary

Ask students to illustrate or cut out pictures of antonym pairs and find matching pairs.

- Mix up the pictures and find the matching pairs.
- Say the antonym pairs.

Word bank

- Create a list of antonym pairs as students learn them—and review often.

- Hang up the list in the classroom.

- Be sure students understand the concepts of *same* and *different* that underlie the concepts of synonyms and antonyms.

Refer to the word bank for assistance.

264   GRADE 2 • VOCABULARY

Notes:

Grade 2

LANGUAGE AREA: Vocabulary

OBJECTIVE: Understand and Use Similes

TIER 1 — Similes

Explain that similes are used to compare two unlike things using phrases that begin with *like* or *as*. For example, if you want to say that somebody *swims well*, you can say they *swim like a fish* because fish swim well.

Read a book about bugs, such as *The Best Book of Bugs* by Claire Llewellyn. Brainstorm a list of bugs. Talk about familiar similes:

- *busy as a bee*
- *pretty as a butterfly*
- *snug as a bug*

Make up new similes about bugs.

TIER 2 — Similes

Completion/Cloze statements

Give the first part of the simile and ask students to complete it aloud:

- *pretty as a _____*
- *slimy as a _____*
- *quiet as a _____*
- *tiny as a _____*
- *shiny as a _____*
- *creepy as a _____*
- *ugly as a _____*
- *deadly as a _____*

Fill in the blank and repeat the simile with your word.

Simplify/Elaboration

Ask students: *How can I say that you run fast? I could say that you run as fast as a cougar. This is a simile.* Continue with *How could I say*

- *a butterfly is as colorful? (as a rainbow)*
- *a weightlifter is as strong? (as an ox)*

Create a simile using *as*.

Ask students, *How can I say that a fly has wings? I could say a fly has wings like an airplane. How could you use a simile to say*

- *a caterpillar is soft (like a pillow)*
- *a mosquito can bite (like a spider)*

Create a simile using *like*.

TIER 3   Similes

Visual dictionary

Show pictures of bugs. Brainstorm a list of adjectives that describe the bugs.

Use the adjectives (*small, colorful, scary, big, creepy*) to create a simile about a favorite bug.

Forced-choice questions

Give students the first part of a simile and ask them to choose between two words to complete the simile.

- *Is a butterfly as colorful as a rainbow or a snail?*
- *Is a caterpillar as soft as a rock or a pillow?*

Choose the word that best completes the simile and use the simile in a phrase or sentence.

Grade
2

| Grade 2 | LANGUAGE AREA: Vocabulary | OBJECTIVE: Understand and Use Homophones |

TIER 1 — Homophones

Explain to students that homophones are two or more words that sound the same but have different meanings and different spellings. Give students examples that can easily be demonstrated:

- *I* and *eye*
- *tail* and *tale*
- *son* and *sun*
- *by* and *buy*
- *won* and *one*

- *aisle* and *I'll*
- *ate* and *eight*
- *aunt* and *ant*
- *cent* and *sent*
- *dear* and *dare*

- *doe* and *dough*
- *do* and *due*
- *for* and *four*
- *hair* and *hare*
- *heal* and *heel*

- *hoarse* and *horse*
- *hours* and *ours*
- *be* and *bee*
- *meet* and *meat*
- *in* and *inn*

Read a book with homophones, such as *Good Night, Good Knight* by Shelley Moore Thomas. After discussing the homophones in the story, pair students with a partner. Pass out index cards on which you have written pairs of homophones.

- Draw a picture to illustrate the pair of homophones on your card.
- Ask other students to guess the pair of homophones.
- Rewrite the homophones under your pictures.

TIER 2 — Homophones

Word bank

Create a list of homophones and their definitions as students learn them. Display the words in an easily accessible word bank.

Refer to the word bank for assistance.

Repeated practice

- Display a different pair of homophones each day.
- Provide opportunities to use homophones in a classroom activity.
- Provide some recognition or reward when students use them independently.

Use the homophone pair in your written and oral class work.

TIER 3	Homophones

Negative practice

- Present sentences in which homophones are used incorrectly.
- Ask students to find the incorrect words and replace them.
  - o *Won day, their was a caterpillar eating sum lovely green leaves.*
  - o *He was glad that there were sew many green things to eat.*
  - o *He exclaimed: "Green is grate."*

Find the incorrect homophone(s) and replace with the correct one(s).

Auditory cues

Give students a description of a homophone pair. For example:

- *This word is a color and also what the wind did on a stormy day. (blue and blew)*
- *This is another name for an ocean and also something you can do with your eyes. (sea and see)*

If necessary provide a verbal cue for the first sound of the word.

Repeat the homophone word meanings and identify the homophones.

Grade
2

GRADE 2 • VOCABULARY   269

Grade 2

LANGUAGE AREA: Vocabulary

OBJECTIVE: Use Words With Greater Depth of Meaning

TIER 1 — Depth of Meaning

Introduce students to semantic sets (related words) from content curriculum such as science. For example:

Dinosaurs	
bone	survival
fossil	backbone
skeleton	head
skull	torso
brain	paleontologists
extinct	relic
spine	archaeologist

- Start a discussion of how these words are the *same* and *different* (*How is a fossil like a relic? How are they different?*).
- Stimulate discussion by asking how these words are used and what they mean.
- Ask students to select two of the words. Write sentences that show their correct use and sentences that show their incorrect use.
- Choose two of the words. Write sentences that show their correct use and sentences that show their incorrect use.
- Place all of the sentences in a pile and take turns reading them aloud.
- Vote on correct/incorrect usage and explain your choice.

TIER 2	Depth of Meaning

Concentrated instruction/Simplify

- Introduce only one semantic set (*dinosaurs*) and start a discussion of how words from the set are the *same* and *different* (*How is a brain like a skull? How are they different?*).

- Stimulate discussion by asking how these words are used.

- Use the prompts below to provide concentrated instruction on the target semantic set:

  o What do you know about (*target semantic set*)

  o Circle the words that go with (*target semantic set*)

  o Brainstorm a list of words you think of about this topic

  o List names of jobs that are connected with (*target semantic set*)

  o Write sentences to tell about what the target does or what you do with (*target semantic set*)

  o Draw a picture of (*target semantic set*)

  o What idioms do you think of with (*target semantic set*)

Discuss what target words mean.

Repeated practice/Visual cues

- Introduce one semantic set (*dinosaurs*) and start a discussion of how words from the set are the *same* and *different*. (*How is a skull like a head? How are they different?*)

- Conduct this activity twice more using a "memory" game with index cards. Each card contains a target word or a function/description/picture of the word.

- Shuffle the cards and lay them out in rows and columns. Take turns turning over two cards to find matches (*fossil* matches *trace of an animal* or *plant*).

- Ask students to select one of the words and write a sentence that shows its correct use.

- Take turns playing the memory game.
- Choose one of the words and write one sentence that shows its correct use.

Grade
2

GRADE 2 • VOCABULARY   271

| TIER 3 | Depth of Meaning |

Concentrated instruction/Simplify/Visual cue

- Introduce one semantic set (*human body*) and discuss the location and function of each body part while pointing to it on a schematic of the human body.

- List the body parts on the board/chart and ask students to write the location and function of each in their notebooks or chart paper.

List the location and function of each body part.

Completion/Cloze statements

- Introduce one semantic set (*human body*) and discuss the location and function of each body part while pointing to it on a schematic of the human body.

- Write incomplete sentences about the location and function of each body part on the board/chart and ask students to complete them (*The location of the brain is _____; the function of the brain is _____*). Write their answers on the board.

- Ask students to read the correct sentences aloud.

Finish the sentences presented by the teacher and read them aloud.

Notes:

Grade 2

GRADE 2 • VOCABULARY 273

				Grade
		Grade	**LANGUAGE AREA:**	**OBJECTIVE:**
		2	Vocabulary	Understand and Use Multiple Meaning Words

TIER 1   Multiple Meaning Words

Explain that some words sound the same but have different meanings.

- Tell the joke, *Why did the Cyclops have to shut down his school? Because he had only one pupil.* (If necessary, explain what a Cyclops is.) Talk about the two meanings of the word *pupil.*

- *When are sheep like ink? When they are in a pen.* Talk about the two meanings of the word *pen.*

Guess the answers to the teacher's jokes.

Multiple Meaning Word List

ball	bank	bark	bat	bend	bowl	can
case	check	date	drop	face	fair	fan
file	fly	grave	hide	jam	kind	light
like	line	mean	mine	miss	order	pen
play	point	present	press	rare	ring	roll
rose	run	ship	sink	star	stick	story
tire	trip	vault	watch	well	yard	deck
lead	lap	might	race	pound	rock	row
sound	state	rap	tap	tick	tip	bowl

⭐ **Bonus:** Talk about how the same word can be a noun or a verb. (*Put the **stamp** on the envelope. **Stamp** your feet. Please give me the **block**. Don't **block** the television.*)

274   GRADE 2 • VOCABULARY

TIER 2 — Multiple Meaning Words

Matching/Auditory cues/Visual cues

- Show students a pair of cards with pictures of words that sound the same but have two different meanings.
- Read a sentence (*The farmer was in the pig pen* or *The farmer wrote with a pen*).
- Ask students to choose the picture that goes with the sentence.
- Continue with multiple pairs of words.

Choose the picture that corresponds to the sentence.

Repeated reading

- Read *Amelia Bedelia* by Herman Parish at least twice, or read only part of the book, emphasizing the words that have multiple meanings.
- Talk with students about each word that has multiple meanings.

Discuss each word with multiple meanings.

TIER 3 — Multiple Meaning Words

Independent practice

- Ask students to draw pictures of targeted words that can have two different meanings (*pound, fall, watch, pet, bat, ring, roll*) or use the website to play a multiple meaning word game at www.quia.com/cb/6344.html.
- Put the students' pictures on a bulletin board and discuss each picture.

- Draw pictures of targeted words.
- Discuss each picture.

Repeated reading/Visual cues

- Read *Amelia Bedelia* by Herman Parish at least three times, emphasizing the words that have multiple meanings and looking at their illustrations.
- Talk with students about each word that has multiple meanings.

Discuss the multiple meaning words.

Grade 2

LANGUAGE AREA: Listening and Speaking

OBJECTIVE: Respond to Multistep Directions

TIER 1 — Multistep Directions

Explain the importance of remembering what is said and of following directions: *Today's activity is going to help us learn how to follow directions. Following directions is important if you want to learn how to play a new game, do your schoolwork, or try other things that you haven't done before.*

The website www.studyzone.org/testprep/ela4/g/directionsl.cfm provides a simple explanation of how to follow directions as well as additional practice in following directions.

- Create a *following directions* activity by giving verbal directions for each student to create her own piece of chalk. The recipe can be found at www.mccormick.com/Recipes/Other/Cooler-than-Classroom-Chalk.aspx.
- Give each student the necessary ingredients (toilet paper tube, plaster of Paris, bowl, food coloring).
- Provide these instructions:
  - *Today we're going to practice following directions to make our own chalk.*
  - *I will tell you what to do for each step and then wait until you've finished that step. Then I'll give the second step. Listen carefully for each direction. Ask for help if there is something you don't understand or didn't hear.*

Follow each direction to make your own piece of chalk.

 Bonus: When new students join the class, use a map of the school and provide multistep directions to help them find their way around. For example, tell the new student to *turn left out of the room and turn at the end of the hall to find the cafeteria; take the stairway up, turn right, and go to the first door on the left to find the library; go to the large room that is the furthest from ours on the first floor to find the main office.*

| TIER 2 | Multistep Directions |

Visual cues/Simplify

Explain that the class is going to make chalk.

Have pictures of all the ingredients (toilet paper tube or paper towel tube cut in half, wax paper or foil, ½ cup water, assorted food colorings, and 1 cup plaster of Paris). Hold up a picture for each step of the direction as you read it.

Additionally, you can print each step of the directions on a card and give students a card for each step.

1. Seal one end of the cardboard tube with foil.

2. Mix water and food coloring in a bowl or disposable plastic container. Add this mixture to the plaster of Paris to make a "pudding" consistency. Stir until the mix starts to thicken. Work fast!

3. Stand your cardboard tubes on end (on wax paper or foil). Pour the mix into the tube.

4. When the mix is firm, peel off the cardboard. Any cardboard left on the chalk can be rubbed off with a gloved finger or scraped off.

5. Dry overnight. Go out to your sidewalk or driveway and start drawing.

Follow each direction to make your own piece of chalk.

Assistive technology/Multiple modalities

Refer to the website www.internet4classrooms.com for second grade skills. The direct link to the skill on following directions is www.internet4classrooms.com/grade_level_help/communication_follow_directions_language_arts_second_2nd_grade.htm. This site requires students to read the directions and follow them. You may read the directions to the students.

The website www.studyzone.org/testprep/e1topic.cfm?topicid=461 provides a simple explanation of how to follow directions and provides additional practice in following directions.

Follow the directions correctly.

GRADE 2 • LISTENING AND SPEAKING   277

| TIER 3 | Multistep Directions |

Repeated practice

Develop a homework activity that allows students to practice following directions at home using the site www.ed.gov/pubs/CompactforReading/pdf/second/s60.pdf.

This activity requires students to

- think about a story;
- draw a picture;
- write a sentence about the picture.

Do the activity in class and then send the practice page home, asking parents to read the directions if students need help completing the assignment at home.

Complete the assignment in class and at home with assistance if necessary.

Simplify/Repeated reading

- Read aloud a series of directions that require the student to write things on a piece of paper. Caution students that directions will not be repeated. For example, say, *Write the number 3 and circle it; draw a square and write the letter c inside of it.*

- If the student does not follow the directions correctly, break each direction into smaller steps and repeat the directions.

Follow the directions correctly.

Notes:

Grade 2

GRADE 2 • LISTENING AND SPEAKING   279

Grade 2

LANGUAGE AREA: Listening and Speaking

OBJECTIVE: Understand and Use Different Types of Sentences

TIER 1 — Different Types of Sentences

Explain the differences between statements and questions. We use statements to give information and questions to get information.

- Use examples from a story or generate a list of statements and questions.
- Talk about statements ending with a period and questions ending with a question mark.
- Write a few examples of each on the board:
  - *Jose is 5 years old.* This is a statement because it tells you something and ends with a period.
  - *How old is Roy?* This is a question because it has an answer and it ends with a question mark.
  - *I had a sandwich for lunch.* This is a statement because it tells you something.
  - *What did you have for lunch?* This is a question because it asks for information.
- Give each student a card with a period and a letter *S* and a card with a question mark and the letter *Q*.
- Ask students to raise the *S* card for statements and the *Q* card for questions.
- Read a list of statements and questions.
- Ask students to generate their own lists.
- Ask other students to indicate which are statements and which are questions.
- Introduce the terms *exclamations* and *commands*. Exclamations are used to express surprise or excitement and commands are used to direct someone's actions.
- Give each student cards with an exclamation point (!) or COMMAND.
- Ask students to say something that can be an exclamation (with an excited voice) or a statement (without an excited voice). For example, say, *I won the prize!* or *I won the prize.*
- Ask students to say something that can be a command (with a commanding voice) or a request (without a commanding voice). For example, say, *Get that ball now* with and without a commanding voice.
- **Raise the appropriate card to show a statement, question, exclamation, or command.**
- **Generate different types of sentences.**

280   GRADE 2 • LISTENING AND SPEAKING

| TIER 2 | Different Types of Sentences |

Comprehension probe/Examples and nonexamples

- Review the characteristics of a question. Give examples, asking if they are questions. Ask students to generate questions.

- If necessary, prompt students with words like *who, what, where, when,* or *how* or ask them, *What would you say if you don't know a person's name? Birthday?*

- Ask a student to say something that is not a question. You may need to prompt with leading statements such as *Tell me what you ate for lunch, Tell me what you did at recess,* or *Tell me who is in your family.*

- Repeat this activity using both statements and questions, asking students to raise the card that corresponds to the correct type of sentence

- Ask students to say a question or a statement when you raise the appropriate card.

- Repeat for exclamations and commands.

- Raise the appropriate card to show a statement, question, exclamation, or command.
- Provide an example of each type of sentence.

Different stimuli

- Give all students sentence strips.
- Ask students to sort the strips into the four categories of statements, questions, exclamations, and commands.

Sort sets of sentence strips appropriately.

Grade 2

| TIER 3 | Different Types of Sentences |

Visual cues

- Provide a set of sentence strips that is color coded. For example, all of the statements can be on pink paper, the questions on green paper, the exclamations on blue, and the commands on yellow.
- Ask students to categorize each sentence strip and read the set of sentences in each category.

Sort the color coded sentence strips appropriately and read all of the sentences from each category.

Repeated exposure

- After you complete the Tier 2 activity, use a current story the class is reading.
- Read the story and pause after each sentence.
- Ask students to say if the sentence is a statement, question, exclamation, or command.

Say if a sentence is a statement, question, exclamation, or command.

Notes:

Grade
2

GRADE 2 • LISTENING AND SPEAKING   283

Grade 2

LANGUAGE AREA: Listening and Speaking

OBJECTIVE: Use Complete Sentences

TIER 1 — Complete Sentences

Explain that a sentence contains a subject (what you are talking about) and a verb or action word (what's happening). Give several examples and nonexamples of sentences and sentence fragments.

- Ask students to say a complete sentence using the following sentence starters.
    - *Three boys _____.*
    - *My friend has _____.*
    - *Next week _____.*
    - *Yesterday _____.*
    - *I went _____.*
    - *I might _____.*
    - *The Little Red Hen _____.*
    - *Tomorrow _____.*

- Continue the activity, selecting sentence starters from a familiar book.
- Divide the class into two teams. For a team to earn a point, students must answer the teacher's question with a complete sentence.
- Model the activity and then alternate between team members as you ask questions.
- Ask students to answer the questions with a full sentence.

- Make complete sentences from the sentence starters that the teacher reads.
- Answer the teacher's questions with a full sentence to receive points for your team.

284   GRADE 2 • LISTENING AND SPEAKING

| TIER 2 | Complete Sentences |

Visual cues

- Make cards containing subjects and verbs and separate the cards into two piles.

- Instruct students to choose a card from each pile and make a complete sentence.

Choose a card from each pile and say a complete sentence using the noun and verb cards.

Different representations

Give students scrambled words and ask them to create a complete sentence.

- *boy, ran, home, the*

- *monkey, bananas, the, ate*

Put the words in the correct order to form a complete sentence.

| TIER 3 | Complete Sentences |

Repeated practice

Ask students questions that stimulate language use. Whenever possible, avoid questions that can be answered by *yes/no* or a nod of the head. If a student does not use a complete sentence, model a complete sentence and ask the student to repeat the model.

- Say: *What did you do in art?* Instead of: *Did you paint today?*

- Say: *What did you do during the holiday?* Instead of: *Did you have a good vacation?*

Respond to the teacher's questions with a complete sentence.

Examples and nonexamples

Give students examples of complete and incomplete sentences, both oral and written.

- Identify which sentences are complete.
- Add words to the incomplete sentences to make them complete.

Grade 2

GRADE 2 • LISTENING AND SPEAKING   285

Grade 2

LANGUAGE AREA:
Listening and Speaking

OBJECTIVE:
Speak for Different Purposes: Describe

TIER 1 — Describe

Discuss how words tell how something feels, tastes, looks smells, or sounds.

- Read the book *Train to Somewhere* by Eva Bunting or a similar story. Choose a character from the story.

- Ask one student to be a police officer. Ask other students to describe the character in the story. The police officer must identify the character from the students' descriptions because he may be a missing person.

Describe characters by giving different characteristics:

- height
- hair color
- gender
- clothing

TIER 2 — Describe

Elaboration/Auditory cues

Ask questions about the character who is missing so that students can practice using descriptive vocabulary:

- *Is he taller or shorter than you?*
- *What does he look like?*
- *Where does he live?*
- *What is the character's age?*
- *How does the character act?*

Answer the questions with words that describe the character.

286   GRADE 2 • LISTENING AND SPEAKING

Advance organizer

- Develop a set of general word webs for each descriptive category. A word web is a graphic organizer with circles, squares, or other shapes that are connected with lines to show the different parts of a word's meaning.
- Ask students to brainstorm words that express
  - o   height
  - o   hair color
  - o   personality traits

Brainstorm words that describe the missing character.

TIER 3   Describe

Multiple choice

- Describe a character from *Train to Somewhere*.
- Provide correct and incorrect words to describe the character.
- Ask students to select that words that correctly describe the character.

Choose the words that describe the character.

Completion/Cloze statements

Talk about a specific character and say the beginning of a sentence that focuses on a characteristic:

- *Tom's hair is _____.*
- *Mary feels _____ at the beginning of the story.*

Fill in the blank with a describing word.

Grade 2

LANGUAGE AREA: Listening and Speaking

OBJECTIVE: Speak for Different Purposes: Ask Questions

TIER 1 — Ask Questions

Talk with students about the importance of being able to ask questions to gain information.

- Tell students you want to know what they like to do after school. You might ask: *Do you play inside or outside? What do you do when you get home from school? Who is at your house after school? When do you do your homework?*
- Ask students to find a partner. Explain to student pairs that they will have a short time to gain information about each other by asking a question.
- Tell students to ask what they want to know about their partner's _____ (*favorite ice cream flavor, favorite animal, favorite after school activity, bedtime, favorite food*).
- Ask students to "turn and talk" to their partners.
- After 1 minute or less, direct all students' attention back to the group.
- Ask several partners to report to the whole group about the question they asked and the answer they received.
- Repeat the activity several times, giving students guidelines about the information they want to know.
- Ask students to "turn and talk" and find out something about their partner by asking any questions they wish.
- Allow groups to share questions and answers.

Share questions you asked and your classmate's answers.

Bonus: Explain to students that news is a report of something that happened recently. News reporters ask questions to gain information about events. Each morning choose one student to say one or two sentences about something that is happening at home or at school. Students act as news reporters and ask questions to gain more information.

TIER 2   Ask Questions

Modeling

- Help students formulate *yes/no* questions.
- Ask a question, such as *Do you like to ride your bike?*
- Ask students to ask *yes/no* questions.

Answer the teacher's question. Ask a classmate the same question.

Turn and talk

Ask students to choose a partner for "turn and talk." Tell them to ask their student partners a question.

Choose a partner and ask that person a question.

TIER 3   Ask Questions

Visual clues

As you ask a question, pair the question word with a gesture:

- *when*—point to the clock to signify time
- *what*—hold palms up
- *why*—give a look of puzzlement
- *where*—look around as if you are looking for something

Ask questions to get more information, using the cues the teacher provides.

Concentrated instruction

Focus on asking only two types of questions until the student understands and successfully expresses these two types. Then focus on the other two types.

Ask questions to get more information about a classmate.

Grade 2

GRADE 2 • LISTENING AND SPEAKING   289

| Grade 2 | LANGUAGE AREA: Listening and Speaking | OBJECTIVE: Speak for Different Purposes: Persuade |

TIER 1 — Persuade

Explain that sometimes we try to persuade someone to think, feel, or act in a certain way. One way to persuade someone is to give good reasons.

- Read *The Great Kapok Tree: A Tale of the Amazon Rain Forest* by Lynne Cherry.

- Ask students to focus on how the animals tried to persuade the woodcutter not to cut down the kapok tree in the Brazilian rain forest.

- Make a list of all the speaking animals in the book.

- Talk about the reasons the animals gave for not cutting down the tree.

- Check for understanding:
  - Determine if students understand *why* questions.
  - Determine if students understand opinions and are able to express their feelings about a familiar topic.

Tell how you would persuade the woodcutter not to cut down the tree.

TIER 2 — Persuade

Role play/Modeling

- Choose one of the animals from the book.
- Reread the part of the story in which this animal is trying to persuade the woodcutter not to cut down the kapok tree.
- Assign the part of the animal and the woodcutter to two students.

Role play the events in the story.

- As the students role play, discuss and write the persuasive reasons on the board.

- Repeat the activity with another animal and ask students to write the persuasive reasons.

Talk and write about the reasons the animals use to persuade the woodcutter not to cut down the kapok tree.

290   GRADE 2 • LISTENING AND SPEAKING

Story starters/Visual cues

Present the student with open phrases about the story, such as

The _____ told the woodcutter not to cut down the kapok tree because _____.

Refer to the story text and complete the story starter.

TIER 3   Persuade

Role play/Different stimuli

- Ask students to find a partner. One plays a student and one plays a parent.
- Ask students to practice persuading their parent to take them to a special place, buy a new toy, and so forth.
- Ask students to switch roles.

- Take the role of the parent or student.
- Practice persuading and give good reasons.

Elaboration/Assistive technology

- Go to a rain forest website such as www.bristolvaschools.org/mwarren/Kapok.htm.
- View a map of the rain forest and talk about animals that live there.
- Ask students to give reasons why rain forests should be preserved.

- Explore the rain forest via the Internet.
- Talk about animals that live in a rain forest in a way that persuades others that rain forests should be preserved.

GRADE 2 • LISTENING AND SPEAKING   291

| Grade 2 | LANGUAGE AREA: Listening and Speaking | OBJECTIVE: Participate in Conversations: Change and End Topics |

TIER 1 — Change and End Topics

Engaging in conversation is a critical skill for social and academic success. Help students develop the following conversational skills:

- providing the right amount of information (not saying too much or too little)
- considering what the listener knows
- staying on topic or changing topics appropriately
- engaging in the conversation by answering or asking questions or making statements
- taking turns
- watching the speaker
- listening
- being relevant
- being concise
- being polite
- being truthful, but tactful
- using appropriate body language
- understanding the vocabulary used

Introduce the idea that we all engage in conversations with others to share information, get new information, problem solve, or just have fun together. There are rules for good conversation that include

- Look at the people who are talking.
- Take turns talking.
- Make comments or ask questions about the topic being discussed.
- Choose words that will not be offensive or confusing to others.
- Get to the point. Don't talk too much or too little.

Practice keeping the conversation going:

- Show that you are listening by leaning forward or nodding your head.
- Ask questions about what the other person has just said.
- Avoid fidgeting, looking away, or yawning.
- Avoid interrupting.
- Don't stand too close or too far away.
- Use body language and facial expressions to match what you want to say (smiling when happy).

Practice closing the conversation:

- Change topics only when everyone seems finished talking about the topic.
- Change to a topic that relates to the topic just discussed.
- Allow everyone to talk.
- Wait for a comfortable break in the conversation to leave or end the conversation (adapted from www.boystownpediatrics.org/ParentingTips/Pages/TeachingchildrenConversationSkills.aspchildren).

- Ask students to watch DVDs of people engaged in conversation (TV shows, movies, web clips, etc.). Give students a feedback form for good conversational habits (see next page).

- As students watch the DVDs, ask them to assign a letter grade to each element on the list. Discuss the results as a class.

Use the list of good conversational habits to grade each conversational sample.

- Choose a number of different settings or scenarios (on the bus, on the playground, in the grocery store, talking to the principal, going to a restaurant, and so forth).

- Have students form small groups and give each group a scenario to role play in front of the class.

- Ask students who are watching the role play to use the feedback form to grade elements of conversation demonstrated by the role play.

- Send the feedback form home as a homework assignment and ask students to evaluate one of their own conversations held outside of school.

- Discuss what they learned as a class after the students return the forms.

- Role play typical conversational activities and/or evaluate role play conversations.
- Use the feedback form to evaluate one of your conversations as a homework assignment.

Conversation Skills Feedback Form

Give each skill listed below a letter grade to show how well it was used in the conversation.

Conversational Skill	Letter Grade (A, B, C, D, E)
Look at people when talking.	
Take turns talking.	
Ask questions about what the other person just said.	
Choose words that will not be offensive or confusing to others.	
Get to the point. Don't talk too much or too little.	
Show that you are listening by leaning forward or nodding your head.	
Avoid fidgeting, looking away, or yawning.	
Don't interrupt the speaker.	
Don't stand too close or too far.	
Use body language and facial expressions to match what you want to say.	
Change topics only when everyone seems finished talking about the topic.	
Change to a topic that relates to the topic just discussed.	
Allow everyone to talk.	
Wait for a comfortable break in the conversation to leave or end the conversation.	

TIER 2	Change and End Topics

Check for understanding

- Show examples of conversations from TV shows, movies, and web clips.
- Pause after each conversational exchange and ask probing questions about specific conversational skills. (*Did they talk too much or too little? Did they change the topic appropriately?*)

Respond to the teacher's questions about the use of specific conversational skills.

Give pairs of students specific conversational skills to model.

Model the specific conversational skill appropriately.

Multiple modality

- Provide students with a short written script that represents a particular setting or scenario (toy store, playground, restaurant, going trick or treating, going to a birthday party).
- Have students take turns reading the conversation and talking about the conversational skills modeled in the script.

Role play a conversation. Observers can use the feedback form to evaluate conversational skills.

Grade 2

GRADE 2 • LISTENING AND SPEAKING   295

| TIER 3 | Change and End Topics |

Completion/Cloze questions or statements

Pair students and ask them to engage in conversation about a specific topic. Provide them with starter phrases or questions to use to maintain the conversation.

Using the teacher's prompts, engage in conversation.

Advance organizer

- Create a spider map (see Appendix F). Place the conversational topic in the center of the web.
- Ask students to provide appropriate words or phrases related to the topic that may be used in a conversation.
- Write the students' suggestions on the web.
- Arrange students in pairs and ask them to have a conversation about the topic, using the spider map to create the content.

Have a conversation about the topic, using the spider map to create the conversational content.

Notes:

Grade 2

Grade 2	LANGUAGE AREA: Listening and Speaking	OBJECTIVE: Adapt Messages to Different Situations and Listeners

TIER 1 Adapt Messages

Discuss how important it is to be polite and talk appropriately in different situations. Explain to students that we use different ways of talking for different people or places. For example, we talk differently on the playground than we do in the principal's office or in the classroom versus in the library. We talk differently to a child than to an adult and we talk differently to a friend than to a doctor.

- Read the story *The Meanest Thing to Say* by Bill Cosby. Act it out as a Reader's Theater to practice using appropriate language.
(See www.literacyconnections.com/ReadersTheater.php for more information about the technique of Reader's Theater.)

- Play a game in which students take turns acting out different situations, such as being polite or impolite, being too noisy, or speaking with the correct volume. For example, act out

  o talking to a waitress in a restaurant

  o talking to the principal

  o talking in the library

  o meeting your friends' parents or grandparents

Act out situations presented by the teacher, remembering to talk appropriately for the situation.

298   GRADE 2 • LISTENING AND SPEAKING

| TIER 2 | Adapt Messages |

Negative practice

- Describe simple scenarios of social interaction, but describe the wrong way to act in each situation.

- Use the situations listed for Tier 1 as well as others such as visiting a museum or going to a wedding ceremony.

- Ask students to tell what was wrong and give examples of what should be said.

Tell what was wrong about the social interaction and provide correct responses.

Grade 2

Check for understanding

- Ask students to form small groups.

- Give students several short stories that demonstrate appropriate behavior and communication for the situation.

- Ask students to talk within their small groups about why the situation was handled correctly.

Acknowledge the correct response and explain why the response was correct.

| TIER 3 | Adapt Messages |

Think-aloud

When students respond inappropriately to a given situation, use the opportunity to teach the correct response by talking through a problem-solving strategy. For example, if you hear a student talking loudly in the library, take her aside and say, *We're in the library, so I'm using my quiet voice. Is that the right thing to do?*

Change behavior in response to the think-aloud.

Repeated exposure

- Throughout the day, point out examples of students using correct communication.

- When you hear examples of inappropriate (unkind, too loud, impolite) communication, model a more appropriate or nicer way to talk.

Communicate in a way that is appropriate for the listener and the situation.

GRADE 2 • LISTENING AND SPEAKING   299

| Grade 2 | LANGUAGE AREA: Listening and Speaking | OBJECTIVE: Understand Nonverbal Signals: Personal Space |

TIER 1 — Nonverbal Signals

Explain how nonverbal signals, such as the use of personal space, help us communicate. Talk about how we all feel comfortable when we're with others who are standing just the right distance away from us (outside our personal space). If people get too close, we feel uncomfortable and sometimes can't even pay attention to them. If they are too far away, we can't see or hear them.

- Bring five students to the front of the room, keeping space between them.

- Ask them to stretch their arms all the way out and turn around in place.

- Tell the class that this shows the area that is your personal space. You shouldn't be closer and you shouldn't be much farther away when talking with someone.

- Talk about what to do when someone is too close or too far away:

  o Move closer or farther away.

  o Ask the other person to move closer or farther away.

  o Use a gesture to indicate movement.

  o Establish a cue in class that will tell your students they're too close or too far away.

- Ask students to stand in pairs around the room and circle arms together to see their personal space.

- Have them experiment with talking to each other when they're too close or too far away.

Practice maintaining personal space and engage in conversation as directed.

TIER 2 — Nonverbal Signals

Visual cues

- Target students who are having trouble understanding the boundaries of personal space.
- Ask them to stand on a large piece of paper and move in a circle with their arms out.
- Draw the circle they make to represent the space visually.

Use the circle to practice keeping the correct distance from conversational partners.

Repeated practice/Visual cues

- Ask a student to stand on the circle representing comfortable personal space.
- Walk toward the student and ask others in the group to say if you're too close, too far away, or just right.
- Alternate with other students who are having difficulty with this concept.
- Take the visual cue away and repeat to determine if students can still accurately indicate if you are too close, too far away, or just right.

With the visual cue, and then without the visual cue, say whether the teacher is demonstrating good personal space rules.

TIER 3 — Nonverbal Signals

Multiple modalities

Use the book *The Chocolate Touch* by Patrick Skene Catling to talk about personal space. Emphasize that anyone who is touching John Midas is violating personal space, which results in a consequence.

Discuss how the character violates personal space and how others may feel or react.

Visual cues

- Provide a small group of students with action figures.
- Ask them to arrange the figures to show appropriate and inappropriate personal space and label what the figures show.

Arrange action figures to demonstrate appropriate and inappropriate use of personal space and label the groups.

Grade 2

GRADE 2 • LISTENING AND SPEAKING   301

Grade 2

LANGUAGE AREA: Listening and Speaking

OBJECTIVE: Understand and Use Tone of Voice to Convey Meaning

TIER 1 — Tone of Voice

Explain that using a different tone of voice can convey a different meaning. Repeat common phrases such as *I'm fine* or *Where are you going?* using a different tone of voice.

- Read the book *Imogene's Antlers* by David Small.
- As you read the book aloud, use tone of voice to convey emotion.
- Stop and say, *Did you hear how my voice showed what the character was feeling (happy, angry,* and so forth)? Continue reading, pausing to ask students what emotion is being conveyed by tone of voice.
- Ask students to read different parts of the book.
- Cue students to convey specific emotions as they read their parts.
- Call on other students to guess what emotion was conveyed by the reader's tone of voice.

- Describe the emotions of the characters as others read.
- Read using tones of voice to show different emotions.

TIER 2 — Tone of Voice

Role play

Give students a phrase and tell them what emotion to use to convey the meaning. If necessary, demonstrate the emotion and ask what feeling is being conveyed.

Say the phrase with the appropriate tone of voice.

Repeated exposure

- Give students a list of words from their spelling word list and ask them to make sentences with the words.
- Make a spinner that has icons for different emotions on each section.
- Spin the spinner to select an icon and ask students to read their sentences in a way that conveys that emotion.

- Create sentences using spelling words.
- Read the sentences using tone of voice to convey emotion.

TIER 3 — Tone of Voice

Assistive technology/Repeated practice

- Go to the website www.storylineonline.net and click on *Sebastian's Roller Skates* by Joan De Deu Prats.
- As the actor reads the story aloud, pause and ask students to talk about the meaning conveyed by the actor's tone of voice.
- Pause whenever Sebastian talks and have students practice talking as he does, and then talking as he wants to talk.
- Discuss how the meaning changes depending on tone of voice.

- Listen to the story as it is read aloud and talk about the meaning conveyed by the actor's tone of voice.
- Try talking like Sebastian talks and how he wants to talk.
- Discuss how tone of voice affects meaning.

Visual cues

- Provide students with pictures of people displaying different emotions such as *happy*, *sad*, *angry*, and *scared*.
- Say a phrase and ask students to point to the picture that shows the emotion conveyed by the tone of voice.
- Repeat with several other phrases.

Point to the picture of a person displaying the emotion conveyed by the tone of voice.

GRADE 2 • LISTENING AND SPEAKING   303

| Grade 2 | LANGUAGE AREA: Listening and Speaking | OBJECTIVE: Understand and Express Feelings |

TIER 1   Feelings

Talk about feelings and how it is important to understand our feelings and to know what others are feeling.

- Brainstorm a list of words that tell about feelings.

- Make a list of what a character or author (for an autobiography) in a book is feeling. For example, read the book, *Listen to the Wind: The Story of Dr. Greg & Three Cups of Tea* by Greg Mortenson and Susan L. Roth. Talk about:

  o How does the main character (the author, Dr. Greg) feel?

  o What caused the author to have these feelings?

  o If you were the author, would you have felt the same way or a different way?

  o Did anything ever happen to cause you to feel the same way as the author?

  o Did anything ever happen to you that was similar to what happened to the people in the book? How did you feel?

  o How does the story make you feel?

  o Did anything in the story surprise you?

  o What takes place in the story that makes you feel happy? Sad? Excited? Scared?

Create a list of words that tell about feelings. Answer the teacher's questions using words from your list of feeling words.

304   GRADE 2 • LISTENING AND SPEAKING

TIER 2 — Feelings

Elaboration

Reread the story.

- Call attention to a specific sentence in the story that explains how a character is feeling.

- Ask students if they have ever felt the same way and what caused them to feel that way?

- Reread the sentence and find the words that tell about how the character is feeling.

- Talk about what happened to you that caused you to feel the same way or different from the character.

Matching

Paraphrase an event in the story. Ask, *How did the character feel?*

Match the story events described by the teacher with a feeling from your emotions list.

TIER 3 — Feelings

Advance organizer

Assist students in making a spider map (see Appendix F). On the lines that radiate from the feeling word in the center, ask them to list things that made the character feel this way.

Complete the spider map about feelings.

Mental imagery

Instruct students to create a visual or mental image of how they would feel in the following situations:

- *Imagine you just got a new bike.*

- *Imagine the lights went out suddenly.*

- *Imagine you lost your homework.*

- Talk about how you would feel in different situations.
- Brainstorm other situations that would make you feel the same way.

GRADE 2 • LISTENING AND SPEAKING 305

Grade 2

LANGUAGE AREA: Listening and Speaking

OBJECTIVE: Ask Questions for Repetition/Clarification

TIER 1 — Clarification Question

Explain to students that we ask questions when we need more information.

- Talk about a situation in which we don't have all of the information we need or haven't correctly heard the instructions. In these situations it is important to be able to ask the right questions to get the information that is missing.

- Prepare a list of 20 sentences similar to the ones below based on topics studied in class.

- Ask one student to read the sentence. When the student comes to the part of the sentence marked with X's, he should muffle the word in parentheses.

- Another student should then use the skills of focused repetition to figure out the part of the sentence that is unclear.

Examples:

- Student A: *The bank is on the X of the street. (right side)*

- Student B: *The bank is on what side of the street? The bank is on the . . . (trailing off)*

- Student A: *Right side of the street.*

- Student A: *Let's meet at X at X Park. (1:40/Central)*

- Student B: *Let's meet when? Where?*

- Student A: *At 1:40 at Central Park.*

Listen to sentences and ask for repetition or clarification when needed.

TIER 2	Clarification Question

Different stimuli

Present any classroom DVD or audio clip to teach asking for clarification.

- Play a portion of the clip and fade the sound out at crucial points where important information is given (phone numbers, addresses, dates, and so forth).

- Ask students to ask questions about information they did not understand.

- Replay the clip or, for ease of administration, read the part they missed from the transcript. This also allows students to confirm what they heard.

Ask questions to get all the important information.

Alternative response mode

- Give students a list of sentences to read, but ask them to distort or omit the critical information as they read the sentences. It may be helpful to underline the critical information.

- Ask a student a question about the missing information.

- Ask students to tell if it was a good question and asked for the right information.

- Read sentences aloud, but muffle some important details so they cannot be understood by your listener.

- When your listener asks a question, tell her if it was a good question for learning about the muffled information.

Grade
2

GRADE 2 • LISTENING AND SPEAKING   307

| TIER 3 | Clarification Question |

Imitation

- Tell students that you are going to do a "following the directions" activity, but that you will sometimes forget to say some important information. Tell them you will stop and have them ask a question about the missing information.

- After you read each instruction (see examples below), pause and call on students. Tell them the question to ask and ask them to repeat that question.
  - *Write your X on top of the paper. (What will I write at the top of the paper?)*
  - *Make an X in a circle in the bottom corner (What color should I use for the circle?)*
  - *Write the letter A (Where should I write the letter A?)*

- Continue practicing with additional directions.

Ask an appropriate question to get the missing information.

Advanced organizer

- Provide students with a list of questions that can be used to ask for clarification/repetition. These questions can include
  - *Where will we?*
  - *How many?*
  - *Which one?*
  - *What color?*
  - *What object?*
  - *In what direction?*
  - *What size?*

- Divide students into pairs. Give one member of the pair (Student A) a simple drawing and ask him to keep the drawing hidden from his partner.

- Give the other member of the pair (Student B) paper and markers or crayons.

- Tell all *A* students that they will begin to describe their object so their partners can draw it.

- After you give just one instruction, tell *B* students that they will need to ask a question to get more information about what they are to draw.

- Cue students to use the question sheet.

Take turns giving directions, or asking questions to get the information needed to successfully complete a drawing.

Notes:

Grade 2

GRADE 2 • LISTENING AND SPEAKING   309

| Grade 2 | LANGUAGE AREA: Listening and Speaking | OBJECTIVE: Understand and Use Logical Order of Events |

TIER 1 — Logical Order of Events

Discuss how important it is to be able to understand and tell about the correct order of things we do every day. Explain that at school, we put these important items on a daily schedule.

- At the end of the day, ask students to tell what they did during each part of the day. Point to the items listed on the schedule as a cue, but ask students to add more details.
- Ask students to write two or three sentences about each activity of the day in the correct order on a blank schedule.
- Encourage students to take home their completed schedules to tell their parents about their day.

Retell the sequence of activities completed during the school day, and then write two or three sentences describing each activity.

TIER 2 — Logical Order of Events

Turn and talk

- Pair students together (perhaps pair students with different strengths). Give each pair a copy of the class schedule.
- Ask each pair to work together to generate two or three sentences describing each activity of the day.

Generate two or three sentences describing each activity of the day.

Role play

- Refer students to the written class schedule and ask them to act out something that they did in each segment of the schedule.
- Ask students to retell what they enacted.

Role play the events of the day, and then tell what you enacted.

310   GRADE 2 • LISTENING AND SPEAKING

TIER 3	Logical Order of Events

Double dose of instruction

- Work with the student one-on-one to determine why he is not being successful in understanding and using a logical order of events. Skills that are necessary to successfully complete this goal include
    - o vocabulary
    - o auditory memory/recall
    - o sequencing
    - o word finding
    - o attending/focusing
    - o grammar
    - o oral language

- Provide instruction in the area needing improvement and then reteach understanding and using a logical order of events.

Tell about the activities of the day in the correct order.

Elaboration

- Provide students with the main idea for each daily activity on the class schedule.
- Ask students to write sentences in the correct order for each daily activity.

Write a full sentence for each element of the schedule after repeating it aloud using the teacher's prompts.

Grade
2

GRADE 2 • LISTENING AND SPEAKING   311

| Grade 2 | LANGUAGE AREA: Listening and Speaking | OBJECTIVE: Understand and Use Fictional Narratives |

TIER 1   Fictional Narratives

Provide definitions for story elements to help students understand narrative structure.

Story grammar elements

1. **Setting:** When and where the story occurs

2. **Main Characters:** Who the story is about

3. **Problem or Conflict:** The focal point of the story

4. **Response:** The main characters' reaction to the problem/complication

5. **Plan:** The main characters' strategy for attaining their goal

6. **Events/Attempts/Actions:** Attempts by the main character(s) to resolve the problem or conflict

7. **Resolution/Solution/Conclusion:** How successfully the characters resolved the problem or conflict

8. **Reaction:** The main characters' thoughts or feelings about the outcome

Introduce the concept of story grammar by using a story map (see Appendix H).

Explain that most stories have certain elements in common that are called the story grammar, and use the following questions to provide explicit instruction on these elements:

Questions to guide discussion

1. **Setting:** *Where does the story occur? When does the story occur?*

2. **Main Characters:** *Who are the main characters?*

3. **Problem or Conflict:** *What major problem do the main characters face? What do these characters hope to achieve?*

4. **Response:** *How do the main characters feel about the major problem?*

5. **Plan:** *What are the main characters' plans for achieving his or her goal?*

6. **Events/Attempts/Actions:** *What do the main characters do?*

7. **Resolution/Solution/Conclusion:** *Do the main characters solve the problem? How?*

8. **Reaction:** *Are the main characters defeated by the problem? Do they learn to live with the problem? How do the main characters feel about the outcome? How does the story end?*

312   GRADE 2 • LISTENING AND SPEAKING

Model the way to use the story map to summarize a story. Provide a blank copy of the story map to each student, and give students guided practice in developing their own story maps, independently or in class.

> Listen as the teacher models the use of the story map. Use the same story to fill in a blank copy of the story map independently or in a small group.

 Bonus: Introduce the concept of *theme* (the main point or moral of the story) and discuss the overall theme of the story with students.

TIER 2 — Fictional Narratives

Comprehension probe

Read the same story multiple times to help students become more familiar with story content as well as story elements. Throughout book reading, engage the class as active participants using the **CROWD** strategy to

- **preview text**—*What do you think this story is going to be about?*
- **facilitate retrieval of story structures schema**—*What do you think will happen next? Why?*
- **monitor comprehension**—Check whether predictions were confirmed.

CROWD is a set of five question types/prompts during book reading. Each targets a different area.

- **C** = comprehension Q's. Target: particular linguistic structures (*Q: What did the bunny do? A: He hopped and skipped.*)
- **R** = recall Q's. Target: story content (*Q: Do you remember what this story is about?*)
- **O** = open-ended Q's. Target: increased amount of talk and detail (*Q: What is happening on this page?*)
- **W** = *wh–* Q's. Target: new vocabulary (*Goldilocks tasted the porridge. Q: What is porridge?*)
- **D** = distance Q's. Target: link between book event and student's own experiences (*Q: Does your family eat porridge?*)

Following this **CROWD** discussion, use a story such as *Crocodile's Tale* by Jose Aruego or *Franklin Is Bossy* by Paulette Bourgeois to have students create a story map individually or in small groups.

> Use the **CROWD** strategy to create a story map.

Different stimuli

- Create a story that has all eight story map elements on the board or chart paper. For example:

  o **Setting and Character**: *Once upon a time there was a girl named Sue who lived in the city.*

  o **Problem or Conflict**: *One afternoon, Sue sneaked into the kitchen to get a cookie out of the cookie jar.*

  o **Response**: *She knew she wasn't supposed to eat sweets before dinner.*

  o **Plan**: *She thought she could be very quiet.*

  o **Events/Attempts/Actions**: *She reached for the cookie jar.*

  o **Resolution/Solution/Conclusion**: *As she grabbed the cookie jar, it fell on the floor and broke.*

  o **Reaction**: *She felt guilty about doing something she wasn't supposed to do.*

- Provide a wordless book and a story map (see Appendix H) for students to use to create their own written stories. Encourage them to include all eight components. Some wordless books that may be appropriate include

  o *Pancakes for Breakfast* by Tomie dePaola

  o *A Boy, a Dog and a Frog* by Mercer Mayer

  o *Full Moon Soup* by Alice Stair Graham

A list of other wordless books can be found at www.acpl.lib.in.us/children/wordless.html.

Create a story containing all eight story map elements.

TIER 3   Fictional Narratives

Visual cues

- Use a book such as *Pecos Bill* by Steven Kellogg. Write a story frame on the board or a chart:

  o **Setting**: *The story takes place in _____.*

  o **Main Character**: *The main person in this story is _____.*

  o **Problem or Conflict**: *The problem starts when _____.*

  o **Response**: *The first thing the main character does is _____.*

  o **Response**: *and then _____.*

  o **Plan**: *The character decides to _____.*

  o **Events/Attempts/Actions**: *The character tries to _____.*

  o **Resolution/Solution/Conclusion**: *The problem is solved when _____.*

  o **Reaction**: *After the problem is solved, the main character feels _____.*

- Use the starting phrases listed above to retell the story with all eight critical elements.

- Ask students to retell the story aloud, and then ask them to write the story. Keep the cues available to them during the writing process.

Retell the story aloud and then write it.

Concentrated instruction/Change response length

- Define each of these elements by providing a sample story.

- As you tell the story, write each sentence on the board and label it.

  o **Setting and Character:** *Sam's parents asked him to stay home to finish his homework before doing anything else.*

  o **Problem or Conflict:** *Sam's friends came over and asked him to play baseball with them.*

  o **Events/Attempts/Actions:** *Sam told his parents that his homework was finished and said he was going out to play baseball. After Sam left, his parents found his unfinished homework.*

  o **Resolution/Solution/Conclusion:** *When Sam returned home, he saw his parents' unhappy faces and realized that they knew he hadn't finished his homework.*

- Help students create a story with five of the critical elements (setting, character, problem, event/attempts, and conclusion).

- Prompt students to create the story using temporal words such as *first, then, next,* and *finally.*

- Write a five-element story after discussing the sample story provided by the teacher.

- First say the story aloud and then write it.

Grade 2

GRADE 2 • LISTENING AND SPEAKING   315

| **Grade 2** | LANGUAGE AREA: Listening and Speaking | OBJECTIVE: Retell a Story or Directions in Correct Order |

TIER 1 — Retell Story

Talk about how important it is to understand and to do things in the correct order. Talk about the order of simple things such as getting ready for school. You can't put your shoes on before you put on your socks. You can't put the toothpaste on the brush after you brush your teeth.

- Have students talk about the sequence of their morning activities.

- Read about something that has a specific sequence (larva turning into a butterfly, a recipe, steps in a game) and ask students to listen for clue words that show the sequence of the story (*first, second, then, last*).

- Write a map of the story using clue words and a few details for each word.
- Read your story map aloud.

TIER 2 — Retell Story

Auditory cues/Memory aid

Reread the Tier 1 story, emphasizing the cue sequence words by saying them louder and with greater emphasis, and pausing after each cue word segment.

Write each cue word and short description on your story map before moving on to the next story element.

Comprehension probe

Reread the Tier 1 story, but pause after each segment.

Retell the segment of the story after the teacher reads it.

Mental imagery

Reread the Tier 1 story, but encourage the students to close their eyes and think of pictures of the Tier 1 story in sequence as you read.

Draw a story map using visual images of the Tier 1 story in sequence.

316   GRADE 2 • LISTENING AND SPEAKING

| TIER 3 | Retell Story |

Visual cues

Reread the Tier 1 story and pantomime each sequence of the story.

Create a story map as it is shown.

Visual cues

- Provide the student with cards on which key phrases are written.
- Reread the story and ask students to place the cards in order as the story is read.

Place the written cues in the correct order as the story is reread.

Grade 2	LANGUAGE AREA: Listening and Speaking	OBJECTIVE: Understand and Use Figurative Language: Metaphors

TIER 1 — Metaphors

Explain that metaphors are figures of speech that use one thing to mean another and make comparisons between the two. The key words here are *one thing to mean another*. The simplest form of a metaphor is *The [first thing] is a [second thing]*.

- Instruct students to look at this example: *The inside of the car was a refrigerator.*

- Say to the students: *When someone says this, we do not understand it literally. Instead, we might think that the inside of the car was very cold.*

- Review other examples of metaphors:
  - *My name is mud.*
  - *He is a sheep.*
  - *Dad was boiling mad.*
  - *Homework was a breeze.*

- Discuss that metaphors are used to help describe something by comparing it with something else. Metaphors make speaking and writing more interesting and get listeners and readers to think.

- Ask students to do a sentence completion task to create metaphors with these phrases:
  - *My legs were _____ after I ran that long race.*
  - *This classroom was a _____ after the party.*
  - *That basketball player is a _____.*

- Ask students to use the Introduction to Metaphors and Making Metaphors worksheets found at www.bogglesworldesl.com/metaphor_worksheets.htm.

Complete the sentences to create metaphors.

318   GRADE 2 • LISTENING AND SPEAKING

TIER 2   Metaphors

Different stimuli

- Provide students with pictures that can be used to generate metaphors.

- Give an example of how to use a picture to create a metaphor.

- Ask students to create metaphors for each picture.

- Ask each student to share his picture and metaphor.

Draw a picture of a metaphor and describe it.

Independent practice

The following sample worksheet questions are reprinted with permission from "English Grammar and Usage: Metaphors," by RHL School, 1999, *English Basics, 3* (26). Retrieved November 2010 from www.rhlschool.com/eng3n26.htm. Copyright RHL School.

1. *Brian was a wall*, bouncing every tennis ball back over the net.

    This metaphor compares Brian to a wall because

    a. he was very strong.

    b. he was very tall.

    c. he kept returning the balls.

    d. his body was made of cells.

2. *Cindy was such a mule*. We couldn't get her to change her mind.

    The metaphor compares Cindy to a mule because she was

    a. always eating oats.

    b. able to do hard work.

    c. raised on a farm.

    d. very stubborn.

3. The poor rat didn't have a chance. Our old cat, *a bolt of lightning*, caught his prey.

    The cat was compared to a bolt of lightning because he was

    a. very fast.

    b. very bright.

    c. not fond of fleas.

    d. very old.

Grade 2

GRADE 2 • LISTENING AND SPEAKING   319

4. Even a student could carry my dog, Dogface, around for hours. *He's such a feather.*

This metaphor implies that Dogface

a. is not cute.

b. looks like a bird.

c. is not heavy.

d. can fly.

Select the correct metaphor.

TIER 3 Metaphors

Restricted-choice questions

- Present a list of phrases that includes some metaphors.

- Ask students to say *yes/no* after each phrase to indicate whether it is a metaphor.

Tell if the phrase presented by the teacher is a metaphor.

Alternative response mode

Provide sentences containing metaphors and ask students to underline the metaphor. Examples:

- *After that game, my name was mud.*

- *His friends think that he is a sheep.*

- *My dad was boiling mad by the time my sister came home.*

- *This science homework was a breeze.*

- *Last August the streets were a furnace.*

- *His legs were rubber after running the marathon.*

- *That football player is a tank.*

- *The wind was howling all night long.*

Use the metaphor practice page at
http://library.thinkquest.org/J0112392/metaphorpractice.html
to allow students to practice choosing the metaphor phrase.

Underline metaphors in sentences.

320   GRADE 2 • LISTENING AND SPEAKING

Notes:

Grade 2

GRADE 2 • LISTENING AND SPEAKING 321

Grade 2

LANGUAGE AREA: Listening and Speaking

OBJECTIVE: Understand and Use Humor in Words and Situations

TIER 1 — Humor

Discuss why humor is important.

- Tell or read a familiar story, such as *The Little Red Hen* by Paul Galdone.
- Explain that you are tired of reading the same story over and over again and it would be fun to change the story to make it funnier.

- Think of a more creative name for *The Little Red Hen*.
- Change the names of the animals in the story.
- Change the tools and objects in the story.
- Reread the story, incorporating your changes.

- Display a selection of commercial products or pictures such as soap, tissues, toothpaste, canned vegetables, and pasta.
- Read the names and ask students to create new, funny names.

Think of funny names for the products.

TIER 2 — Humor

Simplify

Ask students to make a list of actions that the little red hen would never do (*drive, dress, clean, study spelling words*) and to use these action words in silly sentences.

Make a list of action words and use them in silly sentences.

Advance organizer

- Place the name of a familiar product in the center of a spider map (see Appendix F). On the lines that radiate from the center, list words that describe the product.

  ○ *Soap: has bubbles, white, bar, slippery, slimy, changes size.*

- Ask students to create new, funny names.

Use the words on the spider map to think of a funny name for the product.

322   GRADE 2 • LISTENING AND SPEAKING

TIER 3	Humor

Independent practice

- Share a funny experience that happened in your family.
- Ask students to talk with their families about something funny that happened to them.

Share your family's funny experience with your classmates by drawing a picture or telling a story.

Visual dictionary

Show simple comic strips that focus on absurdities and silly situations.

Identify what could or couldn't happen and why it is funny.

Grade
2

| Grade 2 | LANGUAGE AREA: Listening and Speaking | OBJECTIVE: Summarize Stories and Events |

TIER 1 — Summarize

Discuss how important it is to be able to summarize information so you can share ideas, experiences, and events with others.

- Cut out seven paper dog bones for each student.
- Read *Henry and Mudge: The First Book* by Cynthia Rylant as a class read-aloud chapter book.
- After you read each chapter, ask students to summarize the chapter in one or two sentences and then write their summaries on a bone.
- At the beginning of the next reading session, ask students to refer to the bones and summarize the events of the previous chapters.
- After students have recorded summaries for each chapter on the bones, mix up the bones.
- Take turns summarizing the beginning, middle, and end of the story.
- Write a summary for each chapter on a bone.

TIER 2 — Summarize

Visual cues

- Write *who*, *what*, *when*, *where*, and *why* at the top of a piece of paper.
- Read a chapter.
- Ask the student to summarize the chapter.
- Point to one of the *wh–*words to cue the student, if necessary.

Refer to these question words to summarize the chapter.

Concentrated instruction

Focus on the main idea of the chapter.

Listen to the chapter and express the main idea.

TIER 3	Summarize

Previewing

Before you read a chapter in the book, give the students a summary of the chapter.

After the teacher reads the chapter, brainstorm details that support the summary.

Memory aid/Adjust pace

- Read a chapter slowly.
- Ask the student to record one or two words or sketch a picture that will help him remember the important events of the story.

Use your list to recall and summarize the important events of the story.

Grade
2

| Grade 2 | LANGUAGE AREA: Listening and Speaking | OBJECTIVE: Paraphrase Stories |

TIER 1 — Paraphrase

Talk about how important it is to be able to paraphrase or retell information in your own words. It allows you to tell others about your thoughts and feelings, what you've read, and things you've done.

- Read *Miss Nelson Is Missing* by Harry Allard.
- Give each student a piece of paper divided into four sections labeled *first*, *next*, *then*, and *last*.
- Ask students to write a sentence or illustrate a key event of the story in each section. Use the organizer below to discuss and paraphrase the important events in the story:
  - *How do the beginning events affect what happened in the middle of the story?*
  - *What is the problem and when did we find out about it?*
  - *When does most of the action take place?*
- Instruct the students to "turn and talk" to a partner about the important events in the story.

Refer to your story organizer and take turns paraphrasing the story.

TIER 2 — Paraphrase

Elaboration

Demonstrate how to identify the main idea of a story and causal relationships within the story to help students recall information in the correct sequence.

Use your own words to retell the story in the correct sequence.

Repeated practice

Ask students to repeat/paraphrase directions, explanations, or content instructions immediately after they hear them.

Repeat the information given by the teacher in your own words.

326   GRADE 2 • LISTENING AND SPEAKING

TIER 3	Paraphrase

Simplify/Repeated reading

Reread the Tier 1 story, pausing frequently to discuss key events in the beginning, middle, and end of the story.

- Listen to the story and paraphrase the events that happened in the beginning of the story.
- Continue listening and paraphrase the events that happened in each section.

Alternative response mode

List the events that happened in the story.

Arrange the events in logical order.

| Grade 2 | LANGUAGE AREA: Listening and Speaking | OBJECTIVE: Understand and Distinguish Fact From Opinion |

TIER 1 — Fact and Opinion

Define *fact* and *opinion*. Facts can be all or some of the following: proven, true for all people and places, duplicated, observed, and historically true. Opinions refer to a particular person's or group's feeling, thought, judgment, belief, estimate, and/or anything that is not always true and can't be proven.

- Ask students to distinguish between facts and opinions in the following statements:

  o *All people must breathe to live.*

  o *All people love basketball.*

  o *Blue is the best color.*

  o *Abraham Lincoln was a United States president.*

  o *North Carolina is a southern state.*

  o *I don't like broccoli.*

  o *Fire needs oxygen to burn.*

  o *Pizza tastes great.*

  o *Most people have two arms and legs.*

- Ask students to identify books in which facts can be found (encyclopedias, dictionaries, almanacs, atlases, textbooks, *Guinness Book of World Records,* and so forth).

- Ask students to identify books in which opinions can be found (autobiographies, self-help books, novels, journals, and so forth).

- Cut out newspaper and magazine advertisements and separate facts and opinions.

- Ask students to create a fact-finding scavenger hunt, with each student contributing different questions that they've answered.

328   GRADE 2 • LISTENING AND SPEAKING

- Combine everyone's questions to complete the hunt. For example, students can do research about the school, staff, or next unit topic with questions like:

School

- o *When was the school founded?*
- o *How many students attend our school?*
- o *What's the record number of pizzas served in one day?*
- o *Which grade has the best attendance?*

Staff

- o *Where was the principal born?*
- o *Who was Teacher of the Year last year?*
- o *Which teacher has been at this school the longest?*
- o *What college/university did your teacher attend?*

Upcoming unit topics

- o *What is the largest land mammal?*
- o *What were some of the most significant inventions during the Industrial Revolution?*
- o *How long have women had the right to vote?*
- o *What is necessary for fires to burn?*

Create a fact-finding scavenger hunt consisting of questions that you've answered and discuss opinions on the topics.

| TIER 2 | Fact and Opinion |

Different stimuli

- Bring in many newspapers.
- Ask students to say which parts of a newspaper contain factual information and which contain opinions.
- Ask them to color code each section of the newspaper according to whether it contains facts or opinions and then to circle items that are facts and cross out items that are opinions.

Circle items that are facts and cross out items that are opinions.

- letters to the editor
- restaurant reviews
- sports scores
- calendars of events
- wedding announcements
- movie reviews

- advice columns
- astrology reports
- weather forecasts
- birth announcements
- rainfall measurements

- Provide copies of an article in the newspaper.
- Ask students to circle sentences that express facts versus sentences that express opinions.
- Use magazines or other reading material if this task is too difficult for the students.
- Ask students to find an advertisement and distinguish which parts of the advertisement are facts and which are opinions.
- Have students color code each section of the advertisement according to whether it is a fact or an opinion.

Circle sentences that are facts and cross out items that are opinions.

Completion/Cloze statements

- Provide students with sentence starters such as the following and ask them to finish the sentences to create facts:

  o *My friend _____.*

  o *In school yesterday, _____.*

  o *Outside it is _____.*

  o *My dog _____.*

  o *The principal said _____.*

  o *In my backyard _____.*

- Use the same set of sentence starters, and ask them to finish the sentences to create opinions.

Complete the sentences as facts and then as opinions.

TIER 3   Fact and Opinion

Matching

- Provide students with sentence strips and two cards (one card says *fact* and the other says *opinion*).
- Ask students to match the sentence strips and place them in the *fact* pile or the *opinion* pile.

Correctly sort the sentence strips into the correct category.

Examples and nonexamples

- Review the definition of a fact.
- Say a sentence and ask the student to say if it is or is not a fact.
- Continue with more sentences until the student accurately identifies a fact.
- Repeat the exercise, replacing a fact with an opinion.

Indicate if a statement is a fact or an opinion.

| Grade 2 | LANGUAGE AREA: Listening and Speaking | OBJECTIVE: Share Opinions |

TIER 1 — Share Opinions

Explain that an opinion is an idea, thought, or feeling someone has about a topic.

- Read *Ramona Quimby, Age 8* by Beverly Cleary.
- Make a class list of the embarrassing things and events Ramona experiences.
- Invite the students to share embarrassing moments and express why they felt embarrassed.
- Ask the following questions:
  - *Do you think it is important to like your teacher? Why or why not?*
  - *What do you think is the best thing about playing with younger students? Why?*
  - *Do you think Ramona is a show off? Why or why not?*
  - *Would you like to have Ramona for a friend? Why or why not?*
  - *Do you think rainy days make all people feel sad? Why or why not?*
  - *Do you think that you are a brave person? Why or why not?*
  - *Do you think you are a responsible family member? Why or why not?*

Give your opinion and explain why you feel this way.

TIER 2 — Share Opinions

Different stimuli

Have students take a poll of classmates concerning their opinions about a popular TV show, movie, food, and so forth.

Ask your classmates their opinions and record them for later discussion.

Modeling

Ask one of the Tier 1 questions and give your opinion.

Talk about how your teacher feels and how you feel about the question.

332   GRADE 2 • LISTENING AND SPEAKING

TIER 3	Share Opinions

Completion/Cloze statements

Write fill-in-the-blank sentences as a guide for students to answer Tier 1 questions:

- *I think Ramona was brave because she _____.*

- *I think Ramona was not brave because she _____.*

- *I think Ramona was a show-off because she _____.*

- *I don't think Ramona was a show-off because she did not _____.*

- *I am a responsible family member because _____.*

- *I am not a responsible family member because _____.*

Choose a sentence that reflects your opinion and fill in the blanks.

Elaboration

- Brainstorm a list of actions or events that would make you feel brave or responsible.

- Ask students

   o *Do you think you are a brave person?*

   o *Do you think you are a responsible person?*

   o *Do you think Ramona was a show-off?*

- Check for *understanding* by ensuring that students are able to use *why* questions.

- Express your opinion by answering one of the questions.
- Give reasons from the list to explain why you feel this way.

Grade 2

GRADE 2 • LISTENING AND SPEAKING   333

Grade 2	LANGUAGE AREA: Listening and Speaking	OBJECTIVE: Understand and Use Inferences

TIER 1   Inferences

Explain the differences between facts and inferences. Make sure that students understand that you can point to a fact in the text, but an inference is something that you create from hints in the text. Review the website *Inferences vs. Facts* at www.brighthub.com/education/k-12/articles/58029.aspx.

- After reading a story, make a two-column chart on the board with the headings *fact* and *inference*.

- Write various facts or inferences on sentence strips and have students put the strips into the appropriate columns.

- Ask students to point to the text that helps them make the inference.

Point to the text that helps you distinguish facts from inferences.

TIER 2   Inferences

Comprehension probe

- Show students how to use inferences to understand unfamiliar vocabulary words by using nonsense words. For example, write several sentences on the board such as *I didn't want to absculate again this winter. Last time I did it, I broke my arm going down a steep hill.*

- Make a list of facts that students know about the nonsense word *absculate* from reading the sentences; for example, *it can be done in the winter and it involves hills.*

- Have students come up with inferences that they can make about the word *absculate,* such as that *it probably requires snow and involves moving very quickly.*

- Help students extend these inference activities to real-life by choosing a real sentence that contains a difficult word that can be understood from the context.

- Have students use the same process to try to infer what the word might mean.

Read more about inferences at www.brighthub.com/education/k-12/articles/58023.aspx.

Use facts and inferences to define new words presented by the teacher.

Different stimuli

- White out the speech bubbles in several comic strips and photocopy them for the class to use.
- Have groups of students decide what might be going on in each frame of the comic strip.
- Encourage them to share their ideas with the class, as well as why they made those inferences from the pictures.

- Write what you think the characters are saying in the comic strip.
- Tell why you think they are saying those words.

 Bonus: Provide students with comic strips with blank speech bubbles, but use guided practice, explaining what the characters may be saying for one or two of the comic strips. Explain what inferences you made and on what basis you made them. Then, ask students to complete one of the comics independently.

TIER 3 — Inferences

Matching

- Create a worksheet with two columns of sentences. On the right side are the sentences with inferential information. On the left side is a sentence about what was inferred.
- Ask students to draw a line between the sentence and what is meant to be inferred.

- Draw a line between sentences on the right and sentences on the left to show what is inferred.
- Listen to the teacher's explanation; then complete one comic strip.

Multiple choice/Alternative response mode

- Use the comic strips from Tier 2, changing the task to a receptive activity.
- Provide two or three choices about what inferences can be made from the story or comic strip, asking the student to identify the most appropriate choice.

Recall or point to the correct inference.

Grade 2

| Grade 2 | LANGUAGE AREA: Phonological Awareness | OBJECTIVE: Blend Phonemes Into Words |

TIER 1 — Blend Phonemes

Explain to students that a word is composed of sounds blended together.

- Gather three large blocks of different colors to represent sounds/letters of 10 consonant-vowel-consonant (CVC) words that begin with noncontinuant sounds (duck, boot, pen, chick, cup, tooth, bus, kite, cage).

- Tell students that they are going to make a sound train by putting together the blocks. Each block makes a different sound.

- Place the blocks on the table apart from one another. Model the blending activity by saying the sound of each block with a 1-second pause between each sound (d-u-k). Point to each colored block as the sound is said.

- Show the class how to make blocks form a train by slowly blending the sounds together into the word duck, pushing the blocks together as the sounds are merged.

- Repeat the demonstration having students say the isolated sounds and blend them together to form the whole word. Repeat with the remaining nine CVC words.

Say the isolated sounds and blend them together to say a whole word.

TIER 2 — Blend Phonemes

Visual cues

Repeat the Tier 1 activity with colored magnets, each representing one sound (d-u-k).

Say the isolated sounds and blend them to say a whole word as the teacher slides the magnets together.

Visual cues/Concentrated instruction

Repeat the Tier 1 activity but reduce the number of words to five and increase the number of trials per item.

Say the isolated sounds and blend them to say a whole word as the teacher slides the magnets together.

| TIER 3 | Blend Phonemes |

Visual cues/Imitation

- Show a picture of an item.
- Ask students to imitate isolated sounds in a word and then blend them to form a whole word.
- Repeat the activity for five additional items.

Imitate the teacher's word production with sounds isolated and then blended to form a whole word.

Visual cues

- Show a picture of an item.
- Say the first sound of the word (*d-d-d-d*) with a prolonged duration and have students finish the word (*uk*) as you point to the item.
- Repeat the activity for five additional items.

When you are shown a picture and the first sound of a word, complete production of the word.

Grade
2

Grade 2

LANGUAGE AREA: Phonological Awareness

OBJECTIVE: Substitute Sounds in Words

TIER 1 — Substitute Sounds

Explain that words can be changed by replacing a sound within a word.

- Ask students to listen carefully to a pair of words (*map/tap*).
- Ask students to guess which sound was different between the first and second word.
- Repeat with 10 additional word pairs

Initial Sound	Final Sound
map/tap	nice/night
sit/pit	bag/back
hot/pot	gate/game
mad/bad	cap/cat
bat/fat	lame/lake

Guess which sound was different in the two words that were presented.

 Bonus: Use words with multiple syllables (*funny/bunny*) and CVC words that have different vowels (*cut/cat*).

338 • Grade 2 • Phonological Awareness

| TIER 2 | Substitute Sounds |

Different stimuli

- Introduce the *Name Change Game*. Explain that a person's name can be changed by replacing the first sound with another sound.

- Ask a student to say his name out loud. Write the student's name on the board and ask students to guess what the new name would be if the first sound was changed to an s. Provide an example (*Matthew* would become *Satthew*).

- Write the two versions of the name on the board and ask students to say both versions.

- Go around the room and repeat the activity with five other students' names and different initial sounds.

- Repeat the two versions of each name.
- Guess a student's new name after the initial sound is changed.

Repeated practice

Double the number of items to 10 in the *Name Change Game*

- Repeat the two versions of each name (Matthew, Satthew) after the teacher.
- Guess a student's new name after the initial sound is changed.

| TIER 3 | Substitute Sounds |

Imitation

- Repeat the Tier 2 activity.
- Provide a model of a student's new name after the critical sound is changed.

Imitate the teacher's production of a student's new name.

Different stimuli/Restricted-choice questions

- Provide students with two options for the name change (*Is it Matthew or Satthew?*) and write those options on the board.

- Ask students to point to the correct pronunciation when this student's name begins with an s sound.

- Repeat the activity with 10 other students' names using the target phoneme.

Point to the correct version of the name.

GRADE 2 • PHONOLOGICAL AWARENESS   339

| Grade 2 | LANGUAGE AREA: Print Knowledge | OBJECTIVE: Understand Concept of Paragraph |

TIER 1 — Paragraph

Explain that sentences are made up of words and stories are made up of paragraphs.

- Present a short paragraph from a textbook, write it on the board, and explain that it is called a *paragraph*.

- Define the term *paragraph* (a group of sentences about the same topic) and explain that paragraphs have a beginning, middle, and end.
  - *Beginning:* A statement is made (**topic sentence**: what the paragraph is about).
  - *Middle:* The statement is explained (**supporting details**: why?).
  - *End:* The thought is ended (**concluding sentence**: what the topic sentence is about).

- Place the key words next to each sentence in the paragraph.

- Select another paragraph and ask students to identify each sentence with one of the key terms (*topic sentence, supporting details, concluding sentence*).

- Ask students to write a paragraph called *My Favorite Season of the Year*, remembering to put in all three parts.

- Ask one or two student volunteers to share their paragraphs. Write them on the board.

- Ask all students to identify which key term goes with each sentence and fill in or help to rearrange the sentences in the correct order.

- Identify the key terms (topic sentence, supporting details, and concluding sentence) of a paragraph.

- Write a paragraph on a specified topic and identify which key terms go with each sentence of the paragraph.

340   GRADE 2 • PRINT KNOWLEDGE

TIER 2 — Paragraph

Matching/Visual cues

Explain the concept of *paragraph,* name the parts of a paragraph, and provide an example of a paragraph on the board.

- Present three word cards, each containing the name of a part of a paragraph.

- Ask students to match a card with the correct sentence in the paragraph.

Match cards to the correct part of the paragraph.

Double dose of instruction

Double the amount of time spent on the Tier 2 matching activity.

Match cards to the correct part of the paragraph.

TIER 3 — Paragraph

Modeling

Explain the concept of *paragraph*, name the different parts of a paragraph, and provide an example of a paragraph on the board.

- Select a word card and match it to the correct sentence of the paragraph, explaining the reason for the selection.

- Repeat this activity at least three times with the same paragraph.

Observe as the teacher models the matching activity.

Repeated practice/Multiple choice

Explain the concept of *paragraph,* name the different parts of a paragraph, and provide an example of a paragraph on the board.

- Present three word cards, each containing the name of a part of a paragraph.

- Ask students to select the correct card as each sentence of the paragraph is read.

- Repeat this instructional activity at least three times with the same paragraph.

As each sentence of the paragraph is read, select the word card from a set of three that corresponds to the name of that part of the paragraph.

References

Assessments

Boehm, A. E. (2000). *Boehm Test of Basic Concepts, Third Edition*. San Antonio, TX: Pearson Assessments.

Bracken, B. A. (1998). *Bracken Basic Concept Scale—Revised*. San Antonio, TX: Pearson Assessments.

Wiig, E. H. (2004). *Wiig Assessment of Basic Concepts*. Greenville, SC: Super Duper Publications.

Resources

Books

Aliki (1971). *The story of Johnny Appleseed*. New York, NY: Simon & Schuster.

Allard, H. G. (1977). *Miss Nelson is missing* (J. Marshall, Illus.). Boston, MA: Houghton Mifflin Books for Children.

Aruego, J. (1976). *A crocodile's tale* (A. Aruego, Illus.). New York, NY: Scholastic.

Bourgeois, P. (1993). *Franklin is bossy* (B. Clark, Illus.). New York, NY: Scholastic.

Bunting, E. (2000). *Train to somewhere* (R. Himler, Illus.). New York, NY: Houghton Mifflin.

Cherry, L. (1990). *The great kapok tree: A tale of the Amazon rain forest*. Boston, MA: Houghton Mifflin Harcourt.

Cleary, B. (1992). *Ramona Quimby, age 8* (T. Dockray, Illus.). New York, NY: HarperCollins.

Cleary, B. P. (1999). *A mink, a fink, a skating rink: What is a noun?* (J. Prosmitsky, Illus.). New York, NY: Lerner.

Cosby, B. (1997). *The meanest thing to say* (V. P. Honeywood, Illus.). St. Louis, MO: Turtleback Books.

De Beer, H. (1994). *Little polar bear*. New York, NY: North-South Books.

De Deu Prats, J. (2005). *Sebastian's roller skates* (F. Rovira, Illus.). San Diego, CA: Kane Miller.

dePaola, T. (1978). *Pancakes for breakfast*. New York, NY: Harcourt.

Galdone, P. (1973). *The little red hen*. New York, NY: Houghton Mifflin

Graham, A. S. (2003). *Full moon soup: A wordless book that's brimful of stories*. London, UK: Chrysalis Books.

Holland, G. (1998) *Johnny Appleseed* (K. Palmer, Illus.). New York, NY: Houghton Mifflin

Kellogg, S. (1986). *Pecos Bill* (L. Robb, Illus.). New York, NY: William Morrow.

Kellogg, S. (1998). *Johnny Appleseed*. New York, NY: HarperCollins.

Lindbergh, R. (1990). *Johnny Appleseed* (K. J. Hallquist, Illus.). New York, NY: Little, Brown Books.

Llewellyn, C. (1998). *The best book of bugs*. New York, NY: Kingfisher.

Mayer, M. (1992). *A boy, a dog and a frog*. New York, NY: Penguin

Morris, A. (1998). *Work*. New York, NY: HarperCollins.

Mortenson, G., & Roth, S. L. (2009). *Listen to the wind: The story of Dr. Greg & Three Cups of Tea* (S. Roth, Illus.). New York, NY: Penguin.

Muldrow, D. (Ed.). (2001). *The little red hen* (J. P. Miller, Illus.). New York, NY: Random House Children's.

Parish, H. (1991). *Amelia bedilia* (F. Siebel, Illus.). New York, NY: HarperCollins.

Rylant, C. (1996). *Henry and Mudge: The first book* (S. Stevenson, Illus.). New York, NY: Simon & Schuster.

Skene, P. S. (2006). *The chocolate touch* (M. Apple, Illus.). New York, NY: HarperTrophy.

Small, D. (1988). *Imogene's antlers*. New York, NY: Random House Children's.

Thomas, S. M. (2002). *Good night, good knight* (J. Placas, Illus.). New York, NY: Puffin.

RTI in Action:
Appendices

Appendix A:
Cultural Competence Checklist.. 346

Appendix B:
Developmental Milestone Checklist 347

Appendix C:
Progress Monitoring for Individual Students.. 350

Appendix D:
Progress Monitoring for Classrooms..351

Appendix E:
Intensity Grid 352

Appendix F:
Graphic Organizer—Spider Map.. 353

Appendix G:
Graphic Organizer—Venn Diagram... 354

Appendix H:
Graphic Organizer—Story Map.. 355

Appendix I:
Graphic Organizer—Definition Map 358

Appendix A

Cultural Competence Checklist: Personal Reflection

This tool was developed to heighten your awareness of how you view students from culturally and linguistically diverse (CLD) populations.* There is no answer key; however, you should review responses that you rated 5, 4, and even 3.

Ratings:

1 Strongly Agree	4 Disagree
2 Agree	5 Strongly Disagree
3 Neutral	

____ I treat all of my students with respect for their culture, even though it might be different from my own.

____ I do not impose my beliefs and value systems on my students, their family members, or their friends.

____ I believe that it is acceptable to use a language other than English in the U.S.

____ I accept my students' decisions as to the degree to which they choose to acculturate into the dominant culture.

____ I provide services to students who are GLBTQ (gay, lesbian, bisexual, transgender, or questioning).

____ I am driven to respond to others' insensitive comments or behaviors.

____ I do not participate in insensitive comments or behaviors.

____ I am aware that the roles of family members may differ within or across culture or families.

____ I recognize family members and other designees as decision makers for services and support.

____ I respect non-traditional family structures (e.g., divorced parents, same-gender parents, grandparents as caretakers).

____ I understand the difference between a communication disability and a communication difference.

____ I understand that views of the aging process may influence the students'/families' decision to seek intervention.

____ I understand that there are several American English dialects. I recognize that all English speakers use a dialect of English.

I understand that the use of a foreign accent or limited English skill is not a reflection of:

____ reduced intellectual capacity

____ the ability to communicate clearly and effectively in a native language

I understand how culture can affect child-rearing practices such as:

____ Discipline
____ Toileting
____ Self-help skills
____ Communication
____ Dressing
____ Feeding
____ Expectations for the future

I understand the impact of culture on life activities, such as:

____ Education
____ Religion/faith-based practices
____ Alternative medicine
____ Employment
____ Views of wellness
____ Family roles
____ Gender roles
____ Customs or superstitions
____ Perception of time
____ Views of disabilities
____ The value of Western medical treatment

I understand my students' cultural norms may influence communication in many ways, including:

____ Eye contact
____ Use of gestures
____ Turn-taking
____ Asking and responding to questions
____ Greetings
____ Interruptions
____ Decision-making roles
____ Interpersonal space
____ Comfort with silence
____ Topics of conversation
____ Use of humor

Reference this material as: American Speech-Language-Hearing Association. (2010). *Cultural Competence Checklist: Personal reflection.* Available from www.asha.org/uploadedFiles/practice/multicultural/personalreflections.pdf.

*While several sources were consulted in the development of this checklist, the following document inspired its design: "Promoting Cultural and Linguistic Competence Self-Assessment Checklist for Personnel Providing Services and Supports in Early Intervention and Childhood Settings," by T. D. Goode, 1989 (rev. 2002).

© Copyright 2010 American Speech-Language-Hearing Association. All rights reserved.

Appendix B

Developmental Milestones for Listening, Talking, Reading, and Writing: Kindergarten to Second Grade

Children learn at different rates. We expect children to achieve certain skills in each grade. Some children reach these milestones later. Or they may need help to reach them. These checklists show what most children can do by the end of kindergarten, first grade, and second grade in the areas of listening, talking, reading, and writing.

Kindergarten

Has your child finished kindergarten? Use this checklist to mark off your child's skills.

Listening Skills

By the end of kindergarten, my child:

- ❏ Follows one or two directions in order, like *Choose a book and come sit on the couch.*
- ❏ Understands short conversations.
- ❏ Listens to and understands short books written for kindergarten children.
- ❏ Understands what's taught in class.

Talking Skills

By the end of kindergarten, my child:

- ❏ Answers *yes* or *no* questions like *Did you finish your lunch?*
- ❏ Answers open-ended questions like *What did you have for lunch?*
- ❏ Speaks clearly. Most people can understand him.
- ❏ Retells a story or parts of a story.
- ❏ Takes turns and stays on topic when talking.
- ❏ Talks about things that happened during the day.
- ❏ Uses many different types of sentences—asks and answers questions, asks for information, and makes comments.
- ❏ Shows interest in what others are saying.
- ❏ Starts conversations with people.

Reading Skills

By the end of kindergarten, my child:

- ❏ Knows that you read books in English from front to back, top to bottom, and left to right.
- ❏ Knows that words are made up of sounds.
- ❏ Finds words that rhyme, like *cat* and *bat*.
- ❏ Knows that some words have the same sounds in them, like *sun, soup,* and *sand*.
- ❏ Knows some sight words. Sight words are words that children see a lot in books like *cat, the,* and *with*.
- ❏ Finds uppercase (CAPITAL) and lowercase letters.
- ❏ Knows that letters stand for speech sounds. Can match many sounds to letters—for example, the letter *B* sounds like *buh* in the word *bus*.
- ❏ "Reads" a few picture books from memory.
- ❏ Tells a story by looking at the pictures in a book.

Writing Skills

By the end of kindergarten, my child:

- ❏ Prints her first and last name.
- ❏ Writes uppercase and lowercase letters.
- ❏ Draws a picture that tells a story. Names and writes words about the picture.

RTI in Action • APPENDIX B   347

Appendix B

Developmental Milestones for Listening, Talking, Reading, and Writing: Kindergarten to Second Grade

First Grade

Has your child finished first grade? Use this checklist to mark off your child's skills.

Listening Skills

By the end of first grade, my child:

- ❏ Remembers facts taught in class.
- ❏ Understands what's taught in class.
- ❏ Follows two or three directions in order, like *Get a piece of paper, find your pencil, and write your name.*

Talking Skills

By the end of first grade, my child:

- ❏ Answers harder *yes* or *no* questions, like *Did the girl take her puppy into the house with her?*
- ❏ Says all speech sounds clearly.
- ❏ Tells and retells a story in the right order.
- ❏ Uses complete sentences to talk about different ideas.
- ❏ Uses most parts of speech, or grammar, correctly.
- ❏ Asks and answers *who, what, where, why,* and *when* questions.
- ❏ Stays on topic and takes turns when talking with people.
- ❏ Gives directions.

Reading Skills

By the end of first grade, my child:

- ❏ Makes up rhyming words.
- ❏ Finds all the sounds in short words.
- ❏ Blends separate sounds to make words.
- ❏ Matches spoken words with written words.
- ❏ Identifies letters, words, and sentences.
- ❏ Sounds out words.
- ❏ Recognizes about 100 common words.
- ❏ Easily reads first-grade stories.
- ❏ Shows that she understands what she reads.

Writing Skills

By the end of first grade, my child:

- ❏ Prints clearly.
- ❏ Spells commonly used words correctly.
- ❏ Starts sentences with a capital letter.
- ❏ Ends sentences with a period, question mark, or exclamation point.
- ❏ Writes short pieces like stories and journal entries.

Appendix B

Developmental Milestones for Listening, Talking, Reading, and Writing: Kindergarten to Second Grade

Second Grade

Has your child finished second grade? Use this checklist to mark off your child's skills.

Listening Skills

By the end of second grade, my child:

- ❑ Follows three or four directions in order, like *Stay in your seat, wait for the bus to stop, and don't forget your backpack.*
- ❑ Answers questions about a story.
- ❑ Understands words about place and time, like *on top of, behind, next to, before, after, today,* and *yesterday.*
- ❑ Understands what's taught in class.

Talking Skills

By the end of second grade, my child:

- ❑ Answers more complex *yes* or *no* questions, like *Was the boy in the story telling the truth when he said he was going to his friend's house?*
- ❑ Explains words and ideas.
- ❑ Gives directions with three or four steps.
- ❑ Starts and ends conversations properly.
- ❑ Stays on topic and takes turns when talking with people.
- ❑ Uses more complex sentences when speaking.
- ❑ Talks for a variety of reasons—to comment about something, to convince someone, and to make someone laugh.

Reading Skills

By the end of second grade, my child:

- ❑ Knows all the letters and the sounds they make.
- ❑ Knows many sight words.
- ❑ Links speech sounds with written words.
- ❑ Finds and uses spelling patterns in words. For example, the word *cat* has the *at* sound. The word *that* has the same *at* sound. He knows how to spell *that* by putting together the sounds from *cat*.
- ❑ Uses clues, like pictures, titles, or facts, to figure out what words mean.
- ❑ Reads words again and makes corrections as needed.
- ❑ Finds facts to answer questions.
- ❑ Explains the main parts of a story, like the main idea, main characters, and plot.
- ❑ Predicts what will happen in stories.
- ❑ Reads and retells a story in the right order.
- ❑ Reads second-grade stories, poetry, or plays—silently and out loud.
- ❑ Reads smoothly—doesn't need to sound out words a lot.
- ❑ Reads for fun.

Writing Skills

By the end of second grade, my child:

- ❑ Writes neatly.
- ❑ Uses many types of sentences in journals, poetry, and short stories.
- ❑ Uses capital letters and basic punctuation like commas, periods, and question marks correctly.
- ❑ Writes stories that have a beginning, middle, and end.
- ❑ Spells common words correctly.
- ❑ Begins to spell more words correctly.
- ❑ Spells name and recognizes letters on the computer.

RTI in Action • APPENDIX B 349

Appendix C

RTI Progress Monitoring—Individual Student

Enter data in each column for the student at the agreed upon intervals, adding comments for each goal.

Student: _____

Progress Key: (1) Mastered (2) Good—70%–85% accuracy (3) Fair—55%–69% accuracy (4) Poor—below 55% accuracy

Goal	Date/Mastery Level (e.g, 12/5-3)								Comments

© Copyright 2010 American Speech-Language-Hearing Association. Permission for individual/educational use of photocopies not required.

RTI Progress Monitoring—Classroom

GOAL: _____

List all students who are demonstrating a weakness on the targeted goal. Enter data in each column for individual students at the agreed upon intervals, adding any relevant comments.

Progress Key: **(1) Mastered** **(2) Good—70%–85% accuracy** **(3) Fair—55%–69% accuracy** **(4) Poor—below 55% accuracy**

Student	Date	Date	Date	Date	Date	Date	Date	Date	Date
Comments									
Comments									
Comments									
Comments									
Comments									

© Copyright 2010 American Speech-Language-Hearing Association. Permission for individual/educational use of photocopies not required.

Appendix E

RTI Intensity Grid

Student's Name _____   Grade _____   Student's Birth Date _____

Classroom
Teacher _____   Date of Initial
Referral for Intervention _____

Beginning Date
of Intervention _____   Ending
Date _____   Delivered
By _____

Intervention Strategy	Frequency/Intensity	Progress Monitoring Frequency	Outcome	Recommendations	Professional Responsible
Tier 1					
Tier 2					
Tier 3					

© Copyright 2010 American Speech-Language-Hearing Association. Permission for individual/educational use of photocopies not required.

352   RTI in Action • APPENDIX E

Appendix F

Spider Map

Instructions:
- Use the "body" or circle to write your central idea or topic.
- Use the slanted "legs" or branches to write main ideas.
- Write details on the horizontal lines.

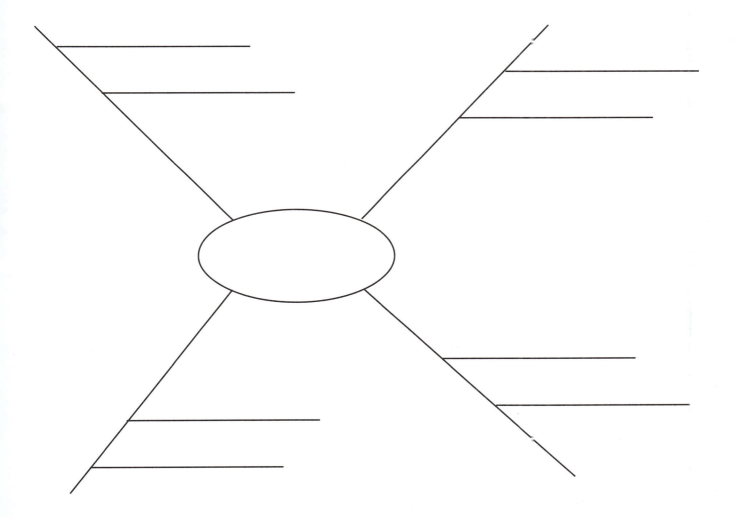

© Copyright 2010 American Speech-Language-Hearing Association.
Permission for individual/educational use of photocopies not required.

Appendix G

Venn Diagram

Instructions:

- Place the name of the items that you are comparing in the spaces above the two circles.
- Write the details about how the <u>items are different</u> in the outer portion of the circles.
- Write about how the <u>items are the same</u> in the area where the two circles overlap.

Compare and contrast the items by referring to the Venn diagram and discussing how the items are different and the same.

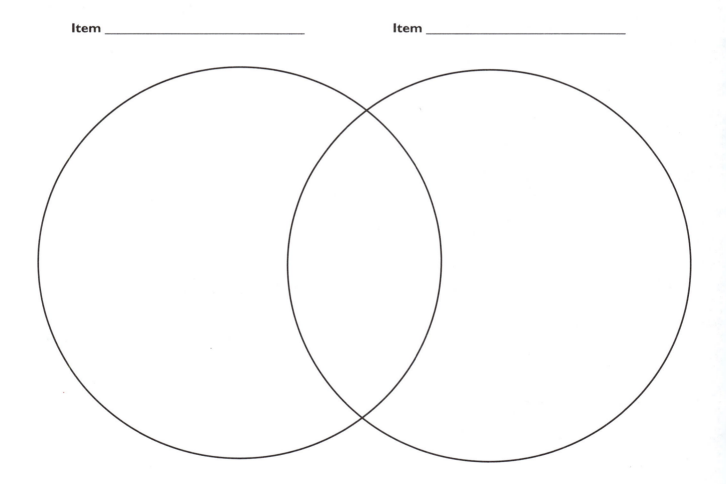

© Copyright 2010 American Speech-Language-Hearing Association.
Permission for individual/educational use of photocopies not required.

354   RTI in Action • Appendix G

Appendix H

Story Map–1

Instructions:

Use the labeled boxes to write the information about the story you are reading.

Setting

Main Characters

Problem or Conflict

Events/Attempts/Actions

1.
2.
3.
4.

Resolution/Solution/Conclusion

© Copyright 2010 American Speech-Language-Hearing Association.
Permission for individual/educational use of photocopies not required.

RTI in Action • Appendix H 355

Appendix H

Story Map–2

Instructions:

Use the labeled boxes to write the information about the story you are reading.

Setting
_____
_____

Main Characters
_____
_____
_____
_____

Problem or Conflict
_____
_____
_____
_____

Response
_____
_____
_____
_____

© Copyright 2010 American Speech-Language-Hearing Association.
Permission for individual/educational use of photocopies not required.

Appendix H

Story Map–2 (continued)

Plan
_____
_____
_____
_____

Events/Attempts/Actions
1. _____
2. _____
3. _____
4. _____

Resolution/Solution/Conclusion
_____
_____
_____
_____
_____

Reaction
_____
_____
_____
_____
_____

© Copyright 2010 American Speech-Language-Hearing Association. Permission for individual/educational use of photocopies not required.

Appendix I

Definition Map

Instructions:

- Fill in the map with the target word, and then, using the other shapes, provide a synonym, characteristics, examples, and relational words about the target word.
- Once the Definitions Map has been completed, use the filled-in map to formulate a definition.
- Put the definition in context by reading a paragraph from text.
- Use comparison elements and fill in words that are similar in meaning; discuss common and uncommon properties.

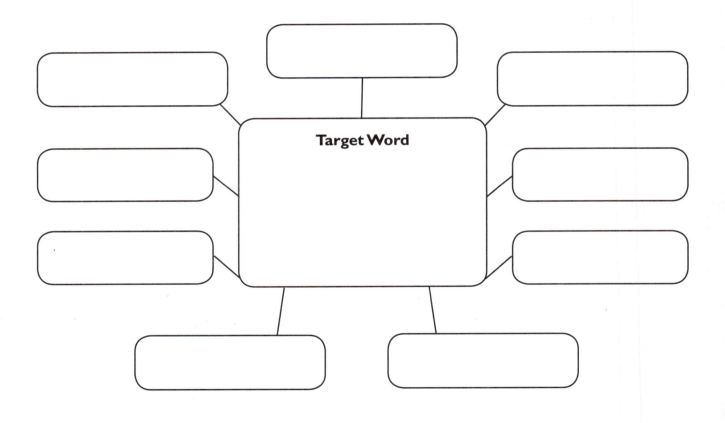

Definition: _____
_____
_____

© Copyright 2010 American Speech-Language-Hearing Association.
Permission for individual/educational use of photocopies not required.